THE GENERAL PRINCIPLES OF ENGLISH LAW

THE GENERAL PRINCIPLES OF ENGLISH LAW

by

W. F. FRANK

LL.B., B.Com., M.Sc.(Econ.), Dr.jur.

formerly Head of the Department of Legal Studies
Lanchester Polytechnic

Co-Author of
"*The Legal Aspects of Industry and Commerce*"

SIXTH EDITION

HARRAP LONDON

First published in Great Britain 1957
by George G. Harrap & Co. Ltd
182–184 High Holborn, London WC1V 7AX

Reprinted 1958

Second edition, revised, 1961

Reprinted: 1961; 1962; 1963

Third edition, revised, 1964

Reprinted: 1964; 1965; 1966; 1967

Fourth edition, revised, 1969

Fifth edition, revised, 1971

Reprinted 1973

Sixth edition, revised, 1975

Reprinted 1976; 1978

ISBN 0 245 52662 5

Composed in Baskerville type and printed by
Western Printing Services Limited Bristol
Made in Great Britain

Contents

Preface

THIS book has been written for one specific purpose, and that is to be of help to students preparing for examinations in the General Principles of English Law, set by one or another of the professional bodies including this subject among their examination syllabuses, particularly the Chartered Institute of Secretaries and Administrators, the Institute of Bankers, and the Institute of Transport. The book should also be useful to students preparing for the National Certificates and Diplomas in Business Studies and Public Administration.

It must be emphasized that this book, unlike most of the existing ones on the subject, is not intended for university students or law students in general. This accounts for the method of presentation. Footnotes have been avoided as far as possible, and detailed case-references have been limited to the Tables of Cases and are not otherwise found in the text.

For many readers this must be the first book on law which they have read. The author strongly recommends those who come quite fresh to the subject to read through the whole book once before starting on a detailed study of its contents. It is only in this way that they will grasp the interconnections of the subject. The author has tried, as far as possible, to avoid cross-references; but to some extent these are unavoidable.

Students with whom the author has discussed his plans for this book have told him that they find difficulties in understanding some of the legal terms. All such terms used in the present book have been explained to the best of the author's ability, but in order to help students in this respect Appendix I contains a glossary. It was, of course, impossible to include more than a selection of such terms; but students who find difficulties with any other terms should try to consult a good legal dictionary in their local library.

Appendix II contains a selected list of questions on the subject-matter of this book, as set in various public examinations. The questions are arranged in sections corresponding to the chapters of the book. This should help students who are not attending regular courses of lectures to test their knowledge by trying to answer the questions appropriate to any chapter after having studied it in detail. The author would like to use this opportunity of thanking the professional bodies concerned for their kindness in permitting the reproduction of the questions.

Readers who wish to study any of the topics in greater detail will find a reading list in Appendix III.

The author would welcome comments from teachers as well as from students about difficulties encountered in studying with the help of this book.

W. F. F.

Note to the Sixth Edition

IN the three years that have passed since the fifth edition of this book was published some significant changes have taken place in the administration of justice in England and Wales. Some of these were foreshadowed in an Appendix to chapter two of the book, but the opportunity has now been taken to rewrite this chapter completely. Other changes in the book have become necessary because of the legal implications of Britain joining the European Economic Community. Furthermore, the main readership of this book has always been among those students preparing for ONC or OND Business Studies examinations and the guide syllabus in General Principles of English Law for these examinations has also been radically revised with effect from 1973. This was in part taken care of by the inclusion of a special supplement in the fifth edition of the book, but the author has used the present revision to embody this material in the text of the book. Seventeen years have passed now since this book was first published and the very fact that it is still in demand indicates that it meets the needs of its readers. As in the past, the author still welcomes comments from readers and is grateful to those who have taken the trouble of writing to him.

W.F.F.

CHAPTER ONE

The Nature and Sources of English Law

The Meaning of Law

In view of the large number of books that has been written on legal subjects, it is perhaps at first sight surprising that there does not exist any generally accepted definition of 'law.' Leaving aside the many intrusions of philosophy into this field, one of the main reasons for this inability to find a definition is the duality of meaning of the concept of law. We have to be careful to distinguish between 'a law' and 'the law.' A law is a rule of conduct which differs from other rules of conduct, such of those of ethics, good manners, or of sport, in that it is supported by sanctions administered by the State. The rule that spitting is forbidden in railway trains is a good rule of hygiene. It becomes a legal rule, and thus in a sense 'a law' if the State is prepared to enforce obedience to this rule by administering punishment to those who break it. There is no single answer to the question why certain rules of conduct have become laws while others have not. By and large it is society itself which decides this by means of its pressure on the law-makers to raise rules of conduct to a higher level where society has a direct interest in seeing that these rules are complied with. It is not that there is something inherently fair and just about legal rules which distinguishes them from other rules of conduct; indeed, there have been, and there probably still are, many laws in existence which, on a majority vote of the population, would be held to be unfair. Laws are amoral—that means that they are binding irrespective of whether they are morally just.

The law of a country is primarily the sum total of all the separate laws in existence there; but it is more than that, just as a wood is more than just a large number of trees arbitrarily thrown together. Most forests which have been planted show a certain design or symmetry, which is the work of the foresters who have been responsible for them. Thus, also, the law of a country works on certain general principles which give sense to some of the legal rules making up the law. The law is as much a living thing as a people's language, their clothes, or their habits. It grows as the country's economy changes and it adapts itself to ever-changing tasks. In the same way in which the philologist has to study the language of the past in order to understand that of the present so also the student of law cannot properly appreciate the law of his country as it exists to-day without paying some attention to its history.

The Nature of English Law

This book is concerned with the law of England and Wales. The law of Scotland has its own history and differs in many respects from English law. Much of recent legislation has been common to both England and Scotland, but the basic legal concepts of the two countries vary to such an extent that it would be a superhuman task to create a unified British Law.

English law possesses certain general features which mark it out from the legal systems of other countries.

1. *Continuity.* English law represents an excellent example of an ancient legal system which has grown and thus adapted itself to modern conditions. Although it has grown, it should be noted that old legal rules, the reasons for which have long disappeared, remain a part of English law until they are expressly repealed. No legal rule will cease to be operative merely by reason of disuse. Thus, in *Ashford* v. *Thornton*, a murder trial in the early nineteenth century, the defendant was allowed to take advantage of the medieval procedure of trial by battle, which had not been used for centuries but had never been expressly repealed. Needless to say, Parliament repealed it shortly afterwards.

In its continuity English law differs from most Continental legal systems, which are the work of nineteenth-century legal reformers.

2. *Absence of codification.* English law has never been codified —*i.e.*, assembled into one or two simple codes, or digests. In view of the antiquity and the bulk of English law, this has always been too formidable a task, though one or two attempts have been made to codify certain sections of it. The most that has been done has been the consolidation of some small branches of our law by means of consolidating Acts of Parliament (*e.g.*, the Sale of Goods Act 1893; the Companies Act 1948). The main difference between codification and consolidation is that in the former event the existing law is not only collected together but is at the same time also altered. A code is thus more than a mere collection of existing law, it represents in part a major piece of law reform. Consolidation, on the other hand, merely means bringing together in statute form legal rules which are spread widely in judicial decisions, customs, and statutes.

3. *The Judicial Character of English Law.* English law is basically judge-made law. Acts of Parliament represent to-day a fair proportion of it; but Acts have been passed only where it was felt necessary to fill in gaps in judge-made law or where judge-made law was con-

sidered to be out of date and incompatible with modern ways of thinking about social and allied questions.

4. *No Reception of Roman Law.* The legal systems of most Continental countries, and even that of Scotland, have been built on the foundations of Roman law. Surprisingly, however, Roman law has had very little influence on English law, except in those matters where up to the last century the courts of the Church possessed jurisdiction (*e.g.*, wills) and in the law relating to shipping, which is derived from the customs of the seafaring merchants of the Middle Ages, most of whom were of Mediterranean origin.

The Sources of English Law

When we talk about the sources of law we may be referring to one of two things. We may be thinking in the first place of where rules of law may be found, such as law reports, copies of Acts of Parliament, law text-books, and other written material. On the other hand, the search for the sources of law may lead us to investigate from where law comes—that is to say, where and how the legal rules which to-day govern our conduct originated. It is in this latter meaning that we shall be discussing the sources of English law. The main sources of English law in this sense are: (*a*) Common law; (*b*) Equity; (*c*) Legislation; (*d*) Law Merchant; (*e*) Custom.

The Common Law

The term 'common law' also has two meanings. In its broadest sense it means the unwritten law of England—*i.e.*, the whole of English law except that which has been enacted by Parliament. In its narrower, and technically more correct, sense it is the law which before the passing of the Judicature Acts 1873–75 was administered by the common law courts. It is called 'common' because it was, and is, the law which is common to the whole of England and Wales as distinct from mere local customs which apply to parts of the country only. In order to understand how common law developed we have to review briefly its history.

When William the Conqueror established his control over England he tried to forestall any possible rebellion of his native subjects by providing them with what one could call an early example of a welfare state. Under the weak governments of his predecessors the people of this country had never enjoyed much security, and it was quite clear to William that unless he could gain their confidence in his desire to administer law fairly and without favour a state of internal war would continue. There existed at that time nothing remotely resembling English law. Different parts of the country had their own customs, the provisions of which differed widely. Even these customs were not fairly applied, as many of the King's poorer subjects were unable to get justice in the manorial courts. In order that all his subjects should be able to enjoy fully their legal rights, William and his successors on the throne of England sent royal commissions round the country. Henry II was the first to make this a regular procedure.

The primary purpose of the commissions (eyres) was to keep a watchful eye on local administration and on tax collection, but in addition the commissioners were also given judicial powers. The judicial powers became gradually more important than the others, and the frequency with which the commissioners visited the various parts of England also increased. Three judicial commissions, or tasks, were generally issued: the *commission of gaol delivery*, the purpose of which was to clear the gaols by trying all the persons found in local gaols; *the commission of oyer and terminer*, by which the commissioners were instructed to hear and determine all cases of major crime committed since their last visit to the area; and, lastly, the *commission of assize*, which ordered the commissioners to try civil cases also. Civil cases should have been tried before the Royal Courts at Westminster, but the commissioners (also known as itinerant justices) were allowed to try them locally for the convenience of the parties and witnesses. These civil trials were known as trials at *nisi prius*. When a date was fixed for the hearing of a civil action at Westminster it was stated that the case would come up for trial at such and such a time unless before (nisi prius) the justices had heard the case in the county where it had arisen.

With the gradual increase in the judicial character of the commissions there came also a change in the personnel of the commissioners. Originally many of the commissioners had been clergymen, as they were the only people able to write and also because they usually had some understanding of the tasks of a judge. It was only much later, when a legal profession had developed and had gained respectability, that the commissions were issued to lawyers holding specific judicial offices.

At first the itinerant justices applied local customary law at their hearings. This meant that the justices had the double task of finding out what the customs were and then applying them to the case before them. They received in this the help of juries, introduced during the twelfth and thirteenth centuries, whose functions differed from the modern jury. The juries were made up of local citizens who had to report to the justices on the facts of the cases coming up before them and also on the local customs which were relevant to a decision of the dispute.

Between their tours of the country (circuits) the justices were sitting in the Royal Courts at Westminster. It was inevitable that they must have exchanged impressions of their visits to the four corners of England, with special reference to the diverse legal customs which they had encountered. Although we do not know for certain what happened, we may surmise that they must have agreed that certain customs were to be preferred to others. When they then went on circuit for the next time they began to rely less on the recollection of the local juries as to what the local law was and preferred to apply legal rules of their own, which were based on the customs of some part of the country. This was a lengthy process, but gradually all local customs were replaced in the Royal Courts, both at Westminster and on assize, by legal rules collected and agreed upon by the justices. Thus a legal system came into existence which, though built on local custom, owed its existence to the activity of the justices in selecting the best customs from all over England and merging them into a coherent entity, the common law of England.

Among the central Royal Courts at Westminster the oldest was the *Court of Exchequer*. This court had split off from the Department of State dealing with financial matters, and was at first concerned solely with disputes affecting directly the royal revenue. Later on, however, the Barons of the Exchequer (as its judges were known) began to extend the jurisdiction of this court and started to hear all kinds of common-law actions, the connection of which with the royal revenue was a remote one. Another Royal Court was the *Court of Common Pleas*, which dealt with all kinds of disputes between citizens. The youngest, but in many ways the most important, of the Royal Courts was the *Court of King's Bench*, so called because the King used occasionally to join his judges on the bench of the court. Because of the close connection that existed between this court and the King's Council (*Curia Regis*), the King's Bench was able to exercise a measure of supervision over the activities of inferior courts by means of the *prerogative writs*. (See page 53.) Bearing in mind that the income of the judges and of the other court officials depended on the amount of business done in their courts, it was not surprising that there existed a large measure of competition between the courts and that each of them tried to extend its jurisdiction so as to attract more parties to bring their disputes to it.

Proceedings in the common-law courts started with the issue of an original writ which had to be obtained—that is to say, bought—from the main royal office, the Chancery. The writ consisted of an order addressed to the sheriff of the county in which the defendant resided, commanding him to secure the presence of the defendant at the trial and also outlining the plaintiff's cause of action. For every cause of action (legal wrong complained of by the plaintiff) there existed a separate writ, and these writs were collected in a register of original writs. The remedies which the court might grant to the plaintiff depended on the writ with which the case started. The common-law judges had to pronounce both on the correctness of the writ and also on the merits of the case. If an action had been started with the wrong kind of writ the judges at once threw out the case and did not go into its merits at all. The Chancery officials who made their living from the sale of writs were, of course, keen on accommodating all prospective plaintiffs and were thus prepared to make out new kinds of writs to deal with new situations for which no writ was found in the existing register of writs. At first the common-law judges tolerated this procedure and accepted the new writs; but by the middle of the thirteenth century their attitude began to harden and they refused to accept new writs for which no precedent existed. The Provisions of Oxford (1258) prohibited the creation of new writs. This meant that a person who had been wronged in a way which did not fall within the terms of an existing writ was unable to obtain even a hearing in the common-law courts. The Statute of Westminister II (1285) provided a partial remedy. It laid down that where a situation arose similar to one for which a writ was already in existence a new writ could be made out to meet the new case. These writs were known as writs *in consimili casu* (in a similar case). Even so, it remained difficult at times to obtain redress at common law, and this led to the development of a new type of law, namely equity.

Equity

When a citizen could get no redress in the common-law courts, or when he felt that his case had not been fairly tried, it was quite natural that he would petition the King for his personal intervention in the matter. The common-law judges were, after all, administering law in the King's name, and the King had, through his Council, taken a personal interest in legal matters. When such petitions reached the King he would bring them to the meetings of the Council, and he would ask the member of the Council most likely to have some understanding of legal issues to deal with them. This member was the Chancellor. The Chancellor was not only the King's personal secretary and his Minister for all departments, he was also a clergyman and, as such, the King's personal chaplain and in the language of the day the Keeper of the King's Conscience. As the petitioners generally appealed to the King's conscience, reminding him that his conscience surely could not suffer wrongs to be done to his loyal subjects, the Keeper of the King's Conscience was even more so the obvious person to deal with their complaints.

Three main types of situations could give rise to an appeal to the King. Either common law provided no remedies at all for certain wrongs (*e.g.*, breaches of trusts); or such remedies as the common-law courts were prepared to grant were inadequate to meet the real demands of the situation (*e.g.*, only damages could be obtained, where what the petitioner really wanted was that the other party should be made to carry out something which he had undertaken); or it was alleged that the judge had been under the influence of the other party and had failed to behave impartially.

The Chancellor had one great advantage compared with the common-law judges and that was that he was not tied by any rigid rules of procedure. His main task was to get to the bottom of the matter and to discover the truth. No writs were needed to initiate proceedings before the Chancellor, and he could enforce the attendance of the parties by means of the *writ of subpoena*, where refusal to attend would be followed by the imprisonment of the recalcitrant party and the confiscation of his property. It should also be recalled that the Chancellor was a clergyman, who felt himself responsible not only for the King's conscience but also for that of any other man. He tried, therefore, to get the parties to unburden their consciences, and he felt that if, in order to make them do so, he had to use the threats of imprisonment and loss of property he was really protecting their own souls, as a person who had a wrong on his conscience could not possibly find peace with God. Having found out for himself by a cross-examination of the parties where justice rested, the Chancellor would order the party whom he considered to be wrong to undo the wrong which he had done. If the party was not willing to co-operate the Chancellor was again prepared to use compulsion in the interests of that person's conscience. In coming to his decision, the Chancellor did not follow any set rules. This approach had some obvious disadvantages, which were clearly seen by the seventeenth-century lawyer, John Selden, who commented in his *Table Talk* as follows:

> Equity is a roguish thing, for Law we have a measure, know what to trust to, Equity is according to the conscience of him that is Chancellor and as that is larger or narrower so is Equity. 'Tis all one as if they should make the Standard for the measure, we call a Chancellor's Foot, what an uncertain measure would this be? One Chancellor has a long foot, another a short foot, a third an indifferent foot. 'Tis the same thing in the Chancellor's Conscience.

Early equity was thus not a coherent system of law at all. It was based on the personal consciences of successive Chancellors, on what they individually considered to be just and fair. Such a situation could not persist for long. As the Chancellor's jurisdiction became more popular with petitioners, a separate Court of Chancery was set up, to which parties directly sent their petitions (known as bills). This happened towards the end of the fifteenth century. The oral examination of the parties by the Chancellor was also gradually replaced by an exchange of written contentions, thus sowing the seeds for the paper battles which characterized the procedure in the Court of Chancery later on. The Chancellor also had to appoint assistants (Vice-Chancellors), who would take off his shoulders some of the work of the court. With equity now being applied by more than one judge at a time, it became necessary to create some general rules to be observed by all of them. General principles were established as to the conditions in which the special remedies of equity would be available and as to the kind of person to whom they would be granted. Equity became thus a body of rules, fairly rigidly applied, and no longer depending on the judge's conscience or his particular sense of values.

Equity may be defined, then, as the body of rules applied by the Court of Chancery before its abolition by the Judicature Acts 1873 and 1875. In this, its modern, sense equity has no longer any connection with fairness as an ideal of justice. As the Court of Chancery dealt with those cases only where common law either provided no remedy or only insufficient remedies, equity was never a complete legal system in the way that common law was. If equity had never come into existence the common-law courts could have provided us with a legal system of sorts, but equity without common law would be unimaginable. This is the reason why Professor Maitland referred to equity as a 'gloss on common law,' meaning that to understand equity it is necessary first to study common law, since every rule of equity is somehow related to a defect or deficiency in common law.

The general principles of equity are often stated in the form of legal maxims which reflect the spirit underlying this branch of our law. This was that people should do what they were in conscience bound to do. Unfortunately, in its maturity equity became so formalized that the maxims were often applied with little respect to their original reason.

The main differences between equity and common law were:

1. Until 1875 equity and common law were administered by different sets of courts. This meant that parties who wished both legal and equitable remedies had to apply for them at separate courts. If an action was started at the wrong kind of court the action was dismissed at great expense to the plaintiff.

2. Common law, as we have seen already, was a complete system of law, while equity was merely made up of a number of isolated principles, stating when and how a court of equity would grant specific equitable remedies or when it would not allow a person to take advantage of his rights at common law.

3. It is said that equity *acts in personam* while common law *acts*

in rem. This means that equitable rights were and are valid against those persons only who are in conscience bound to recognize them, while legal[1] rights are valid against the world as a whole. As an example, we might mention the difference between equitable and legal forms of property. If someone steals a book of which I am the legal owner I am able to reclaim it from anybody who has acquired it, even if he bought it for value and in good faith. On the other hand, the beneficiary under a trust whose interest in the trust property is merely equitable will be able to reclaim trust property unlawfully disposed of by the trustee from such persons only who either knew or should have known that they were acquiring trust property in breach of a trust. These people are in conscience bound to recognize the better title of the beneficiary.

4. A person who has a right of action at common law must exercise it within the time-limits laid down by the Limitation Act 1939. Equitable remedies will be granted only if they are applied for promptly, and it is a question of fact in each case whether this has been done. The maxim that 'delay defeats equities' is the basis of what is known as the doctrine of *laches.*

5. All equitable remedies are discretionary. This means that, in contradistinction to the practice with legal remedies, the court is not bound to grant an equitable remedy merely on proof that the conditions for it exist. Every breach of contract entitles the innocent party to claim damages (a remedy of common law), but it is not every breach of contract which will entitle him to demand that the court should order the specific performance of the contract (a remedy of equity). To-day the discretion which the court exercises in granting or refusing these remedies is applied in accordance with definite rules described below. The main remedies of equity are specific performance and injunction.

A *decree of specific performance* is an order addressed by the court to a party who has undertaken some legal obligation and who refuses to honour it. He is ordered by the court to perform what he has agreed to do. This decree is granted by the court in the following circumstances only:

1. It is never granted where, in the opinion of the court, the plaintiff's interests would be sufficiently protected by awarding him monetary damages.

2. It is not awarded where constant supervision by the court would be necessary. For instance, the court would not order specific performance of a contract, the performance of which is spread over a period of time.

[1] The adjective 'legal' is used in two meanings. In its broader sense it means 'pertaining to law', while in its narrower sense, as in the above passage, it means 'relating to *common* law.'

3. Specific performance is not granted to enforce a contract for personal work or services, such as a contract of employment.

4. A *valid* contract must exist, even if it is not enforceable at common law because of the absence of some formal requirement.

5. The contract must impose mutual obligations on the parties. Thus, specific performance will not be granted where the contract is voidable at the option of one of the parties—*e.g.*, in the case of contracts made by minors (*i.e.*, persons under eighteen).

An *injunction* is an order granted by the court for the purpose of restraining the doing, continuance, or repetition of some wrongful act. The act may be wrongful either because it is opposed to the general law, such as a tortious act, or because it would involve the breach of a contract. Injunctions are granted subject to the following conditions:

1. Where an injunction is applied for in order to prevent the breach of a contractual obligation, the obligation must be one expressed in negative terms. Thus, if X, having the choice of doing either A or B, agrees with Y that he will do A and then sets about doing B, Y will be unable to obtain an injunction to restrain him, as X has never expressly agreed *not* to do B, even though in the circumstances this might have been implied from the contract between the parties.

2. An injunction will not be granted if monetary damages would be a sufficient redress for the damage done to the plaintiff.

3. Injunctions will not be granted where the court could not enforce obedience to its orders.

Both a decree of specific performance and an injunction will be enforced by the court by contempt proceedings. A person failing to act in accordance with the court's order shows contempt to the court, and may be fined or sent to prison until such time as he is prepared to 'purge his contempt' by carrying out the court's order.

Injunctions are divided into *mandatory* and *prohibitory injunctions*. A mandatory injunction is one where a person is ordered to do something positive in order to restore a previous situation which he has wrongfully disturbed. A person who has agreed not to erect a certain kind of structure on his land and has done so may be ordered to pull it down again. A prohibitory injunction is one restraining the defendant from doing something which he should not do. Where the court may wish to take its time in deciding whether or not to grant a prohibitory injunction, the plaintiff may ask the judge to grant in the meantime an *interim* (or *interlocutory*) *injunction*. This injunction restrains the defendant from commencing or continuing the acts to which the plaintiff has objected, but, of course, only until the court has finally decided the matter. The court may ask the plaintiff to provide some monetary security out of which damages could be paid to the defendant for the delay if eventually the injunction is not granted. Where the matter is so urgent that the plaintiff cannot even wait until the case comes up before the judge in open court, he may ask the judge in chambers (*i.e.*, out of court) for an *ex parte injunction*, so called because the judge has not had an opportunity of hearing the other side. Needless to say, these injunctions will be granted in exceptional cases only.

The Judicature Acts 1873 and 1875

We have seen already that early English law was burdened with a multiplicity of courts. Not only was this a wasteful duplication of judicial work, but it also caused great inconvenience to the parties concerned in finding the court which would hear their particular complaint and grant the remedy which they wanted. Apart from the common-law courts and the courts of equity, there were also the ecclesiastical courts, which had, among other things, jurisdiction over matrimonial matters and over wills. This jurisdiction was, however, transferred to a separate Divorce Court and a Probate Court in 1857. Then there was also the court of Admiralty, which administered maritime law. Practising lawyers specialized in the different branches of English law and had access to their particular type of court only.

The Judicature Commission, which had been set up in 1867, recommended the replacement of all the superior courts in England (county courts were not affected by this recommendation) by one single court. The recommendations of the Commission were embodied in the Judicature Act 1873, which came into operation on November 1, 1875. The common-law courts, the Court of Chancery, and the Admiralty Court were abolished and were replaced by the Supreme Court of Judicature, consisting of the Court of Appeal and the High Court of Justice. The High Court of Justice was divided into five divisions—namely, the Queen's Bench Division, the Chancery Division, the Probate, Divorce, and Admiralty Division, the Exchequer Division, and, lastly, the Common Pleas Division. In 1881 the two last-mentioned divisions were merged into the Queen's Bench Division, thus reducing the number of High Court divisions to three.

All divisions of the High Court may apply both common law and equity, and may also grant both kinds of remedies. Any division may try any kind of legal issue, though the business of the court has been divided out among them for administrative reasons roughly on the basis of what their independent predecessors used to deal with before 1875. The organization of the courts after 1875 will be further discussed in the next chapter.

It cannot often enough be stressed that the Judicature Acts did not bring about a merger of common law and equity. What they did was to merge the *administration* of law by the courts, but the rules of common law and those of equity have not been directly affected by this legislation. The origin of a rule of English law is still important to-day, since equitable remedies will not be granted unless the conditions mentioned above are fulfilled. One legal writer compared the situation as it exists after 1875 to two streams which used to flow in their own beds. Now they are sharing the same river-bed, but the waters have not mixed.

The Doctrine of Judicial Precedent

We have shown already that both common law and equity are judge-made law. It remains now to consider how it is that the principles applied by one generation of judges in dealing with the cases coming before them are followed by their successors. It is an unwritten, but nevertheless basic, principle of English law that judges should stand by their decisions and by those of their colleagues. This is known as the principle of *stare decisis*. If there is one thing which is more important than that law should be fair it is that it should be certain; and how could law be certain if judges could deal with problems coming before them without having regard to the way in which other judges have dealt with similar problems in earlier cases? It is, however, only in fairly recent times that the principle has become accepted in this country that judges are *bound* to be guided by the decisions of their predecessors. Such earlier decisions, or precedents, have always been studied with respect by judges; but in past centuries judges reserved for themselves the right to deviate from them if they felt that they could not agree with the conclusions reached. The stricter rule prevailing at the present time is certainly explainable in part by the much better system of law reporting, which makes it possible to ascertain what a judge has really said, while in earlier law reports the opinions of the judge were often hopelessly mixed up with the comments of the reporter.

The position to-day then is this: when a judge decides a case he not only disposes of the immediate problem before him, but he also lays down a legal principle which other judges will have to follow, subject to the reservations discussed below. The legal principle on which the judgment rests and which thus represents the core of the decision is called the *ratio decidendi*. This has to be distinguished from the remainder of the judge's decision, in which he may have discussed matters which were not directly relevant to the problem before him—*e.g.*, he may have discussed what would have been the legal position if the facts had been different. The parts of the court's decision which are not essential to the judgment are known as *obiter dicta*. It is only the *ratio decidendi* which operates as a precedent. No comments which a judge might make, however great his reputation, will be precedents unless they were part of the decision of an actual case in court.

The decision of all judges will be studied with respect, but some of them are *binding precedents* and must be followed irrespective of what the judge applying them thinks about their wisdom, while other decisions are mere *persuasive precedents* and need be followed only if the judge approves of the reasoning underlying the decision. The decisions of the House of Lords are binding on all courts, but not on the House of Lords itself. This means that once the House of Lords has laid down a new principle this principle will have to be applied by all courts unless Parliament decides to abolish it by statute. Until 1966 the House of Lords could not overrule its own decisions, but in that year the Lord Chancellor announced that in future this would no longer be the case. Decisions of the Court of Appeal are binding on all courts, including the Court of Appeal,[1] but not on the House of Lords. Decisions of High Court judges are not binding precedents at all, though they may persuade by their reasoning. Similarly, decisions of foreign courts, even if they are applying law similar to English law (U.S. courts or Commonwealth tribunals), are not binding precedents in England. This also applies to the decisions of Scottish and Irish courts. The decisions of county court judges are not even as a rule reported, so that they have no binding force either.

When a judge hearing a case is told that there exists a precedent his task is not as simple as it might appear. History never repeats itself entirely, and it is therefore unlikely that the facts of the current case are exactly the same as those that came before the earlier judge. Our judge has therefore to determine whether the essential legal issue in the case is the same as in the earlier decision. If he is satisfied that this is so, he still has to find the *ratio decidendi* of his predecessor. A judgment is generally fairly long, and it is not easy to glean from the report why the judge decided the case as he did.

It is quite evident from reading law reports that a judge is occasionally none too keen to apply a precedent where he feels that it might do injustice in the case before him. He may refuse to follow the past decision if that decision has been given *per incuriam*, which means that the court giving the decision had omitted to consider some relevant Act of Parliament or some decision which was binding on it. Another way of avoiding the necessity of following a precedent is by claiming that there exists some material difference between the

[1] Some judges in the Court of Appeal have claimed that they should enjoy the same right as the House of Lords—*i.e.*, to change their minds. These views have not so far found favour with the House of Lords.

facts in the earlier case and those applying in the case before the court now. Often such differences are artificially introduced in order to avoid having to follow an unpopular precedent.

From what has been said so far it might appear that judges make law as they go along. Every decision dealing with a hitherto undecided point of law adds something to the bulk of English law. This is not, however, the way in which it appears to the judges themselves. They claim that the task of a judge is to find law which is there already, to discover law rather than to invent it. We have seen already that those who proclaim this theory are underrating the work of the judges. The so-called declaratory theory may have been valid in the early days, when the task of the judges was limited to the discovery of existing customs; it hardly represents a fair description of their present task.

Judicial law, or case law, has many advantages compared with the legal systems of other countries, where more reliance is placed on Acts of Parliament and where the decisions of judges have no future binding force. Case law is more practical in that there exists no legal rule for which there cannot be found a practical illustration—*i.e.*, the case in which the rule has been first developed. Case law is more flexible than statute law. If statute law is to be altered lengthy Parliamentary proceedings are required, while changes in case law are effected gradually by the judges finding distinctions between the existing rules and new situations which are presented to them.

On the other hand, however, we must not close our eyes to some of the defects of the system of case law. It tends to add to the quantity of legal rules. Hundreds of decisions having binding force are given each year. This means that it becomes more and more difficult to know the whole of the law. Such a situation may act to the prejudice of the ordinary citizen, especially since by a fiction of English law everybody is supposed to know the law. This maxim—*ignorantia juris non excusat*—*i.e.*, ignorance of the law is no excuse—does not mean that it is seriously assumed that anyone, even a trained lawyer, masters the full intricate details of our law. It means simply that it is the duty of the citizen to find out what the law is concerning any matter in which he is interested, and if he is to be able to do that he and his legal advisers should thus not be faced with insuperable difficulties in ascertaining the true state of the law.

Jeremy Bentham referred to case law as 'dog's law'. He said that we learn our legal duties in the same way in which a dog learns to understand his master's wishes. If the dog does something which the master does not like he will punish it so that the dog learns by experience. Similarly, where a new point of law is involved, the parties do not really know what the law is until the highest court has decided the dispute for them and the loser in this dispute will have to pay the costs of finding out what the law is.

The very existence of binding precedents has encouraged judges to think out some rather artificial distinctions in order to avoid having to follow a precedent which they disapprove of. Where this happens, the reputation of law and of the lawyers applying and enforcing it is bound to suffer.

It is probably too late now for the principle of *stare decisis* to be radically reformed, but Parliament and various Law Reform Commissions set up by the Lord Chancellor have done a lot towards removing some of the worst defects of our case law by legislation, especially by consolidating such parts of the law where this has proved to be possible.

Statutory Law

Statutes, or Acts of Parliament, have been always a secondary source of English law. In the same way in which equity developed as a gloss on common law, adding to it where common law fell below certain ideal standards of justice, so statute law has been used as a means of supplementing case law, remedying its defects and consolidating its provisions where this had become necessary. In more recent years statute law has become the main tool of the social reformer, especially in altering the economic structure of our society.

Modern constitutional doctrine proclaims that Parliament has unlimited legislative powers. A bill which has been properly passed by both Houses of Parliament and which has received the Royal Assent will be a source of good law, however ill-conceived or badly drafted it may be. Courts of law cannot interfere with the sovereign power of Parliament to make law, and judges have to apply statutes even if they do not approve of their intentions or wording. Statutes do not lose their force by reason of age. As long as an Act of Parliament has not been repealed it remains good law. While judges cannot declare a statute to be void, they may do much towards nullifying the intentions of the legislature by the interpretation which they place on the words used in the statute. Parliamentary draftsmen do their best to see that statutes are clear (at least, to the legally trained reader), but even then it may be necessary to decide some points where the meaning of a section is doubtful. Judicial practice and legislation (the Interpretation Act 1889) have co-operated in laying down certain general principles of interpretation, the most important of which are the following:

1. The meaning of a statute must always be derived from its wording. No account may be taken of any extraneous information, such

as Parliamentary reports, Ministerial pronouncements, or memoranda or anything of that sort.

2. The words of a statute should always be interpreted according to their literal meaning (*e.g.*, as given in the *Oxford Dictionary*) unless this were to lead to a manifest absurdity or unless this meaning appears to clash with the intention of the legislature as gathered from the statute itself. This principle is known as the *Golden Rule of Interpretation.*

3. Words should always be interpreted in the context in which they appear, and not in isolation.

4. Where the words used are ambiguous, the statute should be considered as a whole to discover the purpose which the legislators had in mind when they passed it (the *Mischief Rule*).

5. There exists a presumption against an alteration of the common law. This means that, where an Act of Parliament may be interpreted in two ways, one of which involves a change in the existing law while the other is compatible with common law as it stands, the court will adopt the latter interpretation. If, therefore, the legislature wish to alter existing common law rules they will have to make sure that the Act clearly indicates their intention.

6. Where in an Act of Parliament general words are used following specific words, the general words will be construed as applying to persons or things of the same kind as described by the specific words. Thus, where the Electricity Regulations 1928 demanded that certain premises should be adequately lighted to prevent "danger" and "danger" was defined as "danger from shock, burn, or other injury," it was held that this did not include danger from tripping, since the specific words related to forms of danger resulting from contact with electricity (*Lane* v. *London Electricity Board*).

7. Conversely, if in an Act of Parliament specific words are used *not* followed by general words the Act will apply to those situations only which are specifically described and not to other, though similar, ones.

Delegated Legislation

Parliament has the monopoly of legislation in this country, but Parliament may delegate its powers to other persons or bodies. Where this happens, we speak of delegated legislation. The main instance of delegated legislation is the transfer of legislative powers to individual Ministers of the Crown or to Her Majesty in Council. Ministers exercise their powers by making regulations or orders, while in the latter case delegated legislative powers are used by making Orders in Council. Similar powers are also given to local authorities (for the making of bye-laws) or even to certain professional organizations (*e.g.*, the Law Society) for the purpose of regulating the conduct of their members. Ministerial orders and regulations and Orders in Council are published by H.M. Stationery Office in a series of statutory instruments.

The main reasons for the delegation of legislative powers by Parliament are:

1. Parliament is generally short of time and cannot therefore discuss all Bills in sufficient detail. Frequently an Act contains only the framework of a certain legal measure, the filling-in of the details being left to the Minister whose Department is responsible for the subject-matter. Thus, the National Insurance Act 1965 contains only the basic principles of the system of national insurance, the details being contained in some hundreds of regulations which have been made by the Minister of Health and Society Security.

2. Quite apart from shortage of time, Parliament may not wish to deal with details of legislation where the subject-matter is one which is so technical that few members of either House of Parliament would feel competent to discuss it.

3. In a situation where some legal rule has to be changed quickly it is very convenient if this can be done by Ministerial order rather than by Act of Parliament. For instance, at the time of food rationing it would have been impossible to wait for Parliamentary sanction before the ration of any one commodity could be altered. Such changes were effected by Ministerial order.

One important difference between Parliamentary legislation and delegated legislation has to be noted. Courts of law may not question the validity of an Act of Parliament on the grounds that Parliament has exceeded its powers. This is impossible, since there are no legal limits to the powers of Parliament. The position with delegated legislation is different. The Minister or the local authority making a legal rule are acting merely on the basis of authority given them by Parliament. If they exceed the authority given to them, whether by making an order for a purpose for which they had no power to make orders, or by not complying with the conditions laid down by Parliament as to the procedure to be followed in making the order, the order will be void, being *ultra vires* (outside the powers of) the Minister or local authority concerned. The courts of law may therefore examine every order which they are asked to apply with a view to determining whether it falls within the scope of the delegation of legislative power by Parliament. It stands to reason that, since delegated legislation is derived from Parliamentary legislation, it is impossible to amend or repeal an Act of Parliament by the exercise of delegated legislation unless the Act of Parliament itself permits it.

The volume of delegated legislation has increased enormously during and since the last war. In the course of a Parliamentary session rarely more than sixty statutes are passed, but the number of items appearing in the series of statutory instruments has on occasions exceeded two thousand in one year. It is not surprising, therefore, that fears have been expressed by many lawyers about this trend of events. Delegated legislation is just as much part of the law of the land as is the common law or Parliamentary legislation. The enormous quantity of statutory instruments makes the task of the people to know the law even more difficult. Indeed, not only is the task more difficult, but frequently it may be impossible, since, because of the large number of the instruments involved, some may be out of print for a time and the law may thus be inaccessible to those looking for it.

It is sometimes suggested that the growing importance of delegated legislation is a symbol of the growing powers of the civil service, since civil servants draft these instruments and the Minister only signs them. This is not entirely true, as Parliament has reserved for itself powers of control over delegated legislation. Under the Statutory Instruments Act 1946, Ministerial orders and regulations must be submitted to Parliament when made, and either will cease to be operative if either House of Parliament resolves so within forty days or, in the case of the more important of these instruments, will not be operative at all unless they have been first approved by both Houses of Parliament.

Law Merchant

Law Merchant, another source of our law, was the medieval law applicable to commercial transactions. Most of the rules applying to commercial transactions had been imported from abroad by foreign traders who came to England on business and brought their law with them. In order to attract these traders, special courts were set up for them in the main ports frequented by them, the *Courts of Staple*, where they were able to have their legal problems settled according to the law of their own country.

Domestic trade had its own customs developed from commercial practice. Trade was generally conducted at the annual fairs, and most of these had their own courts sitting during the fair where disputes between traders or between them and local customers could be decided on the spot. This was necessary, as the traders never stayed long enough in any one place to allow the slower procedure of the ordinary courts to become effective. These commercial courts were known as *piepowder courts*, because the traders used to come to court with their feet still dusty (*pieds poudrés*) from the market.

After the seventeenth century most of these courts disappeared, with the exception of the Court of Admiralty, which dealt with maritime law and which survived until the reforms of the nineteenth century. When the special commercial courts lapsed the customs which they had been applying were gradually absorbed into the common law, mainly under the influence of two of the greatest English judges of all time, the Lords Chief Justices Holt and Mansfield.

Custom

Common law was originally based on local custom. Custom may, however, even to-day be considered as a source of law, though not a very important one. The only customs that have any legal importance to-day are local customs. The main examples of such local customs, or, better perhaps, customary rights, are local rights of way and rights of common. Every legal custom necessarily represents an exception from the general law of the land and will as such be accepted by the courts only if the following conditions are given:

1. The custom must have existed since times immemorial. Since the sixteenth century it has been accepted that this meant that the custom must have been operative already at the time of the accession to the throne of Richard I in 1189. Naturally, it would be quite impossible to prove to-day that any custom existed already as far back as that, and so it is sufficient for the party wishing to establish the existence of the custom to prove that it has existed for as long as living memory reaches. If that is so it is presumed that it existed already in 1189, and the burden of proving that this has not been the case rests then with the person opposing the existence of the custom.
2. The custom must have existed without interruption. If it can be shown, for instance, that a right of way *could not* have existed at some time in the sixteenth century because what now is a footpath was then a river the custom will be defeated.
3. The terms of the custom must be reasonably certain, and they must not be in opposition to some fundamental principle of English law.
4. People observing the custom must have done so because they felt that they were bound to observe it. Mere social or ceremonial customs are not sources of legal rights or duties.
5. The custom must not have been exercised by force or violence.

It should be noted that trade usages are not a form of legal custom. Such usages are binding, not because they are a source of law, but because they are considered to be implied in contracts between persons who may be presumed to be acquainted with them.

Community Law

When the British Parliament passed the European Communities Act 1972 it decided that as from 1st January 1973 when Britain became a full member of the three European Communities (the European Economic Community, the European Coal and Steel Community and the European Atomic Energy Community), Community law should be applicable throughout the United Kingdom. Unlike other international treaties negotiated by the United Kingdom which impose solely duties on the government and grant it certain rights against the governments of other countries, adhesion to the European Communities has affected all individuals within the country in as much as they have acquired rights and become subject to obligations as outlined in the Community legislation. Where this legislation is in conflict with the established rules of English (or indeed Scots) law, the law of the Community would prevail and this law has to be applied by the courts of the United Kingdom in the same way as domestic law.

The law-making powers within the Community are vested in the so-called *Council of Ministers* on which each of the nine member states has one representative. If there exists a disagreement among the members of the Council and a particular matter has to be put to a vote, their voting rights are not equal, so that in effect a vote by two of the four main member states (France, Germany, Italy and the United Kingdom) could block the passing of a proposed law.

The law-making functions of the Council are exercised by means of regulations, directives and decisions. A *regulation* has general application and resembles thus an Act of Parliament. It is directly applicable in all member states of the Communities. A resident in this country could therefore apply to an English court if he were to feel that his rights under a Community regulation had been infringed.

A *directive* of the Council is, on the other hand, not directly applicable in the member states. It merely decrees that member states should by domestic legislation achieve certain results, leaving the detailed implementation to domestic legislatures and governments. National governments are then compelled to enact provisions or modify their existing laws to give effect to the directive. Directives may be issued not only by the Council of Ministers of the Community, but also by the European Commission, consisting of full-time commissioners selected from the various member states but owing allegiance to the Community and not to their national governments. The Commission is in a way the government of the Community since each commissioner is responsible, like a minister in a national government, for a particular aspect of Community affairs (e.g. foreign relations, agriculture, etc.).

A *decision* of the Council of Ministers or the European Commission, unlike a regulation or a directive, is not of general application but settles a particular concrete case which has been brought before the Council or the Commission. Decisions are generally of an administrative nature, implementing Community law by granting exceptions to particular Community laws or imposing fines on those who have broken their legal obligations.

CHAPTER TWO

The Judicial System of England and Wales

The Civil Courts

The courts of law of this country may be divided into civil and criminal courts. Some courts have both civil and criminal jurisdiction (*e.g.*, the Petty Sessions, the Queen's Bench Division of the High Court, the Court of Appeal, and the House of Lords); but otherwise there exist separate courts to deal with civil and criminal matters respectively. Civil courts deal with disputes between individuals as to property and legal obligations. Criminal courts exist in order to decide whether an accused person has committed a criminal offence and, if so, what punishment should be imposed. A hard and fast distinction between criminal and civil matters is impossible, but basically the difference is one between granting redress (compensation or restitution) for some wrong (civil jurisdiction) and punishing a person who has done wrong (criminal jurisdiction).

The diagram on page 33 illustrates the structure of the courts as it is at present.

CIVIL COURTS

The High Court of Justice

The origins of this court have been discussed already in the preceding chapter. More has to be said now about the work of the three divisions.

The Queen's Bench Division

The Queen's Bench Division consists of the Lord Chief Justice of England and of over forty puisne (subordinate) judges. This division of the High Court has the largest number of judges attached to it, because not only has it the largest volume of work to get through, but it is also responsible for finding some Crown court judges. Its main functions are the following:

1. All civil actions are tried before a judge of the Queen's Bench

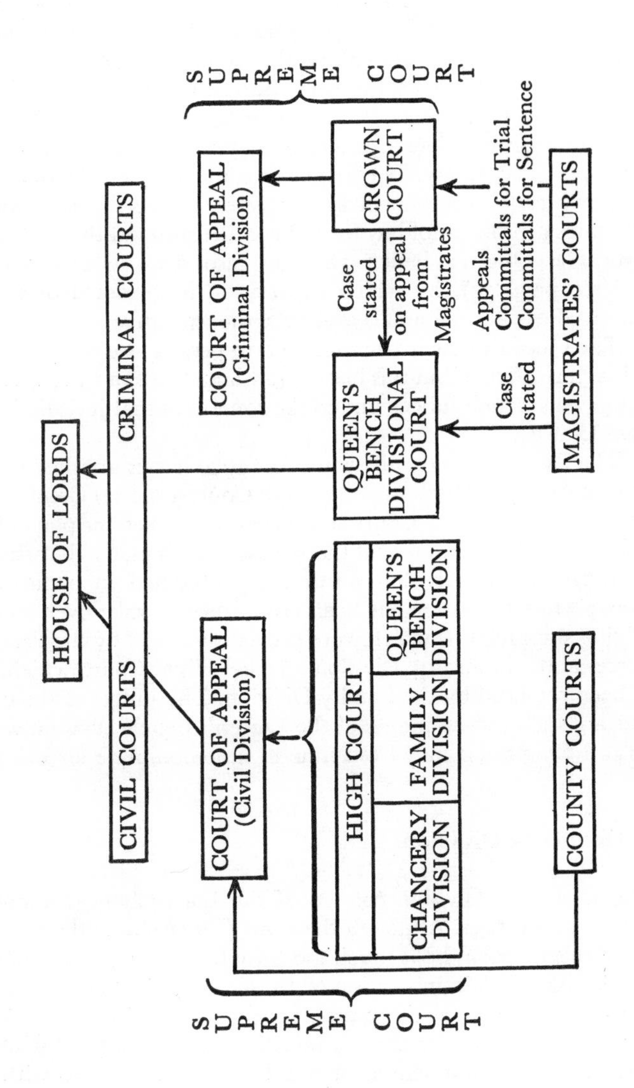
HOUSE OF LORDS
CIVIL COURTS
CRIMINAL COURTS
COURT OF APPEAL (Civil Division)
COURT OF APPEAL (Criminal Division)
SUPREME COURT
HIGH COURT
CHANCERY DIVISION
FAMILY DIVISION
QUEEN'S BENCH DIVISION
QUEEN'S BENCH DIVISIONAL COURT
CROWN COURT
SUPREME COURT
Case stated on appeal from Magistrates
Case stated
Appeals
Committals for Trial
Committals for Sentence
MAGISTRATES' COURTS
COUNTY COURTS

Division, except those which are specifically assigned to another division.

2. The Queen's Bench Division has retained a certain amount of appellate jurisdiction. In its capacity as an appeal court the Queen's Bench Division sits as a Divisional Court—*i.e.*, two or three judges sit together to hear the appeal, while the ordinary cases come up before one judge sitting on his own. Most of the appeals thus heard are appeals from the lower criminal courts—*e.g.*, the Petty Sessions and also the Crown Courts, where the latter have themselves acted in an appellate capacity. These appeals come on questions of law by means of a procedure known as *case stated*, where the subordinate court states a problem of law for the consideration of the Divisional Court. The Queen's Bench Division also deals with *prerogative orders* (see page 53), by which supervision is exercised over subordinate courts and tribunals and over the executive.

3. The Queen's Bench Division used to possess also some original criminal jurisdiction, but this has by now largely disappeared, except that Queen's Bench judges undertake some criminal jurisdiction at Crown Courts.

4. The Administration of Justice Act 1970 has established within the Queen's Bench Division of the High Court a special Commercial Court and an Admiralty Court. The former has taken the place of the previous so-called Commercial List of cases which used to be assigned to a judge of the Division particularly qualified in commercial matters; while the latter has been established to take over matters involving shipping law which were previously heard by the Probate, Divorce and Admiralty Division of the High Court which has now been replaced by the Family Division. The judges of these two courts are such puisne judges of the Queen's Bench Division whom the Lord Chancellor may from time to time nominate for this purpose.

The Chancery Division

The Chancery Division consists of the Lord Chancellor and of eleven puisne judges. Although the Lord Chancellor is the nominal head of this division, he is much too busy to take any direct part in its work and the Administration of Justice Act 1970 has authorized him to appoint one of the puisne judges of the Division as Vice-Chancellor to look after the organization and management of the Division. The main functions of this Division are to deal with the following matters:

1. The administration of the estates of deceased persons.
2. The dissolution of partnerships or the taking of partnership or other accounts.

3. Mortgages and charges on land.
4. Trusts, including charitable trusts.
5. The sale of property subject to any lien or charge.
6. The rectification or cancellation of deeds or other written instruments.
7. Questions of company law.
8. Specific performance of contracts.
9. Partition and sale of real estates.
10. Wardship of infants.
11. Revenue matters.
12. Bankruptcy.
13. Contentious probate matters.

The reader who may find difficulties in understanding the above functions will find most of them fully explained in later parts of this book.

The Family Division

The Family Division of the High Court was set up by the Administration of Justice Act 1970 in place of the former Probate, Divorce and Admiralty Division.

The Family Division has the following functions:

1. Business at first instance:

(a) All proceedings consisting of a matrimonial cause, including the dissolution of marriages and proceedings for a decree of presumption of death.

(b) Proceedings in relation to the wardship of minors.

(c) Proceedings under the Adoption Acts 1958 and 1968.

(d) Proceedings to obtain the court's consent to the marriage of a minor.

(e) Proceedings to determine the title to property in disputes between spouses and proceedings where a spouse claims the right to continue occupying the matrimonial home.

(f) Proceedings in connection with maintenance orders.

2. Appellate business:

(a) Appeals from magistrates' courts in connection with adoption orders, maintenance orders and affiliation orders.

(b) Appeals from county courts in connection with orders under the Guardianship of Minors Act 1971.

The Family Division has also retained responsibility for non-contentious probate business while contentious probate business now goes to the Chancery Division.

The Division consists at present of a President and sixteen puisne judges.

The Restrictive Practices Court

This court, set up by the Restrictive Trade Practices Act 1956, is treated as a superior court, and is therefore in line with the High Court of Justice. It is made up of five judges, three from the English High Court, one from the Scottish Court of Sessions, and one from the Supreme Court of Northern Ireland. The Lord Chancellor selects one of these judges to act as President of the Court. In addition to the judicial members of the court, the Crown also appoints, on the recommendation of the Lord Chancellor, up to ten other members who are chosen from among persons experienced in industry, commerce, or in public affairs. These additional members, who may be paid for their services, are appointed for a period of three years and may be removed by the Lord Chancellor on the ground of misconduct. The court may sit in divisions, the quorum for a division consisting of one judge and two lay members. On matters of law the opinion of the judge will prevail, while in other matters the court decides by a majority of the members hearing the case.

The task of the court is to decide whether a restrictive trading agreement is against the public interest. Such agreements have to be registered with the Director General of Fair Trading, a new post set up by the Fair Trading Act 1973, and he may bring any such agreement before the court for a decision as to its validity. In reaching its decision the court is applying mainly its judgment as to the likely economic effects of the agreement, and this accounts for the inclusion of laymen among its members.

The National Industrial Relations Court

This court, which was equal in status to one of the Divisions of the High Court, was set up by the Industrial Relations Act 1971. It is sometimes referred to as the Industrial Court, but should not be confused with the pre-1971 Industrial Court (now renamed the Industrial Arbitration Board).

The NIRC consisted of judges nominated by the Lord Chancellor from among judges of the High Court and the Court of Appeal, one of whom is nominated as President of the court. The first President of the court was Sir John Donaldson. In addition to judicial members, the courts consisted of a number of lay members appointed by the Queen. The lay members of the court were selected from persons having close personal experience of industrial relations in this country. A court consisted generally of one of the judicial members together with two to four lay members. The court had its office in London and generally sat there, but it could, if convenient, sit also in any other place in the United Kingdom.

The court had a wide jurisdiction in matters concerning industrial relations. It had power to approve agency shop and closed shop agreements and sole bargaining agencies and heard most complaints about alleged unfair industrial practices. The court was also empowered to hear applications from the Secretary of State for Employment for a "cooling-off" period in a threatened industrial dispute and for ordering a ballot of union members to ascertain whether they approve of industrial action. The NIRC heard appeals from industrial tribunals in connection with claims for redundancy payments or for compensation for unfair dismissal of an employee. Appeals from the decisions of the NIRC went to the Court of Appeal (Civil Division).

Following the general election in 1974, the new Labour Government introduced the Trade Unions and Labour Relations Act 1974 which abolished the NIRC.

Magistrates' Courts

These courts deal mainly with criminal offences, but they have also a limited civil jurisdiction, mainly in connection with family matters. In particular, they are entitled to make separation, maintenance and custody orders and also deal with affiliation cases and the guardianship of minors. Outside the family sphere, they have important functions in connection with the licensing of premises for the sale of alcoholic drinks. In family matters, appeals from the Magistrates' Courts go to the Family Division of the High Court.

The County Courts

The county courts were first established in 1846, taking the place of earlier local courts with a more limited jurisdiction. The main reason for their creation was to make cheap and speedy justice available to everyone in the country, without their having to travel long distances. There are over four hundred county courts in existence in England and Wales, and they are staffed by circuit judges. Some judges are in charge of a number of courts, these courts being for this purpose grouped into special county court circuits. In the Metropolitan area circuits consist of one court only, while in the provinces a circuit may embrace as many as ten courts. The jurisdiction of the county courts is as follows (County Courts Act 1959–65):[1]

1. Actions founded on contract or tort up to £1000.
2. Equity matters (trusts, mortgages, etc.) up to £5000.
3. Recovery of land and questions of title to land where its net annual rateable value does not exceed £400.
4. Bankruptcies.

[1] As amended by the Administration of Justice Act 1969.

5. Probate proceedings where the value of the deceased's estate is estimated to be under £1000.
6. Winding-up of companies with a capital of under £10,000.
7. County courts also have jurisdiction under much of our social legislation. It is their task, for instance, to enforce the Rent Restriction Acts; they supervise the adoption of children, etc. Certain county courts have also jurisdiction in Admiralty matters.

The Court of Appeal (Civil Division)

The Court of Appeal consists of the Master of the Rolls and of up to 16 Lords Justices of Appeal. Other judges of superior courts are *ex officio* members of the court, but they do not usually participate in its work. Three judges sitting together make up the court for hearing appeals from the High Court or from a county court. Appeals are possible from decisions of High Court judges on either questions of fact or questions of law. Appeals from county courts are possible on points of law and in certain cases also on points of fact. Where the Court of Appeal decides to allow the appeal, it may either order a new trial or amend or reverse the decision of the lower court. Findings of fact by the lower court are, however, rarely reversed, as the lower court had an opportunity of hearing the evidence directly, while the Court of Appeal decides on the basis of the judge's record only.

The House of Lords

The House of Lords is the highest court of appeal for the United Kingdom in both civil and criminal matters. It consists, for judicial purposes, of the Lord Chancellor and of up to eleven Lords of Appeal in Ordinary (known for short as Law Lords) and any other members of the House of Lords who have held high judicial office—*e.g.*, former Lord Chancellors. The Law Lords are life-members of the House of Lords who have been appointed as members of the House because of their legal or judicial experience. One at least of the Law Lords is a person with experience of Scots Law, and another comes from Northern Ireland. The House generally hears appeals with five of its members present. Appeals to the House of Lords from the Court of Appeal are possible only either if the Court of Appeal allows the appeal because of the general importance of the legal issue involved or if the appellant-to-be is able to persuade the House of Lords to allow him to appeal to them. The Administration of Justice Act 1969 has introduced the principle of 'leap-frogging' by permitting, in certain cases, appeals from the High Court to go direct to the House of Lords, thus by-passing the

Court of Appeal. A High Court judge may certify that a sufficient case for an appeal direct to the House of Lords has been made out to justify application for leave to bring such an appeal. Such a certificate will be granted only where a point of general importance is involved. This must relate wholly or mainly to the construction of a statute or a statutory instrument and must have been fully argued in the High Court proceedings. Alternatively, the point of law must be one in respect of which the High Court judge is bound by an earlier decision of the Court of Appeal or the House of Lords.

The Judicial Committee of the Privy Council

The Judicial Committee of the Privy Council is the final court of appeal from the highest courts of British colonies, protectorates, trust territories, and such of the Dominions as have not abolished the right of appeal to the Committee. It is also the final court of appeal from ecclesiastical courts in England. When hearing appeals from other parts of the Commonwealth, the Committee consists of Law Lords and of Privy Counsellors with special experience of the law of the territory from which the appeal comes. There is no automatic right of appeal to the Committee; the prospective appellant has to petition the Crown for leave to appeal, and the judgment of the Committee, where leave to appeal has been granted, is in the form of a recommendation to Her Majesty to grant or to reject the appeal. Since the Judicial Committee is not, strictly speaking, an English court, its decisions are not binding precedents, but the composition of the court ensures that an English court will not readily deviate from any legal principle laid down by the Judicial Committee.

CRIMINAL COURTS

Magistrates' Courts

Magistrates' Courts, also known as courts of summary jurisdiction, are staffed by justices of the peace. These may be either lay magistrates or stipendiary magistrates. Lay magistrates are appointed on the advice of the Lord Chancellor (or the Chancellor of the Duchy of Lancaster in respect of the county of Lancashire). In the appointment of county magistrates the Lord Chancellor acts on the advice of the Lord Lieutenant of the county concerned and the Lord Lieutenant is himself advised by an advisory committee. Where the appointment of borough magistrates is concerned the Lord Chancellor acts directly on the advice of a local advisory committee. A magistrate is appointed for a particular area and must reside within fifteen miles of that area.

Magistrates are unpaid, but are entitled to claim travelling, subsistence and financial loss allowances. In the past, magistrates did not require any special training, but this is now compulsory for newly appointed magistrates. At the age of seventy, a magistrate is generally transferred to the so-called supplemental list of magistrates, which means in effect that although he stays a magistrate he will no longer be called upon to sit in court proceedings.

Stipendiary, or paid, magistrates are appointed by the Crown on the recommendation of the Lord Chancellor from among barristers or solicitors of at least seven years' standing. They are appointed for some of the larger towns where the volume of work makes it desirable that a full-time and professionally qualified magistrate should be appointed. Stipendiary magistrates may sit on their own, while lay magistrates generally sit in threes.

Courts of Magistrates have two main functions in criminal proceedings: they may conduct a summary trial and they may act as so-called examining magistrates in committing an accused for trial at a superior court. In a summary trial, which is generally for a minor criminal offence, the magistrates may impose a sentence of up to six months' imprisonment or a fine of up to £400. Should they feel that the offence proved against the accused is one which would merit a more severe sentence they may commit him to the appropriate Crown Court for sentence.

Where an accused is charged with a more serious offence, which by law is triable on an indictment, he will still appear in the first place before the magistrates for a preliminary hearing. The function of the magistrates in this case is not that of finding the accused guilty or not guilty, but of determining whether on the evidence submitted to them there exists a *prima facie* case for the defendant to answer. Witnesses may be heard by the magistrates and their evidence is taken down in so-called depositions which will be available at the subsequent trial of the accused and thus provide a check on the memory of the witnesses, bearing in mind the fact that the committal proceedings before the magistrates are likely to have taken place not too long after the alleged offence, while there may be some delay before the actual trial comes up for hearing. If the defence claims at the committal proceedings that there is no *prima facie* case against the defendant and the magistrates agree, the accused will be discharged. If the court decides, however, that there is a case for the accused to answer, he will be given an opportunity to make a statement in his defence or to produce witnesses or other evidence. Should he decide to do so, the magistrates will consider again whether he should be committed for trial. The accused may, however, prefer not to show his hand at this stage but to reserve his defence for the actual trial at the appropriate Crown Court.

Juvenile Courts

Juvenile Courts are Magistrates' Courts with jurisdiction to hear cases against children (persons between ten and fourteen) and juveniles (persons between fourteen and seventeen). Justices are generally specially selected for the juvenile bench and there must be at least one woman among them. In order to avoid the impression that the Juvenile Court is an ordinary court, it is provided that it may not sit in a room in which other court sittings either have been held one hour before or will be held one hour after the juvenile proceedings. In order to protect the children and juveniles from undesirable publicity, proceedings are conducted in private with only authorized persons admitted to the court room and restrictions exist on the reporting of the proceedings in the press in as much as the names of the juveniles may not be made known without the permission of the court.

Crown Courts

The Administration of Justice Act 1971 abolished the Courts of Quarter Sessions, the Assize Courts, the Crown Courts of Manchester and Liverpool and a host of minor criminal courts and replaced them with a single Crown Court. The Central Criminal Court in London (the Old Bailey) survived, however, and has become the Crown Court for the City of London. The Crown Courts are organized in circuits based on London, Birmingham, Manchester, Leeds, Cardiff and Bristol, and may sit anywhere within the circuit area.

Two High Court judges are attached to each circuit as senior judges. In addition, each circuit has a number of circuit judges whose qualifications and method of appointment will be explained later. Furthermore, the circuits have attached to them a number of part-time judges, known as Recorders, who are appointed by the Crown on the recommendation of the Lord Chancellor from amongst barristers and solicitors of at least ten years' standing. The terms of appointment specify the length of time for which each Recorder will have to be available for his judicial duties. This generally amounts to at least twenty working days in each year. The retiring age for Recorders is seventy-two, but their appointment may be terminated earlier for reasons of incapacity or misbehaviour.

Crown Courts in the major provincial centres are referred to as first tier centres, of which there are twenty-four. They are served by High Court judges, circuit judges and Recorders and have jurisdiction in both civil and criminal matters. Second tier centres number nineteen and are similarly staffed, but deal with criminal matters only. Third tier centres (forty-six in number) are staffed by circuit judges and Recorders and deal with criminal cases only.

As far as the criminal jurisdiction of Crown Courts is concerned, offences are divided into four classes:

Class 1 offences, which include cases of murder and offences under the Official Secrets Act, are reserved for High Court judges.

Class 2 offences, including cases of manslaughter and rape, must also be tried by a High Court judge unless by order of the presiding judge a particular case has been released for trial by a circuit judge or a Recorder.

Class 3 offences, which include all other indictable offences, are listed for trial by a High Court judge but may by leave of the presiding judge for the circuit be transferred for trial by a circuit judge or Recorder.

Class 4 offences, being those which may be tried either on indictment or summarily, are normally listed for trial by a circuit judge or Recorder.

Where a circuit judge or Recorder is in charge of a criminal trial he is assisted by two to four justices of the peace.

Divisional Court of the Queen's Bench Division

An appeal from a decision of the Magistrates' Court will go to the Crown Court if it is an appeal against conviction or the sentence imposed. In general, it is the accused only and not the prosecution who may appeal. In addition, however, either side may appeal to the Divisional Court of the Queen's Bench Division "by way of case stated". In this case, at the request of either side, the magistrates will *state a case—i.e.*, outline their findings of fact and give a summary of the rival contentions, their own decision and the grounds for it. It is then up to the Divisional Court to decide whether the magistrates reached a proper decision on the facts before them. The Divisional Court may then either affirm the decision of the magistrates or reverse it or return the case to them for amendment with instructions as to where they had gone wrong in their interpretation of the facts. If the Divisional Court certifies that the case involves a point of law of general public importance either party will have the right of further appeal to the House of Lords.

Court of Appeal (Criminal Division)

The Criminal Division of the Court of Appeal was set up in 1966 to replace the earlier Court of Criminal Appeal. It consists of the Lords Justices of Appeal, but the Lord Chief Justice may, after consultation with the Master of the Rolls, invite any judge of the Queen's Bench Division to sit in the court. For the hearing of appeals the court must consist of an uneven number of judges, normally at least three in number.

The Court of Appeal (Criminal Division) hears appeals from persons convicted in a Crown Court either against conviction or against the sentence imposed. An appeal against conviction is as of right where a point of law is involved but where the appeal is on some issue of fact the leave of the Court of Appeal must be obtained unless the trial judge has certified that the case is one where a right of appeal would be desirable. An appeal against sentence always requires the preliminary leave of the Court of Appeal.

Where the appeal is one against a sentence imposed, the Court of Appeal may reduce it but not increase it. On an appeal against conviction the Court of Appeal may quash the conviction if in their opinion there has been a mistake of law, or a material irregularity in the proceedings or if it is considered unsafe to allow the conviction to stand. Even if any of the above are proved, the court will allow the sentence to stand if in their opinion no serious miscarriage of justice has taken place.

House of Lords

A further appeal from the Court of Appeal (Criminal Division) to the House of Lords is possible either by leave of the Court of Appeal or of the House of Lords. This will be given only if either of them is satisfied that a point of law of general public importance is involved which ought to be considered by the House of Lords. These appeals are fairly rare.

The Judiciary

All senior judges are appointed by the Queen on the recommendation of the Prime Minister. This includes the Law Lords, the Lord Chief Justice, the Master of the Rolls, the President of the Family Division, and the Lords Justices of Appeal. The qualification necessary for appointment as a Law Lord is fifteen years' experience at the bar or the holding of a high judicial office for two years.

The Lords Justices of Appeal either must have had fifteen years' experience at the bar or they must have been High Court judges for at least one year. Puisne judges are appointed by the Queen on the recommendation of the Lord Chancellor, from among barristers with at least ten years' experience.

The Lord Chancellor is a Minister of the Crown who, apart from his judicial duties, also presides over the House of Lords in its legislative capacity and may act there as a Government spokesman. In practice he has therefore little time left for his purely judicial duties, which in his absence may be undertaken by his predecessor in office or by one of the Law Lords.

Circuit judges are appointed by the Crown on the recommendation of the Lord Chancellor from amongst barristers of at least ten years' standing or from Recorders of at least five years' standing. Since Recorders may be selected from practising solicitors it is now for the first time possible for solicitors to join at least the lowest level of the full-time judiciary. All former county court judges became automatically circuit judges as from 1st January 1972. Judges of higher courts may also sit in county courts with their consent and at the request of the Lord Chancellor, but this is unlikely to happen frequently.

All judges are appointed "during good behaviour." This means that they are removable from office only either by the Queen for misconduct in their official position or on a joint address by both Houses of Parliament. Since 1959 all judges of the High Court retire when they reach the age of seventy-five; this does not apply to those judges who held office when the Judicial Pensions Act 1959, was passed. Circuit judges are subject to retirement on reaching the age of seventy-two, but the Lord Chancellor may in exceptional cases extend their period of office until they reach the age of seventy-five. They may be removed from office by the Lord Chancellor for inability to do their work or for misconduct.

Judges of superior courts are immune from civil actions for anything which they may say or do in court, while judges of inferior courts[1] only enjoy immunity when acting within their jurisdiction.

PROCEDURE IN THE COURTS

Procedure in the High Court

Procedure in the High Court is normally initiated by the issue of a *writ*. A writ is a command by the Queen to the defendant to enter an appearance to the action within eight days of its service on him. Printed forms of writs are available from law stationers. They are completed by the plaintiff's solicitor and taken to the central office of the Supreme Court or to one of the district registries where the writ is sealed on payment of an appropriate fee. The writ specifies the division of the High Court to which the plaintiff wishes to assign his action and carries on the back a statement of the plaintiff's claim. The writ has then to be served on the defendant or, where he is represented by a solicitor, service may be made to the latter. Where it is impossible to serve the writ on the defendant because his present

[1] *i.e.*, circuit judges and magistrates.

address is not known, an order for "substituted service" will have to be obtained from the court which allows the writ either to be sent to the last known address or to be advertised.

If the defendant wishes to contest the action he will have to *enter an appearance* by delivering to the central office of the Supreme Court or to the district registry a memorandum in a prescribed form. Should the defendant not enter an appearance the plaintiff may obtain a default judgment against him. If the defendant has entered an appearance but the plaintiff believes that the defendant has no real defence and is merely playing for time, the plaintiff may take out a summons asking for judgment on the ground that the defendant has no real defence to the action. The defendant must then either satisfy the court by an affidavit (sworn statement) that he has a real defence or allow judgment to be given against him. The decision on whether the defence thus disclosed is or is not hopeless rests with a court official, known as a Master of the Supreme Court, from whose decision it is possible to appeal to a judge.

If it appears that the defendant has a case, the next step is the exchange of *pleadings*. The purpose of the pleadings is gradually to narrow down the matter at dispute between the parties so that, when the case eventually comes up for trial, the essentials are clear to the judge and he will be saved the trouble of separating the wheat from the chaff. The rules of procedure state that every pleading shall contain only a statement in summary form of the material facts on which the party pleading relies for his claim or his defence as the case may be, but not the evidence by which they are to be proved.

Where the action is one for the payment of a definite sum of money, the defendant may at any time after entering an appearance pay into court whatever sum he admits to owing to the plaintiff. If the plaintiff refuses to accept this sum in settlement of his claim and proceeds with the case and subsequently is not awarded by the court more than had already been paid in by the defendant, the plaintiff will have to bear the cost of the further proceedings.

Finally, when all the pleadings have been exchanged and assuming that the parties have not been able to settle their dispute out of court, the action will be entered for trial. At the trial, counsel for the plaintiff will open the proceedings by stating the plaintiff's case and will then call witnesses to prove those points of fact which have not been admitted by the defence or have not been proved by documentary evidence. Each witness is examined by plaintiff's counsel, cross-examined by counsel for the defendant, and then re-examined by plaintiff's counsel. The defendant may then, if he wishes, call witnesses of his own who will be examined in the same way. If he decides to call no witnesses, plaintiff's counsel will sum up the case for the plaintiff and counsel for the defendant will reply. If the defence has called witnesses, defendant's counsel will make the first closing speech after the witnesses have been examined and plaintiff's counsel will reply. The judge will then give his findings of fact and his decision on the points of law involved.

Procedure in the County Courts

While the High Court has jurisdiction over the whole of England, the jurisdiction of the county courts is of a local nature and the plaintiff has to commence proceedings in the county court in whose district the defendant carries on business or resides, or in the county court in whose district the cause of action arose.

A plaintiff commences proceedings in a county court by submitting to the court office a statement of his claim, the parties involved and the exact nature of the claim. The county court registrar will then issue to the plaintiff a *plaint note* containing a reference number for the plaint, the title of the action, and the date and time of the hearing. He will also issue a summons to which are attached the details of the plaint. The summons must be delivered to the defendant at least fourteen days before the hearing. The summons could be served on the defendant by the plaintiff or his representative, but is more usually served by the county court bailiff.

The defendant is expected to react to the summons within eight days of service. He may do one of the following:

(a) He may pay into court the whole or part of the amount claimed together with costs on a fixed scale. If he pays less than the full amount claimed, the plaintiff will be informed and may then either accept this sum in settlement of his claim or proceed with his action, in which case, as in High Court proceedings, he risks having to pay the costs if in the end he is awarded no more than the defendant had already paid into court.

(b) If the defendant admits the claim but desires time for payment he will have to inform the court as to how he proposes to effect payment. If the plaintiff accepts this proposal judgment will be entered in his favour on these terms, while if he refuses the action will proceed to trial.

(c) If the defendant denies liability or wishes to raise a counterclaim he will, within the eight days, file a form of defence, a copy of which will be served on the plaintiff. The case will then proceed to trial.

(d) If the defendant has not filed a form of defence, he may still contest the plaintiff's claim at the trial of the action, but he will be responsible for any additional costs that the plaintiff may have incurred because of the defendant's failure to file a defence.

Unless the action has been disposed of in one of the above ways, it will come up for trial on the date stated. If the defendant fails to appear, the case may proceed in his absence and judgment could be entered against him. Where the value of the plaintiff's claim is under £100 the trial will normally be held before the registrar, while if it is above that figure the case will be heard by the judge.

In many cases where the plaintiff claims a liquidated sum and it is unlikely that his claim will be seriously contested, the plaintiff may commence a *default action* instead of an ordinary one. The advantage to him is that if the defendant fails to contest the action, judgment may be entered against him without the need for a trial. A default action is commenced in the same way as an ordinary action except that a special form of default summons is used. This summons contains no date for a hearing, but such a date will be fixed if the defendant delivers a defence or a notice of counterclaim at the court office within eight days. If he fails to do so within this period, the plaintiff may, on proving service of the summons, obtain immediate judgment against the defendant.

Costs in Civil Proceedings

There are two types of costs. Each litigant is contractually bound to his solicitor to pay the costs of the case which are worked out on the basis of a scale laid down by the Law Society. On the other hand, the court in civil proceedings may order one of the parties, generally the one who has lost the case, to pay the costs of the other party, in addition of course to having to pay his own costs. The costs which an unsuccessful party has to pay the other have to be "taxed"—*i.e.*, assessed by a court official—and will not as a rule cover all the costs which the successful party is contractually bound to pay to his own solicitor. When a judge gives his judgment on the matter before him he will also decide whether the losing party has to pay all or part of the costs of the successful party. This order is discretionary, however, and the judge may well show his disapproval of the conduct of one of the parties, particularly where he feels that an action has been frivolous, by not awarding the party his costs, even though he has been successful in his action. Generally speaking, however, "costs go with the event" which means that the successful party will be awarded his costs, subject of course to "taxation" by the so-called "taxing master" of the court. The taxing master has to decide which cost items were incurred reasonably. This means that if a party to civil proceedings indulged in some unnecessary luxuries, such as securing the services of some expensive counsel in comparatively simple proceedings which could easily have been handled by a cheaper man, he will not be awarded the amount which he will actually have to pay but some smaller sum which the taxing master considers would have secured for him the kind of legal representation which he needed for his kind of case. If the successful party to whom costs have been awarded is dissatisfied with the taxation of his bill of costs he may apply to the taxing master for a review and if still dissatisfied might apply to a judge in chambers for a further review.

Enforcements of Judgments in Civil Proceedings

A judgment creditor who has been awarded a sum of money against the defendant may, unless the defendant has obtained a stay of judgment pending appeal, proceed to enforce the judgment by one of the following means:

(a) *Writ of fieri facias*. This is a writ addressed to the sheriff of the county in which the defendant has some property commanding him to seize enough of that property to realize a sum which will cover the judgment debt with interest and costs. The sheriff may then seize such property of the defendant as he is able to find and have it sold by public auction to realize the necessary sums for the plaintiff.

(b) *Garnishee proceedings*. The purpose of these proceedings is to enable the judgment creditor to have assigned to him the benefit of debts owed by third parties to the judgment debtor—*e.g.*, the balance on the debtor's bank account.

(c) *A charging order*. The judgment creditor may apply for an order imposing a charge on land, interests in land, securities or money standing to the credit of the judgment debtor.

(d) *Appointment of a receiver*. A receiver may be appointed by the court at the request of the judgment creditor in order to intercept certain types of income before they reach the judgment debtor so as to avoid the possibility that they might be spent before they could be applied to the satisfaction of the outstanding debt.

(e) *Committal order*. In very exceptional cases the judgment debtor might be committed to prison for contempt of court arising out of his failure to satisfy the judgment given against him. This is most likely to happen where the debtor has some funds at his disposal which the court is unable to touch by any of the means discussed above and where some action by the debtor himself is called for—*e.g.*, in cases where the debtor has resources outside this country which are therefore not within the jurisdiction of an English court.

County court judgments are generally enforced by the issue of a writ of *fieri facias* addressed to the county court bailiff who is instructed to enter on the defendant's (debtor's) property and seize sufficient goods to satisfy the warrant or alternatively take "walking possession" of them in which case the goods would stay on the debtor's premises but be suitably marked so as to indicate that the debtor is not entitled to dispose of them. If the debt has not been settled, the goods will have to be sold, generally by public auction. It should be noted that a judgment obtained in the High Court for the payment of money may be executed in the county court.

The Legal Aid Scheme

Being involved in legal proceedings is an expensive matter and while in the past the courts were open and available in principle to all comers, in practice only those who could afford the costs involved were able to take advantage of the facilities offered. This position has now, in part at least, been remedied by the Legal Aid and Advice Act 1949, the Legal Aid Act 1964 and the Legal Advice and Assistance Act 1972. In outlining the provisions of these Acts we have to distinguish between legal aid in civil and in criminal proceedings.

Legal Aid and Advice in Civil Proceedings

A person wishing to secure legal aid in civil proceedings which he proposes to take or to defend will have to apply in the first place to a local certifying committee for a civil aid certificate. The legal aid scheme is controlled by a series of committees set up by the Law Society and consisting mainly of solicitors with the inclusion, however, of some barristers as well. The certifying committee will have to be satisfied that the applicant has a good *prima facie* case for commencing or for defending proceedings and in addition also that he is eligible for assistance under the scheme. On the first point, the committee has to be satisfied that the applicant has a reasonable chance of success though of course they are unable to predict the outcome of the proceedings. In respect of the eligibility condition no-one would be entitled to legal aid if he has a disposable income of over £1380 or disposable capital in excess of £1200. A person with a disposable income of under £440 and disposable capital of under £250 would be entitled to free legal aid, while those whose disposable income or capital fall between the two figures would be expected to make a contribution towards legal costs. The meaning of the terms "disposable income" and "disposable capital" is defined in regulations and involves the deduction from a person's actual income or capital of certain essential expenses and assets respectively. Disposable income is arrived at after deductions for dependants maintained by the claimant, and income tax and rates payable by him have been made, while disposable capital is arrived at after the value of a dwelling house up to £6000, household furniture, tools of trade and a limited amount of cash have been deducted from the gross amount. The actual assessment of disposable income and capital is made by the Supplementary Benefits Commission who will indicate to the certifying committee the maximum contribution that the claimant may be expected to make. The actual contribution that may be expected of him will of course depend on the actual costs incurred on his behalf and this may well fall below the maximum contribution. The claimant will be informed of the maximum contribution that may be expected of him and he will then have to decide whether he wishes to continue with the proceedings.

It has been contended that the legal aid scheme may work rather harshly against a non-assisted person involved in a dispute with an assisted party in as much as the non-assisted party, even if successful, might not be able to recover any costs from the assisted party and would thus be left to pay his own costs. The Legal Aid Act 1964 has partly remedied the situation by allowing the court to award costs to a non-assisted party to be paid out of the Legal Aid Fund. This award is, however, discretionary as far as the court is concerned and must in its opinion be just and fair in the circumstances and furthermore the court must be satisfied that the non-assisted party would suffer serious financial hardship if the order were not made.

Provisions also exist for the granting of legal advice—*i.e.*, advice by a solicitor independent of any pending legal proceedings—but the person wishing to secure such advice will have to make a nominal payment to the solicitor, the amount of which is again governed by regulations.

Legal Aid in Criminal Proceedings

Any court concerned with a criminal case may grant a legal aid order where it appears to the court that it is desirable to grant it in the interests of justice. The order will not be granted, however, unless the means of the accused are such that in the opinion of the court he requires assistance to secure legal representation. Where an order is made it will cover the cost of employing a solicitor and counsel. Notwithstanding the availability of legal aid on the above basis, the old procedure of obtaining a "dock brief" is still extant. This allows a prisoner who is about to stand trial on an indictment to instruct from the dock any counsel present in court, provided the prisoner is able to produce in cash the sum of £2·22½—*i.e.*, £2·10 for the defending barrister and 12½p for his clerk.

The Legal Advice and Assistance Act 1972 has introduced the so-called *£25 scheme* in order to enable poorer members of the public to obtain legal advice without too many formalities. A person is eligible under the scheme if his disposable income does not exceed £28 p. wk. or his disposable capital £125. Regulations provide for the usual 'disregards' in assessing a person's disposable income. Some of the parties will have to make a limited contribution towards the cost of the advice. A solicitor, under this scheme, may give oral or written legal advice on the application of English law and on the proceedings which a client might usefully take to enforce his legal rights, but the schemes does not cover assistance in actually taking such action. The solicitor is expected to work out for himself whether or not the client is entitled to qualify under the scheme without the necessity of having his income assessed by the Supplementary Benefits Commission. If, however, the cost of advice to be given is likely to exceed the £25 limit or if the solicitor is expected to take action in the court on the client's behalf, the normal procedure involving an application to the local committee and the assessment of the client's income will have to be gone through.

Small Claims Procedure in County Courts

A new set of procedures in county courts to deal with small claims (under £100) has been introduced as from October 1973. Under the new system a county court registrar has power to refer such a claim to arbitration or indeed a larger claim where both parties to the dispute are in agreement. The arbitrator will generally be the registrar or in the case of larger claims the judge.

The advantage of arbitration proceedings is that they are informal (*e.g.*, the arbitrator does not wear his official robe), they are conducted in private, and strict rules of evidence may be dispensed with. Either party may ask for arbitration and unless a charge of fraud has been made against one of the parties, the court may order it whether or not the other party agrees. The award of the arbitrator will be entered as the judgment and there is generally no appeal, except that the award could be set aside as other arbitration awards if it has been secured by wrongful means. Under the new rules, the arbitrator is also empowered to refer technical questions (*e.g.*, about the efficiency of a piece of equipment) to experts for enquiry and report.

The question as to how the costs of the proceedings are to be dealt with is generally left to the decision of the arbitrator. Where the value of the subject matter does not exceed £100 no costs other than those connected with the issue of the summons will be allowed, unless a difficult question of law or a question of fact of some complexity is involved.[1] Legal representation is thus not excluded, but by means of the rule about the awarding of costs is discouraged unless there is a good reason for it. The whole small claims procedure has, of course, been devised to assist claimants in 'consumer cases', *i.e.*, those where a disappointed buyer of a consumer good wishes to take action against the party who supplied the article in question.

[1] Or in personal injury claims where damages awarded exceed £5.

Administrative Tribunals

Courts of law are competent to deal with matters where some definite point of law is involved so that the judge's task is limited to applying the law to the facts presented to him in evidence. Since the beginning of the present century much social legislation has been passed, the effect of which is to circumscribe the rights of the individual in the interests of the community. As examples of this type of legislation we may mention rent-control, wage-fixing, compulsory military service, and many others. The characteristic feature of many of these statutes is that in their application a great deal is left to the discretion of those enforcing them. For instance, a person who had conscientious objections to military service could escape the call-up to the Forces. It was in that case necessary to decide whether his objections were sincerely ones of conscience. Similarly, where a trade union is pressing for a wage increase for their members and the employers are not prepared to grant it, it is desirable in the national interest to have the dispute settled for them so as to avoid interruption of work by strike action. Now, all these disputes could conceivably be tried before the ordinary courts—and, indeed, some of them (*e.g.*, under the Rent Restriction Acts) are—but this would tend to add enormously to the work of the courts and delay the hearing of other disputes. It has, therefore, become customary for separate tribunals outside the general judicial system to be set up to hear and decide these cases. The decisions of these tribunals frequently are a mixture of expediency and justice, where conflicting interests have to be reconciled with but little guidance from the statute which has set up the tribunal in the first place. While, therefore, the rights of individual parties may be seriously affected by the decisions of these tribunals, it should be noted that these bodies do not really apply fixed rules of law; they use their discretion in disposing of the disputes before them, subject only to a very general guidance by Act of Parliament. The number of these tribunals is legion; they include the Rent Tribunals as created by the Furnished Houses (Rent Control) Act 1946; the National Insurance Commissioners appointed in accordance with the National Insurance Acts 1948, and many others.

The main reasons why separate tribunals have been set up in these cases in place of the ordinary courts of law are:

1. The procedure before the tribunals is in general quicker and cheaper than that before the courts of law.

2. The tribunals are staffed by persons who have intimate knowledge of the problems which come before the tribunal for decision.

Administrative tribunals have been attacked because:

1. Frequently no reasons are given for the decisions. This is perhaps understandable, since if a decision is based on the exercise of

discretion it is impossible to give any hard and fast explanation of how the decision was arrived at.

2. The rules of procedure before many of the tribunals do not permit parties to be represented by professional legal advisers.

3. Appeal facilities are frequently non-existent.

4. Many tribunals decide the issues before them on facts which a court of law would regard as insufficient or unsatisfactory.

5. Some tribunals have to decide on disputes to which the Minister who has appointed the members of the tribunal is a party.

Judicial Control over Administrative Tribunals

The Queen's Bench Division of the High Court possesses certain common law powers which allow it to examine the exercise of judicial powers by administrative and other subordinate tribunals, as well as the exercise of executive powers by Ministers of the Crown, civil servants, and local authorities. These powers of control have been exercised for centuries by means of *prerogative writs* which are now (since the Administration of Justice (Miscellaneous Provisions) Act 1938) known as *prerogative orders*. There are three of these, namely the orders of *mandamus*, *certiorari*, and *prohibition*.

Mandamus is an order commanding the performance of a duty. This order, the making of which is at the discretion of the court, is mainly intended to enforce the performance of administrative duties, but it may be also used in the control of the judicial functions of administrative tribunals if they decline jurisdiction which they should exercise.

Prohibition is an order addressed to an inferior court or tribunal with a view to preventing it from exceeding its jurisdiction.

Certiorari is an order requiring an inferior court to place before the High Court any matter which it has decided or which is pending before it, so that the High Court may make sure that no excess of jurisdiction has taken place and also to allow it to ascertain whether the principles of natural justice have been complied with in the hearing before the subordinate court. Much has been written about the principles of natural justice, but there exists no complete agreement as to what they entail. It is suggested, however, that the principles of natural justice have been disregarded if any of the following circumstances can be proved:

1. that the judge (or tribunal) has been biased or has decided the matter even before the hearing;
2. that one of the parties has not been able to present his case before the judge or tribunal;
3. that the decision was given on incomplete facts.

It should be noted, then, that, while administrative tribunals are not bound to follow the procedure of the courts of law, they must not deviate from what are considered to be general principles of justice.

Judicial control is, unfortunately, not always fully effective, since Parliament occasionally gives the administrative tribunals such a wide measure of discretion as to rule out practically the possibility of judicial control. This is well illustrated by the leading case of *Liversidge* v. *Anderson*, where Liversidge's internment had been ordered by the Home Secretary under powers granted to him by the Defence (General) Regulations 1939. The House of Lords decided that the courts had no power to order the Home Secretary to give the reasons for which he had ordered Liversidge's internment, as the Regulations empowered the Home Secretary to detain any person "whom he had reasonable cause to believe to be of hostile origin or associations." The House of Lords decided that the wording of the Regulations gave the Home Secretary subjective discretion, which could not be questioned by the courts.

Tribunals and Inquiries Act 1958

This Act was passed following on the publication of the report of a committee—chairman, Lord (then Sir Oliver) Franks—which had investigated the main complaints against administrative tribunals. The Act has set up a Council on Tribunals which is instructed to keep under review the constitution and the working of some of the more important administrative tribunals.

The chairmen of the various tribunals to which the Act applies are to be selected by the appropriate Minister from a panel of names suggested by the Lord Chancellor. This is intended to ensure that the chairmen of tribunals are persons of sufficient ability and independence of outlook. The Council on Tribunals may make recommendations to each Minister concerning appointments to the Tribunals for which the Minister is responsible. The membership of a person serving on an administrative tribunal may not be terminated without the consent of the Lord Chancellor. The Act also insists on legal qualifications for the members of certain tribunals and grants a right of appeal to the High Court from the decisions of some of the tribunals. Another important improvement in procedure brought about by the Act is that the tribunals to which the Act applies must give reasons for their decisions if they have been requested to do so before the announcement of the decision.

Among the more important tribunals to which the Act applies are the Road Traffic Commissioners, the appeal tribunals under the National Insurance Acts, the rent tribunals, and the Lands Tribunal.

Domestic Tribunals

Apart from administrative tribunals set up by Parliament or under Parliamentary authority, there also exist similar bodies set up by private organizations for their own internal purposes without the authority of Parliament. These domestic tribunals exist for the purpose of deciding questions which are of direct importance to the members of the organization which has set them up. Trade unions, for instance, have their disciplinary committees, which may expel a member for breach of the union's rules; and trade associations have also set up similar tribunals to decide on charges of unfair trading made against any of their members.

Domestic tribunals are set up by the members of the organization concerned, and by subscribing to the rules of the organization these members agree to abide by the decisions of the tribunal. The courts of law will not intervene in the operation of these domestic tribunals as long as they do not exceed their jurisdiction as laid down in the rules by which they were set up, and as long as they follow the principles of natural justice. Where they exceed their jurisdiction a court of law would be prepared to come to the assistance of a member whose interests have been affected. Thus, a trade union may be restrained from expelling a member for a reason not covered by the union's rules, and if the wrongfully expelled member has sustained a financial loss he may be awarded damages against the union. (*Bonsor* v. *Musicians' Union.*)

Much more attention has been paid by the courts to the work of domestic tribunals in recent years than before, because the practical power of the tribunals has increased greatly. Expulsion from a trade union or a trade association to-day is not just expulsion from a private organization: it may mean the loss of the livelihood of the expelled member, where the trade union enforces a closed shop or where the trade association forbids its members to deal with non-members.

A court of law cannot stop a domestic tribunal (as long as the tribunal has acted within its powers) from expelling a member merely because this will cause hardship to him. If the rules of the organization endow the tribunal with powers of discretion the possibilities of intervention by the courts are limited. The courts cannot be excluded, however, where the tribunal has dealt with a matter which is a question of law. Thus, in *Lee* v. *Showmen's Guild* the plaintiff had been expelled from the defendant association on the ground of having engaged in unfair competition. The court granted him an injunction restraining the association from expelling him, because the court disagreed with the interpretation of the term "unfair competition" which the domestic tribunal of the association had used in reaching their decision to expel the plaintiff.

Although domestic tribunals are not courts of law, they are nevertheless acting in a judicial capacity and are therefore expected to comply with what are known as the *principles of natural justice.* These principles may be summarized as follows:

1. A person charged before a domestic tribunal with some breach of the rules of the organization to which he belongs must be informed of the charge that has been made against him.
2. He must also be given an opportunity to answer the charge and must therefore be informed of the date and time and place of the hearing, which must not be arranged in such a way as to make it practically impossible for him to attend. If the accused has been given reasonable notice of the hearing but fails to attend without good reason, the hearing could proceed in his absence.
3. The composition of the tribunal must be such as not to create the suspicion of bias against the accused and must therefore not include anyone who would be unable to consider the case without bias.

In the event of a breach of any of these principles, the person affected could seek the assistance of a court of law to have the decision of the domestic tribunal set aside. These principles of natural justice are so fundamental that they could not be excluded by any rule which might appear in an association's rule book.

The Court of Justice of the European Communities

The Court of Justice consists of eleven judges, selected from all the member states, assisted by three Advocates-General. The latter represent a type of official well known in French law. The Advocate-General is not a member of the court as such—*i.e.*, he does not participate in its discussions and decisions, and his main task is that of acting as *amicus curiae* by putting before the court reasoned submissions on all matters which are up for decision. Being independent of the parties to the dispute, he may examine the subject-matter and submit for the court's consideration issues not submitted by the parties themselves.

Proceedings before the court may be initiated by member states, the Institutions of the Community and also by natural or legal persons. Proceedings may be taken against member states or against the Institutions of the Community.

Proceedings against member states may be taken either by the Commission or by another member state on the ground that the defendant state has failed to fulfil an obligation under the Treaty. Where proceedings are taken against an institution of the Community this may be in order to secure an annulment of some binding act of that institution or to obtain a judgment of the court on the ground that the institution in question had failed to act.

The grounds for which a decision of the institution may be annulled are:

1. Lack of jurisdiction—*i.e.*, that the institution has acted *ultra vires*.
2. Violation of the basic procedural rules laid down by the relevant Treaty.
3. Infringement of the Treaty or of any rule of law made under its provisions.
4. Misuse of power (known in French law, from which this concept has been taken, as *detournement de pouvoir*). This happens when an authority uses its lawful power to achieve an object for which these powers were never intended.

Since Community law applies in all member states it is of course essential that the interpretations given to it by national courts should be identical as well. Where, therefore, the question of the validity or the interpretation of one of the Treaties is under question before a national court, that court may request the Court of the European Communities to give a preliminary ruling on the point at issue. It is thus possible that when an English court is faced with a dispute to which Community law applies and where the parties and the national court cannot agree on the meaning of the relevant provisions of Community law, the question of interpretation will have to be referred to the Court of Justice of the European Communities. This court will not be concerned with the direct application of Community law to the case before the national court, but merely to a statement of the law which will then have to be applied to the facts of the case by the national court. There does appear to exist, therefore, some similarity between this procedure and the appeals by way of case stated from magistrates courts in this country.

In addition to the matters discussed already the Court of Justice deals with disputes between the Community and its employees. It is also willing to perform the function of an arbitrating body in disputes between member states, connected with the provisions of the treaty, provided that the states concerned are willing to submit the dispute to arbitration.

The Legal Profession

England and certain parts of the Commonwealth are unique in having a legal profession which is divided into two branches—*i.e.*, barristers and solicitors. The reasons for this division are largely historical and need not concern us here. Barristers are primarily advocates appearing on behalf of their clients in court (and referred to in that capacity as counsel) though many barristers are concerned with a good deal of paperwork such as drafting complicated settlements and advising their clients on complicated points of law.

Solicitors, the general practitioners of the law, have also a right of access to courts, but generally the lower courts only, and much of their work is concerned in preparing the ground for counsel by interviewing witnesses, preparing pleadings, etc. They have also a great deal of legal work in connection with matters not concerned with litigation, such as the drafting of documents, the conveyancing of land, the preparation of wills and similar matters.

There are certain other differences between the two branches of the profession. Solicitors, unlike barristers, may enter into partnership. They have a contractual relationship with their clients which means that they may sue for their fees, but on the other hand they themselves may be sued by their clients for professional negligence. Barristers may not sue for their fees, nor are they liable to clients for professional negligence.

The solicitors' profession is controlled by the Law Society which is a chartered corporation. Although membership of the Law Society is voluntary in as much as a practising solicitor need not be a member, the Law Society has statutory powers under the Solicitors Act 1957 to control the training and admission of solicitors. In addition, the Law Society, through its Disciplinary Committee, exercises disciplinary powers over solicitors, whether or not they are members of the Society. Solicitors are officers of the Supreme Court and the court has thus disciplinary powers of its own over solicitors and in addition hears appeals from decisions of the Disciplinary Committee of the Law Society. Although the relationship between a solicitor and his client is a contractual one, the solicitor's charges, particularly in respect of non-contentious business, are governed by statutory orders made by a committee set up under the Solicitors Act.

A person may practise as a barrister only if he has been *called to the Bar* by one of the four Inns of Court: Middle Temple, Inner Temple, Gray's Inn or Lincoln's Inn. The power of the Inns is not based on statute but is derived from the judges. Each Inn has three types of members: the Benchers (who control the affairs of the Inn) and are judges or senior barristers; barristers who have been called to the Bar by the Benchers; and students who have been admitted by the Benchers. In order to be admitted to the Bar a student must have paid the requisite fees, passed the Bar examinations and have "kept" eight terms. Terms are kept by dining in the Hall of the Inn on three occasions during the term, of which there are four in each calendar year. Since 1966 the affairs of the four Inns in respect of the education of bar students, their admission to the Bar and the exercise of certain disciplinary powers are in the hands of the Senate of the Inns of Court which consists of thirty-seven members. The Senate also controls the Council of Legal Education which is in day-to-day control of the education of future barristers and organizes series of lectures in

London and arranges the holding of the Bar examinations. There is also the General Council of the Bar which performs for barristers similar functions to those performed for solicitors by the Law Society in dealing with such matters as remuneration and professional etiquette.

We have stated already that the relationship between barrister and lay client is not a contractual one. One of the most important rules of etiquette concerning barristers is that they may not accept instructions from—*i.e.*, be briefed by—the client in person, but must be briefed by a solicitor representing the client. Negotiations about the barrister's fee are conducted between his clerk and the instructing solicitor and it is up to the solicitor to collect the fee from the client and to forward it to the barrister in due course. The barrister would have no direct claim against the client for his fees. If a solicitor has collected from the client the barrister's fee, it would be professional misconduct on the part of the solicitor if he were not to pay it over to the barrister.

CHAPTER THREE

Legal Persons and Legal Relations

Legal Persons

A legal person is any person who is accepted by law as a subject of legal rights and duties. In England to-day legal personality is practically synonymous with physical personality, in that every human being is a legal person. This has, of course, not always been so. In a slave-owning community, for instance, slaves are not treated as legal persons. In addition there are certain legal persons who are not physical persons: in some Eastern countries Gods or some sacred objects are endowed with legal personality.

In our law legal personality attaches to a human being on birth and ends with death. Dead persons are no longer subjects of legal rights, and an attack on the reputation of a dead person will thus not be actionable by his estate. It is true that for certain purposes within the law of property unborn children may be treated as legal persons, but only on condition that the child is eventually born alive.

Nationality and Domicile

By a person's nationality we understand his allegiance to some state. With the exception of a few stateless persons, everybody is the political subject of some state, to whom he owes allegiance, for whom he may have to fight in times of war, and from whom he will expect protection as against other states. Nationality may be of importance for certain parts of public law—*e.g.*, in connection with the franchise (right to vote in elections); but it is to-day of very limited importance in private law. Our law of contract and property, for instance, applies equally to British subjects and to aliens. The only disability of aliens remaining now is that they may not become owners or part-owners of British ships (ships sailing under the British flag and registered at a British port).

Nationality has to be carefully distinguished from domicile. A person's domicile is the place where he is permanently resident and where he has the intention of making his permanent home. A French citizen living permanently in London has thus French nationality but an English domicile. Domicile is of considerable importance for a person's legal status. For instance, English courts had jurisdiction in divorce matters only where the husband had been domiciled in

England. The Domicile and Matrimonial Proceedings Act 1973 now provides, however, that an English court shall have jurisdiction to entertain proceedings for divorce or judicial separation if either party is domiciled in England at the commencement of the proceedings or if either party was habitually resident in England for a period of at least a year immediately preceding the commencement of the proceedings. This provision takes care of the position of a wife whose husband has deserted her, has gone abroad and settled down there leaving his wife behind in this country but making her domiciled in his new home country even though she may have never set foot there. A person's capacity to marry will depend on the law of the country where he is domiciled. Since every person must have a domicile, a child acquires his domicile at birth (*domicile of origin*). A legitimate child follows his father in this respect, while an illegitimate child follows his mother. A person over the age of 16 may choose his own domicile (*domicile of choice*), and he may do so even before reaching the age of 16, if married. This necessitates taking up residence in the country in question with the intention of making his permanent home there. Married women have no independent domicile. Their domicile depends on that of the husband even if they are not living with him. Whenever the husband changes his domicile, the wife is also assumed to acquire the new domicile, even if she never sets foot in the country in which the husband has chosen to settle down.[1]

A British subject is either a citizen of the United Kingdom and her colonies or he is a citizen of one of the following countries: Canada, Australia, New Zealand, India, Ceylon, Ghana, Nigeria, or one of the other independent Commonwealth countries.

Citizenship of the United Kingdom and her colonies may be acquired in four main ways (British Nationality Act 1948):

1. *By Birth.* Every child born within the United Kingdom or her colonies acquires United Kingdom citizenship from birth, irrespective of the nationality of his parents. The position of children born in one of the Commonwealth countries depends on the domestic legislation of that country, though it should be added that every Commonwealth citizen is a British subject.

2. *By Descent.* A child also becomes a United Kingdom citizen from birth if his father, at the time of the child's birth, was a United Kingdom citizen, irrespective of the place of birth. In such a case it will be necessary, however, to register the birth of the child with a British consulate within one year of birth.

3. *By Naturalization.* An alien acquires United Kingdom citizenship by receiving a certificate of naturalization from the Home

[1] But see the provisions of the Domicile and Matrimonial Proceedings Act 1973 above.

Secretary. For this purpose he has to satisfy the Home Secretary that he has been resident for five out of the last seven years (including the last year before application) within the United Kingdom or her colonies, that he has adequate command of English, and is of good character. The granting of the certificate is entirely discretionary, and the Home Secretary may refuse it without giving reasons.

4. *By Registration.* The wife of an alien who has received a certificate of naturalization need not apply for such a certificate herself. She will become a United Kingdom citizen by registering with the Home Secretary her intention of accepting her husband's new nationality. The same procedure applies also to a woman who has married a United Kingdom citizen.

United Kingdom citizenship may be lost in the following ways:

1. *By Renunciation.* A United Kingdom citizen may renounce his citizenship by making a declaration of renunciation which, in order to become legally effective, will have to be registered with the Home Office. A British woman who marries an alien does not now lose her United Kingdom citizenship on marriage even if she acquires on marriage the nationality of her husband, but she may in that case renounce her citizenship of the United Kingdom.

2. *By Deprivation.* The Home Secretary, on the recommendation of an Advisory Committee, may deprive a naturalized (but not a natural born) United Kingdom citizen of his nationality if by his conduct he has shown himself to be a disloyal subject.

Minors (Infants)

Of the various classes of legal persons infants require special treatment, because law has adopted a fatherly attitude towards them, granting to them certain privileges and immunities which do not equally apply to persons who have reached majority.

An infant, or minor, is a person under the age of eighteen.[1] A minor reaches majority at the first moment of his eighteenth birthday.

The special position of minors in English Law may be summarized as follows:

1. A minor has no voting rights in Parliamentary or local government elections, nor may he be elected to Parliament until he reaches the age of twenty-one.

2. A minor (under 16) follows the nationality and the domicile of his father. An illegitimate minor (who in law has no father) obtains his mother's domicile.

3. A minor domiciled in England has capacity to marry at the age of sixteen (Marriage Act 1949), but he still requires the consent of his parents or guardians. If a minor over sixteen should contract

[1] Family Law Reform Act 1969.

a marriage without such consent the marriage would still be valid, but the minor may have committed a criminal offence where he has given the wrong age. A marriage of a minor under sixteen domiciled in England is absolutely void.

4. No child under the age of ten is in English law deemed capable of committing a criminal offence. Children between the ages of ten and fourteen are also deemed incapable of criminal intent, but this is a mere presumption of the law which may be rebutted by proof that the particular minor was fully aware of doing wrong. Young persons over fourteen are fully accountable for their criminal offences, but the procedure in trying them and the punishments to which they will become subject are specially adapted to the needs of this age-group. Young persons over fourteen are fully exposed to the severity of criminal law.

5. A minor may not be the owner of a *legal* estate in land, but he may hold an *equitable* interest in such property where it is held on trust for him. Minors may own personal chattels.

6. A minor has no capacity of making a will, except where as a serving member in Her Majesty's Forces, being on active service, or as a seaman at sea, he becomes entitled to make an informal, so-called soldier's will.

7. A minor is fully liable for his civil wrongs or torts, except for those which contain intention (or malice) as an essential ingredient, where the minor must be of an age sufficient to justify the imputation of malice to him.

8. Contracts made by minors during their minority are, at common law, voidable at the minor's option. This means that the minor may repudiate the contract, provided he does so either during his minority or within a reasonable time of reaching his majority. The Infants' Relief Act 1874, provides, however, that certain contracts made by minors are absolutely void. This means that no action can be taken, even after he has reached majority, on these contracts made by a minor during minority. The Act refers to three contracts:

(*a*) A contract whereby a minor promises to repay a loan of money.

(*b*) A contract whereby a minor promises to pay for goods supplied to him.

(*c*) An account stated—*i.e.*, a promise by a minor to pay a past debt.

It stands to reason that while the minor's promises are void in these three cases there is nothing to stop him from discharging them voluntarily. Furthermore, if a minor has already paid something for goods supplied to him he will be unable to recover the money paid. In all three cases mentioned above what matters is the minor's actual age at the time of the promise, not the age which he may have given to the other party. A minor who obtains goods on credit by stating that he was over eighteen commits the criminal offence of obtaining goods by deception, but even so it will not be possible for the seller to force him to pay. If, however, the goods are still in the minor's possession he may be made to restore them to the seller.

Certain contracts entered into by minors are valid and may be enforced against them.

(*a*) A minor is bound to pay a reasonable price for necessaries supplied to him. Necessaries are defined as goods or services required for personal use (whether by the minor himself or by members of his family) as distinct from business use. The minor must not be already sufficiently supplied with goods of that description, and the particular things chosen must be appropriate to the minor's social standing. Thus, where a minor bank clerk buys a watch, the watch will be a necessary if he has not got one already and provided the quality and price of the watch selected by him are not excessive in relation to the social standing of a bank clerk. The minor is bound to pay a reasonable price only, irrespective of the price which he may have agreed to pay.

(*b*) The minor is also bound by contracts of apprenticeship or service which, on the whole, are to his benefit. It is important here to consider the whole contract and not merely pick out individual provisions of it which may not benefit the minor. Thus, in *Doyle* v. *White City Stadium*, a minor professional boxer had agreed to participate in a prize fight on condition that he subscribed to the usual rules of the British Boxing Board of Control. He was held to be bound by the contract even though one of the rules provided that a boxer who was disqualified (a misfortune which befell the plaintiff) would forfeit his purse.

9. A minor may be declared bankrupt, but only in respect of debts which are legally binding on him.

Husband and Wife

Marriage, as far as English law is concerned, has been defined by Lord Penzance in *Hyde* v. *Hyde* as "the voluntary union for life of one man and one woman to the exclusion of all others." Three conditions must therefore be present if a marriage is to be valid at law. The union must be a voluntary one so that if either party did not agree to the marriage it will be void. The union must have been entered into for life. This means that the parties intended to enter into a permanent union when contracting the marriage, though the union may be subsequently dissolved by a decree of divorce. Finally, the union must be monogamous. While the marriage continues neither party may enter into another marriage. Because of the influx of people into this country coming from parts of the world where polygamy is legally accepted Parliament found it necessary to pass the *Matrimonial Proceedings (Polygamous Marriages) Act 1972*. Before this Act was passed, matrimonial relief—*i.e.*, a decree of divorce or judicial separation or orders for maintenance—were not available to persons involved in a polygamous marriage. Under the Act a court will not be prevented from granting matrimonial relief because a marriage is actually or potentially polygamous. This of course does not mean that a valid polygamous marriage could be contracted in this country, but merely recognizes the existence of such marriages among many of the recent immigrants into Britain.

Wherever the marriage may have been contracted, it is essential that a party who is domiciled in England must have had capacity to marry according to English law. For this purpose three conditions must be fulfilled:

1. Neither party must be under the age of 16.

2. Neither party must be already married (unless, of course, the marriage has been legally dissolved).

3. The parties must not be related with the prohibited degrees of relationship. The prohibited degrees of relationship may be based either on blood relationship or on relationship through marriage. At present the prohibited degrees of relationship are set out in the First Schedule to the Marriage Act 1949. It would be impossible to enumerate here the entire list, but, among others, a man may not marry the following: his mother, his daughter, his father's mother, his mother's mother, his son's or daughter's daughter, his sister, his wife's mother or daughter, his father's wife, his son's wife, his father's or mother's sister, his brother's or sister's daughter. He may marry, however, his deceased (though not his divorced) wife's sister, his deceased brother's wife, his deceased wife's brother's (or sister's) daughter and his father's (mother's) deceased brother's wife.

A woman may not marry her father, her grandfather, her son or grandson, her brother, her father-in-law, her husband's son, her daughter's husband, her uncle, her nephew. She may marry her deceased sister's husband, her deceased husband's brother, her deceased husband's brother's son, her deceased husband's sister's son.

The Marriage (Enabling) Act 1960 provides now that a valid marriage may be entered into between a man and a woman who is the sister, aunt or niece of a former wife of his (whether dead or still alive) or who was formerly the wife of his brother, uncle, or nephew.

A marriage may be contracted either according to the rites of the Church of England or under a Superintendent Registrar's Certificate. A marriage according to the rites of the Church of England may be solemnized

(*a*) after the publication of banns of matrimony; or
(*b*) on the authority of a *special licence* of marriage granted by the Archbishop of Canterbury; or
(*c*) on the authority of a *common licence* granted by an ecclesiastical authority having power to issue such a licence; or
(*d*) on the authority of a certificate issued by a superintendent registrar.

The banns of matrimony must be published on three Sundays preceding the solemnization of marriage, at morning service (or at evening service if there is no morning service on a Sunday). They must be published in the parish church where the parties are to be married, or if they do not reside in the same parish, then in the parish church of each parish in which they reside. If one of the parties is serving on board a naval ship at sea the banns may be published on the ship at morning service on three successive Sundays.

The following marriages may be solemnized on the authority of a certificate of a superintendent registrar:

(*a*) a marriage in the office of a superintendent registrar;
(*b*) a marriage according to the usages of the Society of Friends (Quakers);
(*c*) a marriage between persons professing the Jewish religion and conducted according to the usages of the Jews;
(*d*) a marriage according to the rites of the Church of England;
(*e*) a marriage in a registered building according to such form and ceremony as the persons to be married see fit to adopt.

A certificate issued by a superintendent registrar remains valid for three months from the date on which the notice of marriage was entered in the marriage notice book. The certificate issued by the superintendent registrar may be accompanied by a licence permitting an authorized person to solemnize the marriage in a building which is registered for this purpose, providing that this building is within his registration district. Where a marriage is solemnized in a registered building (generally a Roman Catholic church, or a church of one of the non-established denominations, a meeting-place of the Society of Friends, or a Jewish synagogue), the ceremony must take place in the presence of two witnesses and of a registrar or of an authorized person whose name has been certified by the governing body of the registered building. The doors of the building must be kept open throughout the ceremony.

No person who is not a member of the Society of Friends may be married according to the usages of the Society unless he is permitted to do so by the rules of the Society.

Where a marriage takes place in a register office, the provisions as to witnesses etc., are the same as those given above. No religious service may be used at any marriage solemnized in the office of a superintendent registrar. The parties to a marriage may, however, add the religious ceremony of the church to which they belong to the marriage which they have already contracted. For this purpose they will have to produce to the minister of the church their certificate of marriage and he may then celebrate in his church the usual marriage service, but this will in no way supersede or invalidate the marriage already solemnized in the superintendent registrar's office.

A husband is bound to provide his wife with the necessities of life. The meaning of this term depends on the standard of living of the family and thus indirectly on the husband's income. The wife loses her right to be maintained by her husband if she commits adultery or if she without reason deserts her husband. At common law the wife had no duty to maintain her husband even if she had the means and he was destitute. The National Assistance Act 1948, provides, however, that spouses are under a duty to maintain each other. If one of them becomes a burden on national assistance the Minister of Social Security may apply to a court of magistrates to recover from the other spouse the cost of keeping the claimant.

As far as public law is concerned, women, whether married (*femes covert*) or single (*femes sole*), have the right to vote and sit on terms of equality with men in the House of Commons and on local councils. The position of married women as to nationality and domicile has been discussed already.

At common law on marriage a woman's legal personality was merged into that of her husband, and she ceased to be entitled legally to own property of her own. Husband and wife were one at law, and the husband was the one. All personal property owned by the wife on marriage or acquired by her afterwards became the husband's property. The husband also controlled his wife's real property and drew the income from it. Having no property of her own, the wife could make no contracts, and the husband became responsible for his wife's ante-nuptial (*i.e.*, contracted before marriage) debts.

By a series of Married Women Property Acts passed between 1882 and 1949 the position of married women was, as far as property rights and contractual capacity are concerned, assimilated to that of single women.

The position to-day is, then, that a woman can freely enter into any contracts and own any property she likes. She may engage in business on her own and may be sued on her debts. If she is unable to pay her debts she may be made bankrupt. It is only for income-tax purposes that the wife's income is treated as being part of the husband's income, but even there the income-tax authorities will be prepared to make separate assessments if they are asked to do so. Husband and wife may freely enter into contracts with each other, being now separate legal persons.

Under the Married Women's Property Act 1964, any money and property derived from a housekeepjng allowance will, in the absence of any agreement to the contrary, be treated as belonging to husband and wife in equal shares. Before this Act, where the wife was able to buy, say a piece of furniture out of savings made by her from housekeeping money, the furniture was deemed to belong to the husband because it was his money that she had been spending and any savings out of the money belonged to him.

The Matrimonial Homes Act 1967, provides that where one spouse is entitled to occupy a dwelling house by virtue of any estate in the land held by him (or her) or by contract or by virtue of any enactment (*e.g.*, the Rent Acts) this spouse may not evict the other spouse or exclude him or her from occupation without having obtained first the leave of the court. Where the other spouse (generally a deserted wife) is not in occupation of the dwelling house, the court may give her leave to enter into and occupy the dwelling house.

The old rules about the wife's legal personality being merged into that of her husband survived until recently in the law of torts. Actions in tort between husband and wife were ruled out except for actions under the Married Women's Property Act 1882, in connection with the protection of the wife's property. The Law Reform (Husband and Wife) Act 1962, provides now, however, that both parties to a marriage shall have the same right of action in tort as strangers, subject to the court's right to stay proceedings if no substantial benefits would accrue from the action, or if the matter could be more conveniently dealt with under the Married Women's Property Act 1882.

The husband is no longer responsible for his wife's debts, except in the following circumstances:

1. Where the wife acted as the husband's agent in entering into contracts on his behalf and with his express authority.

2. Where the wife is deemed by law as having been endowed by her husband with authority, even though this has not been expressly given.

(*a*) If the wife buys necessaries for the household the husband will be bound to pay the supplier, provided that he has not given his wife a sufficient allowance to pay for the goods in cash. Necessaries will be defined here much in the same way as they are for infants. The implied authority referred to here exists only where the husband and wife are living together.

(*b*) The husband will have to discharge his wife's debts where by his words or conduct he has led others to believe that the wife was authorized to charge his credit for certain types of purchases. This implication generally arises from the husband's conduct in settling his wife's bills without protest. On the first occasion he might not have been obliged to do so, provided, of course, the goods obtained by her were not necessaries; but once he has started the practice he cannot without notice stop it. This means that the husband would have to communicate with the traders whose bills he has been paying, and inform them that he would not pay his wife's bills in future. Some husbands do so by means of an advertisement in the local newspaper; but this, standing on its own, will not be sufficient, as the husband could never prove that all the traders affected had read it. It would, therefore, have to be supplemented by personal letters to the people concerned. The only practical value of the advertisement is that it may warn people who have not traded with the wife before against extending credit to her.

Needless to say, the wife is not responsible for her husband's debts, except, of course, where he entered into a contract on her behalf and with her express authority.

Corporations

A corporation is a group of physical persons associated for some common purpose, and which is treated by law as a person in its own right, separate from the personalities of its members. The members of the corporation may either be in existence simultaneously (*a corporation aggregate*) or they may be in existence in succession so that at any time the corporation is represented by one member only (*a corporation sole*). Corporations sole were the creation of medieval lawyers who dreaded the idea that land or other property could be temporarily without an owner. This might have happened in the case of land belonging to a church between the death or retirement of the sitting incumbent and the appointment of his successor. A solution was found by making the parson of the living concerned into a corporation sole, the office itself being the corporation and the holders of it the members of the corporation. Property belonged, then, to the parson as a corporation sole, and this property was quite distinct from any private property which he might own. The corporation, unlike its members, could not die, and there was no danger of the property being left without an owner. The most important corporation sole to-day is the Crown, to be discussed later. All the bishops and parsons of the Established Church are also treated as corporations sole, and further examples have been added by statute. The public trustee (Public Trustee Act 1906) is a corporation sole, and so is the Treasury Solicitor (Treasury Solicitor Act 1876). New corporations sole could to-day be created by Act of Parliament only.

Corporations aggregate are by far the more important type of corporation. They may come into existence in three ways:

1. By the grant of a Royal Charter. This method is restricted to-day to corporations established for educational, charitable, and similar purposes (*e.g.*, universities), and to local government corporations—*i.e.*, boroughs.

2. By Act of Parliament. The various Nationalization Acts have set up corporations to run the industries which have been taken into national ownership (*e.g.*, the National Coal Board and the British Railways Board).

3. The most frequently used method of creating a new corporation is by following the procedure laid down in the Companies Act 1948 (or one of its predecessors) or in one of a small number of other Acts with similar provisions. These Acts make it possible for people who wish to be formed into a corporation to register their intention with a public official (*e.g.*, the Registrar of Joint Stock Companies), and if they satisfy this official that they have complied with the legal requirements he will grant to them a certificate of incorporation.

At common law corporations aggregate could not own land, because law (and even more so the Crown) was opposed to the idea of land falling into the dead hand (mortmain). Land owned by corporations was treated as being held in mortmain, because the corporation could not die and there was thus no chance for the superior landlord to benefit from the usual incidents of tenure. In a feudal society superior landowners derived a regular income from the payments which had to be made by the heirs of subordinate landowners before they were allowed to take possession of their land inheritance. Naturally, the possibility of land being held by a body which could not die was frowned upon. Corporations were thus allowed to own land only if they held a 'licence in mortmain,' granted by the Crown. This rule applied in principle until 1960, in which year the Charities Act abolished the doctrine of mortmain. Thus, non-trading corporations now enjoy the same rights as companies formed under the Companies Act have always enjoyed.

The most characteristic feature of a corporation is that in law it has a separate existence from that of its members. It is, therefore, possible for members of a corporation to make contracts with it and, indeed, to take legal action against it. This is so even if the member concerned holds the largest proprietary interest in the corporation. Thus in *Salamon* v. *Salamon and Co., Ltd.*, S. held all the shares in the company, except for six, which were held by six members of his family. This was necessary, as a public joint-stock company requires a minimum of seven members. S. had also advanced some money to the company and had been given load certificates (debentures) entitling him to repayment before other creditors. The company went into liquidation, and the court held that, although S. was for all practical purposes the owner of the company, legally he and the company were separate persons and there was thus no reason why the company could not be indebted to him. He was entitled to have the debt owing to him paid out of the company's assets before the other creditors, for whom there was nothing left.

The contractual capacity of corporations depends on the method of their creation. No corporation can, of course, enter into contracts which only human beings can enter into—*e.g.*, marriage. With that exception, however, chartered corporations have unlimited contractual capacity and can enter into any kind of contract. Statutory and registered corporations, on the other hand, can enter only into contracts which fall within the objects of the corporation, the objects being stated in the Act of Parliament or in the Memorandum of Association of the registered company. Any contract falling outside the company's objects will be treated as being *ultra vires* (outside the powers of) the company and will thus be void. In *Ashbury Railway Carriage and Iron Co., Ltd.* v. *Riche* the company, whose objects referred only to the manufacture and sale of carriages, purported to buy a railway concession. A meeting of the shareholders was convened to approve this transaction. The court held, however, that as long as the corporation's objects had not been extended it was not capable of entering into such a contract even if every single member had consented to it. In S. 9 of the European Communities Act 1972 (which was passed in order to bring certain rules of English law into harmony with the law of the European Economic Communities) it is now provided that where a person deals with a company in good faith, the power of the company's directors to bind the company shall be deemed to be free of any limitations under the company's memorandum and articles of association.

At common law all contracts of corporations had to be made under the corporations' common seal—*i.e.*, in the form of a deed. This rule would, of course, not be practicable under modern conditions, and law permitted, therefore, corporations to make contracts informally where the contract was one of trivial importance or one of utmost necessity or of everyday occurrence. Other contracts made by corporations required the form of a deed, and such contracts were void unless made in this form. Corporations registered under the Companies Act may make contracts in the same form in which other persons do, and the Corporate Bodies' Contracts Act 1960, has now extended this privilege to all other types of corporations. Thus, as far as the form of contracts is concerned, there exists now no difference between corporations and other persons.

A corporation is liable for the torts committed by its servants in the course of their employment even where the servants were engaged in activities which were outside the corporation's objects. Similarly, corporations may, by statute, be made responsible for certain criminal offences committed by their servants in the course of their employment.

Unincorporated Associations

An unincorporated association is a group of persons associating for some legal purpose where the group is not treated as a legal person in its own right. No more than twenty persons may associate for the purpose of conducting a business (except for solicitors, accountants, and members of the Stock Exchange), unless these persons are formed into a corporation. Unincorporated associations for business purposes are subject to the law of partnership and will be discussed separately.

An unincorporated association not conducted for business purposes may have any number of members. Under this heading fall not only social and sports clubs, but also trade unions, non-established churches, and many professional associations. Such an association is really a group of persons employing common agents for the purpose of conducting their affairs. It has no legal personality and cannot, therefore, either own property or enter into contracts in its own name. Property may be owned on behalf of the members of the association by trustees. Contracts are entered into by the officials of the association, but they will be personally liable on these contracts jointly with those members of the committee who authorized the making of the contract. The general membership of the association are not responsible for such contracts unless the making of the contracts has been expressly authorized by them.

Before the passing of the Industrial Relations Act 1971 one of the most important types of unincorporated association were trade unions. Under the Industrial Relations Act, the term trade union (at least in its proper legal sense) was reserved for registered trade unions and these are treated as corporations possessing all the general attributes of legal persons. Registration took place with the Registrar of Trade Unions and Employers' Associations and was optional. An organization of workers which had failed to register remained an unincorporated association and did not enjoy many of the benefits which accrue to trade unions following on their registration.[1]

[1] But note that the Industrial Relations Act was repealed in 1974. Trade unions once again become unincorporated associations, enjoying, however, certain privileges of corporations—*e.g.*, the right to sue in their own names.

Partnerships

A partnership is defined by the Partnership Act 1890, as "the relation which subsists between persons carrying on business in common with a view of profit." The business need not involve the buying and selling of goods, it may well consist in the provision of services. No particular form is needed for the formation of a partnership. Whenever two or more persons are carrying on a business in common and are sharing profits they will be presumed to be partners. The main features of partnerships distinguishing them from corporations (*e.g.*, joint-stock companies) are the following:

1. A partnership is not a legal person. Thus, contracts made with a partnership are in fact made with the individual members of it, and they accept joint liability on these contracts. If an action has to be brought against a partnership it is brought against its members, and these have to be sued jointly in a single action. If any partner has been omitted from the action he may not be sued later separately. Since the partnership is not a legal person, a partner may not enter into a contract with the partnership, as this would involve making a contract with himself. He may, of course, make a contract with his fellow partners.

2. The maximum number of members in a partnership is twenty. There are no maxima for the membership of corporations, except for private joint-stock companies, where the maximum is fifty.

3. The partners in a partnership are fully responsible for the debts of the partnership up to the extent of their separate properties. Most joint-stock companies are run on the principle of limited liability—under which the liability of their members is limited to the value of the shares which they are holding in the company, so that once a member has paid fully for the shares which he holds he will no longer be liable for the further debts of the company.

4. While companies are administered by their boards of directors elected by the members, all partners in a partnership are, unless otherwise agreed, entitled and indeed bound to participate in the management of the partnership business. Every partner is also deemed to be an agent of all the other partners for the purposes of the partnership business and may therefore enter into contracts on their behalf. A member of a company possesses no similar powers.

Reference must also be made to a rather rare type of partnership—namely, the *limited partnership*. These partnerships, which represent a kind of cross between an ordinary partnership and a limited company, were authorized by the Limited Partnerships Act 1907. A limited partnership is subject to the general rules about the maximum numbers of members of partnerships. Of its members at least one must be a general partner and at least one must be a limited partner. The management of the business rests entirely with the general partner or partners, and these partners also take upon them the full risks of the business. The limited partners contribute fixed sums of money to the partnership and may not be called upon for the payment of any debts of the business. The sum contributed by them represents thus the maximum amount which they may lose if the business should fail. A limited partnership must be registered with the Registrar of Joint Stock Companies.

The Crown

Executive powers are exercised in Britain in the name of the Queen—the Queen being the representative of the corporation sole called the Crown. Government departments and their civil servants are thus acting on behalf of the Crown.

The position of the Crown at common law was formerly characterized by the maxim: "The King can do no wrong." This meant that not only could no action be brought against the Sovereign in his personal capacity, but the Crown could not even be sued for wrongs committed by its servants in the course of their employment. Where a servant of the Crown committed a wrong, an action lay only against him personally, though if judgment was given against him the Crown invariably paid *ex gratia* (as an act of grace) the damages which the court had awarded.

Actions against the Crown for breach of contract were possible only where the Attorney-General on behalf of the Crown assented to the case being brought before the court.[1] This procedure by way of *petition of right* was both cumbersome and unfair to the other party, whose action was permitted only by grace of the Crown's legal representative.

The law as to actions against the Crown has now been fundamentally altered as a result of the Crown Proceedings Act 1947. This Act has not affected the Queen's personal immunity from legal proceedings, but it has made it easier for actions to be brought against the Crown as the symbol of the Government. Actions for breach of contract are now possible against the Crown without the need for obtaining first the Attorney-General's fiat, but civil servants and members of H.M. Forces are still unable to sue for wrongful dismissial or for arrears of pay. Actions in tort against the Crown are possible in the following cases:

1. Where a tort has been committed by a servant or agent of the Crown.

[1] The Attorney-General's consent took the form of the so-called *fiat* (Latin for "let it be").

2. The Crown is responsible to its servants for breach of those duties which an employer owes at common law to his servants (*e.g.*, the provision of a safe system of work).

3. The Crown is liable for the breach of the duties attaching to the ownership and occupation of property (*e.g.*, duties regarding the safety of persons entering Crown premises on business).

4. The Crown is also liable for the breach of such statutory duties as are expressly stated to be binding on the Crown (*e.g.*, the safety provisions contained in the Factories Act 1961).

5. The Crown is liable for an infringement of a patent, trade mark, or copyright.

Where an action is to be brought against the Crown, the nominal defendant is the Minister whose department is concerned in the matter. If it is impossible to pin responsibility on any one Government department the action will have to be brought against the Attorney-General.

The Relationship of Parent and Child

One of the most important relationships known to our law is that of parent and child. The father of a legitimate child has the duty of maintaining the child, and he is entitled to control the child's upbringing. It should be noted that there exists no similar duty of maintenance on the part of the child towards his parents. The mother's duty to maintain a child is ancillary to that of her husband and comes into effect if he either does not or cannot carry out his duty of maintenance.

A legitimate child follows his father's nationality and domicile. As will be shown later, such a child has certain rights of inheritance in the event of the father dying without leaving a will and, even where a will has been left, the child may ask in certain circumstances to be maintained out of the father's estate. Similar rights exist also in relation to the mother's estate.

A child is legitimate if he is born to parents between whom the relationship of marriage existed either when the child was conceived or when he was born or at any time between these dates. If the relationship of marriage did not exist between the parents the child is illegitimate. An illegitimate child has legally no father, though his mother may obtain an affiliation order against the child's putative father, compelling him to make a contribution towards the child's upbringing. An illegitimate child follows his mother in her nationality and domicile. Even the mother of an illegitimate child does not possess the full right of control over him unless she decides to adopt the child. Since the Family Law Reform Act 1969 an illegitimate child has the same rights of sharing in the estate of a deceased parent as a legitimate child and his parents may similarly share in the distribution of the estate of the illegitimate child, should he die intestate.

Legitimation

A child born illegitimate may become legitimate (*i.e.*, he may be legitimated) by the subsequent marriage of his parents. This principle has been introduced in this country by the Legitimacy Act 1926 (as amended by the Legitimacy Act 1959). In order that a subsequent marriage of the parents should have this effect the child's father must have been domiciled in England at the time of his marriage. The Legitimacy Act 1959, provides that the child of a void marriage shall be treated as legitimate if at the time of conception both parents or either parent reasonably believed the marriage to be valid.

A legitimated child is treated for all purposes as if he had been legitimate from birth and will have the same rights to maintenance as a child born legitimate.

A British-born subject or a person whose status as a British subject depends on his legitimate birth may apply to the High Court for a declaration of legitimacy. The making of this declaration may be opposed by persons whose interests would suffer if the application were to be granted.

Adoption

The relationship of parent and child is normally a blood relationship, but it may also be established by a legal process known as adoption. The rules concerning adoption are now contained in the Adoption Acts 1958–64.

A minor may be adopted either by one person (male or female) or jointly by a married couple, provided always that the adoptor is

1. at least twenty-five years old; or
2. a relative of the minor and over twenty-one years old; or
3. the father or mother of the minor irrespective of age.[1]

Where the minor is female an adoption order will only in exceptional cases be granted to a male adoptor.

The adoption is given legal effect by an adoption order made by a court of law. The court concerned may be the High Court, but more usually it is the county court or a juvenile court. Adoption by private arrangement will have no legal effect. While normally the applicant and the minor must be resident in England, the High Court or a

[1] The Children Act 1975 prohibits single person adoption unless there is some reason for excluding the other parent.

county court *may* make an order in favour of an applicant not ordinarily resident in England.

Before making an adoption order the court will have to be satisfied that:

1. Every person whose consent is necessary has consented in fact. The parents or guardians of a minor have to consent. The consent of these persons may be dispensed with by the court either if they have neglected or persistently maltreated the child, or if they cannot be traced. The consent may be given subject to conditions concerning the child's religious upbringing. It is not necessary that the natural parents of the minor should know the identity of the prospective adoptor. Where the minor is adopted by a married person, the spouse of the adoptor will have to consent to the adoption.

2. The minor has consented himself if he is of sufficient age to be able to express an opinion on the matter.

3. No payment or reward has been made in respect of the adoption, except such payments as have been authorized by the court.

4. The child has been in the care of the prospective adoptor for at least three months prior to the hearing of the application for the order. This allows the local welfare authority to inspect the home into which the minor is to be adopted and to report on whether the minor appears to be well settled.

5. Where the minor is under school-leaving age, three months' notice must also be given to the local education authority.

The main effect of the making of an adoption order is that all rights and duties of the minor's natural parents in respect of his custody, maintenance, and education become extinct and are vested now in the adoptor as if the minor had been born as his natural child. If the minor now adopted was an illegitimate child whose father had to make payments towards his maintenance these payments will now cease, except where the minor has been adopted by his mother who is a single person.

If after the adoption the adoptor dies intestate (*i.e.*, without leaving a will) the adopted child will have the same rights in the distribution of the adoptor's property as his natural-born children. Any reference by the adoptor in his will to his "children" will embrace his adopted children, irrespective of when the will was made, since, for the purpose of succession to property, a disposition made by will or codicil is to be treated as made on the day of the testator's death, except where the instrument was made before April 1959 and has not been republished afterwards.

An alien minor adopted by a British subject will acquire British nationality by adoption.

Guardians

Guardians may be appointed in the following ways:

1. The father or mother of a minor may appoint a guardian by will (Guardianship of Minors Act 1971). If the person or persons nominated accept office they will be responsible for the care of the minor jointly with the surviving parent. If the latter objects to the arrangement the court will have to decide between them. The predominating interest will be the welfare of the minor.

2. The High Court, county court, or court of magistrates may appoint a guardian where none has been appointed by will, and the minor has no parent, guardian, or other person exercising parental rights over him.

3. The High Court also has jurisdiction to appoint a guardian where a minor has been made a ward of court. The Law Reform (Miscellaneous Provisions) Act 1949, provides that a minor automatically becomes a ward of court on application being made to the Family Division of the High Court. A divorce court may also initiate proceedings to have the children of a dissolved marriage made wards of court. The effects of a minor having been made a ward of court are:

(*a*) the court is now responsible for the care and control of the minor. All important decisions regarding the minor have to be made by the court, and the guardian named by the court may always turn to the court for advice;
(*b*) any interference with the ward or with his guardian amounts to contempt of court;
(*c*) the ward may be committed for contempt of court if he wilfully refuses to carry out the court's orders;
(*d*) the father or mother of the minor may be made guardians, but they would be exercising the guardian's rights under the control of the court.

Insane Persons

A person suffering from insanity is subject to various disabilities in English law:

1. A marriage contracted by an insane person is void if at the time of contracting it he was unable to appreciate its nature.

2. Contracts made by an insane person are voidable at his option if at the time of contracting he was unable to understand the nature of his acts and the other party was aware of it (but see para. 6, page 79).

3. The position of insane persons in the law of tort is doubtful, but it appears that they are liable for their torts with the exception of those which require an element of malice.

4. Insane persons may make valid wills only during a lucid interval.

5. An insane person is not responsible for a criminal offence committed by him if he was unaware at the time of committing it what he was doing or if he was unaware that he was doing wrong.

6. Under the Mental Health Act 1959, far-reaching powers are given to certain court officials to deal with the property of a mental patient. Such a patient is a person in respect of whom the judge is satisfied that he is "incapable by reason of mental disorder, of managing and administering his property and affairs."

CHAPTER FOUR

The Law of Contract

Definitions

A contract may be defined as an agreement between two parties which is intended by them to have legal consequences. This definition is to be preferred to the one frequently encountered defining a contract as a legally enforceable agreement, since there are some contracts which, for reasons to be discussed, may not be enforceable in a court of law.

A contract forms thus a subdivision of the genus 'agreement,' from which it follows that, while every contract is based on an agreement of the parties, not every agreement between parties is necessarily a contract. In order that the agreement should be a contract the parties must have shown an intention that their agreement should have legal consequences. Sometimes this intention may be expressly declared by the parties, but more often it is necessary to deduce it from the type of agreement or from the general circumstances in which it has been entered into. Family agreements, such as where a husband agrees to pay his wife a certain weekly sum by way of housekeeping money, will not be deemed to be contracts (*Balfour* v. *Balfour*), while agreements of a commercial nature will always be presumed to be contracts. The parties to such an agreement may, however, express the wish that the agreement should not be a contract—*e.g.*, by stating that it should be "binding in honour only" or that it should be a mere "gentlemen's agreement." Many readers will be familiar with the conditions which appear on football-pool coupons providing that an entry should not give rise to a legally enforceable relationship between the parties. Thus, neither party may bring an action against the other in the event of a breach of the terms of the agreement (*Appleson* v. *Littlewood, Ltd.*).

In order that a valid contract between the parties should come into existence certain essential requirements must be fulfilled. They are:

1. The parties must possess legal capacity to enter into contracts.
2. One party must have made a binding offer to the other and the offer must have been accepted.
3. The resulting agreement of the parties must have been a genuine one.
4. The contract must be supported by consideration.

5. In certain exceptional cases the contract must have been made in a particular form.

A contract which does not comply with the above requirements may be either *void*, *voidable*, or *unenforceable*. A contract is void if it lacks one of the essential ingredients, so that in reality it does not exist at all. In a way the expression 'a void contract' is a contradiction in terms, since if the contract is 'void' there is really no contract at all.

A contract which is voidable is one that is valid to start with but which may be brought to an end (or avoided) at the option of one of the parties. If that party exercises this option the contract will cease to be operative from that time.

A contract is unenforceable if it is perfectly valid in all respects except for the fact that it cannot be enforced by an action in law. This will be the case if the party wishing to enforce it lacks some particular type of evidence (*e.g.*, evidence in writing) which is necessary for the enforcement of this type of contract. It should be remembered, however, that except for its unenforceability the contract is still a valid one, so that if the other party performs it he will be unable to recover whatever he may have given or paid, having given or paid it in pursuance of a valid contract.

We shall now proceed to a discussion of the essential ingredients —other than the capacity of the parties, which has been described in Chapter Three—of a valid contract.

Offers

The first step towards the formation of a contract is taken by the party who makes an offer to the other party. The offer must express a definite intention on the part of the person making it (called 'the offeror') to enter into a contract with the person to whom it is addressed (known as the 'offeree'). An offer may be addressed to one particular person, who would then be the only one who could accept it, or it may be addressed to a group of people, any of whose members could accept, or to the world at large, where anyone could accept. An offer of a reward to the finder of some lost property would fall into the third category.

An offer, as an expression of a definite intention to enter into a contract with the offeree, must be clearly distinguished from a mere statement that the person making it is willing to negotiate a contract. Such a statement is referred to as an *invitation to make an offer*. The person making it invites some particular person or perhaps any member of the general public to make an offer to him which he will consider on its merits and accept if he should think fit to do so. Goods exhibited in a shop-window with or without a price-ticket attached to them do not represent an offer by the shopkeeper but merely constitute an invitation to the general public to make an offer. A customer who enters the shop and asks for one of the exhibited articles is making the offer to the shopkeeper, and the latter may accept or reject the offer as he pleases. The fact that a price is indicated on the attached ticket merely gives the customer an idea as to what price he should offer. Exactly the same applies also to goods which are advertised in the Press. The offer comes from the reader who writes to the advertiser and not from the advertiser. In a self-service store the customer selecting goods from the shelves makes the offer which is accepted by the proprietor when the goods are brought to the cash-desk (*Pharmaceutical Society of Great Britain* v. *Boots*).

An offer must always be communicated to the offeree. If a person does something which might constitute acceptance of an offer where, however, he had no knowledge of the offer when he did the act in question, no contract will have come into existence.

The offeror may attach any conditions he likes to the offer, and these conditions will be binding on the offeree if he accepts the offer. It is essential, however, that the conditions should have been properly communicated to the offeree. This means that the offeror must do what is reasonably necessary to bring the conditions to the offeree's notice. If they have been brought to the offeree's notice and he neglects to study them he will be acting at his own risk.

Where, as part of the making of the contract, a printed document is handed by the offeror to the offeree, the conditions will be treated as properly communicated if there is a reference to them on some part of the document where it would be noticed by a reasonably careful person. The application of this rule is particularly important where the contractual document happens to be a ticket, such as a railway or bus ticket. In that case it is obviously impossible for the conditions to be printed in full on the limited space available on the ticket, but it has been held to be sufficient if there is a reference to the existence of conditions on the *face* of the ticket and the detailed conditions are available on request from the person who has issued the ticket. Thus, in *Thompson* v. *L. M. and S. Railway* the plaintiff had bought an excursion ticket. On the front of the ticket the words "For conditions see back" were printed, and on the back of the ticket it was said that the conditions were included in the company's time-table. The passenger made no attempt to obtain a copy of the time-table. One of the conditions provided that the company would not be responsible for injuries suffered by holders of excursion tickets. The plaintiff was injured. Her action failed, the court holding that the conditions had been properly communicated to her and were thus binding on her.

The document containing the conditions (or at least the reference to them) must be a contractual document in the sense that its handing to the offeree represents an essential part of the contract. It may be presumed that the offeree will study such a document with care, and he should thus observe the reference to the conditions. He cannot be expected to study other documents—*e.g.*, receipts—with equal care, and conditions contained on such non-contractual documents will not be treated as having been properly communicated. In *Chapelton* v. *Barry U.D.C.* the plaintiff had hired a deck-chair from the defendants. On the receipt which he was given by the defendants' servant there was a statement that the defendants would not be responsible for accidents suffered by users of the chairs. The deck-chair collapsed and the plaintiff was injured. It was held that the conditions had not been properly communicated to him and that they were therefore not binding on him.

Where a ticket has been issued by an automatic machine the position may be different. This was the situation in *Thornton* v. *Shoe Lane Parking Ltd.* where the plaintiff took his car into an automatic car park which he had never used before. A notice at the outside indicated the charges and stated that cars were parked at owner's risk. T. drove his car to the entrance where a machine produced a ticket which among other items referred to 'conditions'. On a pillar opposite the machine a set of these conditions was displayed which contained one stating that the proprietors would not be liable to a customer for injuries suffered while on their premises. When T. collected his car he was involved in an accident and sustained severe injuries. The plaintiff was awarded damages, the court *holding* that he had accepted an offer when he drove into the garage and that the contract could not be altered by anything printed on the ticket issued to him by the machine.

An offer may be revoked by the offeror at any time as long as it has not yet been accepted by the offeree. The offeror may revoke the offer even if he has given the offeree some time for acceptance. The sole purpose of giving the offeree a time-limit for acceptance is to indicate to him that the offer will lapse automatically if it has not been accepted before this time has expired. Where no time-limit has been set, the offer will also lapse after a reasonable time. What is a reasonable time is a question of fact, depending on the subject-matter of the offer. The more important the subject-matter the longer will be the time which the offeree has for considering the offer.

If the offeree wants to ensure that the offer should not be revoked before a certain time has expired he may do so by obtaining an *option* from the offeror. An option is in effect a separate contract, made between the offeror and the offeree, whereby in return for some consideration the offeror agrees to keep the offer open. Should he in this case revoke the offer before that time has expired, the offeree could sue him for damages on the ground of having broken the option agreement.

Acceptance

If the offeree wishes to accept the offer he must do so unconditionally. Where the offeror has laid down how the offer is to be accepted, the acceptance must comply with the offeror's requirements, otherwise it will not be valid. A conditional acceptance by the offeree amounts in law to a rejection of the offer, coupled with the making of a counteroffer. Where an offer has been rejected, whether expressly or impliedly by the making of a counteroffer, the original offer ceases to be operative, and the offeree cannot later fall back on it and accept it. Thus, if I offer my house to B for £5000 and he replies saying that he will buy it for £4500, no contract has come into existence. B has made a counteroffer to me which I may accept or ignore as I please. If I do not choose to accept it B will be unable to accept my original offer, as this offer is now no longer operative.

The offeree must accept the offer within the time laid down for acceptance by the offeror. If no such time has been fixed the acceptance must take place within a reasonable time. The acceptance is not operative until it has been communicated to the offeror. If it never reaches the offeror there is no contract. There are, however, two exceptions to this rule, where an acceptance becomes operative even though it has not reached the offeror. They are:

1. Where the offer is one which is intended to be accepted by being acted upon, there is no need to communicate acceptance to the offeror. In *Carlill* v. *Carbolic Smoke Ball Co.* the defendants had advertised that they would pay a hundred pounds to anyone who contracted influenza after using their smoke ball (a preparation for which it was claimed that it would prevent the user from contracting influenza). The plaintiff bought a smoke ball in a chemist's shop, used it according to the instructions, and contracted influenza after all. It was held that she was entitled to claim the hundred pounds, since she had accepted the defendants' offer by buying and using the smoke ball, the offer being worded in such a way as to show clearly that the offerors had waived the necessity for communicating an acceptance.

2. Where the parties have agreed that the acceptance should be made by post, the acceptance is operative the moment that the letter of acceptance has been posted, irrespective of whether that letter actually reached the offeror. The agreement of the parties that the acceptance should take place by post need not be an express one; it may be implied from the parties' conduct—such as where the offer has

been made by post or even where the parties are living in different towns and it is reasonable for them to communicate by post.

It is important to note here that, while the acceptance by post is operative from the moment of posting, the offer, or the revocation of an offer, is not operative until it actually reaches the offeree. Thus, if, as in *Henthorn* v. *Fraser*, the offeror sends a letter of revocation to the offeree before the offeree has accepted the offer, but the offeree posts the letter of acceptance before the letter of revocation has reached him, a contract will have come into existence from the moment when the letter of acceptance has been posted.

As the rule about acceptance by post forms an exception to the general principle according to which acceptances are not operative until they actually reach the offeror, it must be applied restrictively, and its application may not be extended to similar cases. An acceptance by telephone or by the modern means of Telex[1] (*Entores* v. *Miles*) will thus be effective only if and when it actually reaches the offeror.

The offeree is always free to ignore an offer completely. The offeror can attach a time-limit to his offer and may consider the offer as lapsed if it has not been accepted within this time, but he cannot consider the offer as accepted if there has been no rejection communicated to him within the time fixed. If, then, a publisher sends me a book and informs me that I shall be expected to pay its price if I do not return it within a fixed period, I can safely disregard this notice and leave it to the publisher to collect his book.

A mere mental acceptance of an offer is also insufficient to complete a contract. The acceptance must have been communicated, and if this has been overlooked there is no acceptance even if the offeree intended to accept. The plaintiff in *Felthouse* v. *Bindley* had written to X offering to buy X's horse for thirty pounds. He added that, if he did not hear from X to the contrary within a day, he would presume that the horse was his. X intended to accept and informed the auctioneer who was holding the horse for sale. Nevertheless the horse was sold. F. sued the auctioneer for damages for conversion; but the action failed, the court holding that F. had never become the owner of the horse, since his offer had not been expressly accepted by X.

The Agreement must not be Vague

The agreement between the parties must be a complete one. This means that in the agreement nothing must be left for future

[1] The Telex service allows the dispatch of messages by means of a teleprinter (operated like a typewriter), the messages being received and printed automatically by a similar instrument at the other end.

negotiation between the parties. If the parties have agreed on the major items of their proposed contract, but there is something of importance which still remains to be done, there is no complete agreement in existence and therefore there is no contract either. Examples of this may be found frequently in transactions involving land or houses where the agreement between the parties for the sale of the property is stated to be "subject to contract." This means in effect that neither party is prepared to be bound until such time as a formal contract has been drawn up (probably by their solicitors) and has been signed by them. There is no certainty, however, that the parties will, in fact, sign the contract when it is prepared, and therefore, there is no binding contract in existence.

Similar considerations apply also in other cases where the agreement between the parties contains other terms which are not definite or capable of being made definite. In *Scammell* v. *Ouston* there was a contract for the sale of a motor-van. Part of the price was to be paid at once, and the agreement provided that the buyer could pay the balance "on the usual hire-purchase terms" over a period of two years. The court held that there were no "usual" hire-purchase terms in existence at that time, so that the agreement was too vague to be a contract.

The legal principle involved in this problem is sometimes stated as that "there can be no contract to make a contract." You cannot bindingly agree that you will make a contract in the future. This sweeping statement has to be interpreted with a grain of salt. It is, in fact, possible to make a contract for the purpose of contracting in the future, *provided* that all the details of the contract to be made in the future are either certain or at least ascertainable. After all, an engagement to marry is a contract to make a contract. As an example of a valid contract providing for the making of future contracts we may quote *Foley* v. *Classique Coaches, Ltd*, where F. had sold some land to the defendants on condition that they should buy all their petrol from him at a price to be agreed between them from time to time. It was provided that if the parties were unable to agree on the price the matter should be submitted to arbitration. The defendants contended now that there was no binding obligation on them to buy any petrol from the plaintiff, but it was held that, as provision had been made for submitting any disputes to arbitration, the future contract was certain enough to be the subject-matter of a present binding agreement.

Mistake

We have stated already that the agreement of the parties must have been a genuine, or real, one. There can be no such real agreement if, because of a mistake, the parties have never really consented to the same thing. Not every mistake of a party made in connection with a proposed contract will necessarily invalidate the contract. Mistakes of law—*i.e.*, mistakes as to what the law provides—are never reasons for the upsetting of a contract, because underlying English law there is the presumption that everyone knows the law. This does not really mean that every person is believed to know all the rules of English law, but law imposes on everyone the duty of finding out the legal implications of anything he proposes to do. He neglects this duty at his own risk. If a mistake is to invalidate the agreement of the parties it must be a mistake of fact, and even then not every mistake of fact will have this effect. The mistake must be an operative mistake, which means that it must be a mistake concerning some really essential part of the contract. It is now generally accepted that an operative mistake must fall under one of three possible headings.

1. *A mistake as to the existence or as to the identity of the subject-matter.* The former mistakes are common mistakes, in the sense that both parties must be mistaken about the same thing; a mistake of one party only would not be sufficient to invalidate the contract. A mistake as to the existence of the subject-matter arises where both parties believed the subject-matter to be in existence when entering into the contract when the subject-matter, in fact, did not exist, either never having existed or having been destroyed before the making of the contract. No contract has come into existence in these circumstances. The subject-matter need not necessarily be a tangible thing: it might be a state of affairs which both parties impliedly accepted as the basis of their contract. Thus in *Galloway* v. *Galloway* husband and wife entered into a separation agreement, under which the husband promised to make a weekly allowance to his wife. Subsequently it was discovered that the parties had never been married, although they had always believed themselves to be married. It was held that the separation agreement was void, as the state of affairs—*i.e.*, marriage—which both parties considered to be the basis of their agreement, did not exist.

A mistake as to the identity of the subject-matter is one where the parties enter into a contract, each believing that the contract referred to a different thing. This is known as a mutual mistake. The leading case is *Raffles* v. *Wichelhaus*, where the subject-matter of the contract was a cargo of cotton described as being on board the ss. *Peerless* in the port of Bombay. Unknown to the parties, there were two ships of the same name in the port, both having cargoes of cotton on board. The seller was thinking of the one which was due to leave later, while the buyer only knew of the ship which was due to sail earlier. The court held that there was no contract.

It is important to note in respect of both the types of mistake discussed above that the mistake must be one affecting the subject-matter as such, and not merely its quality. If I buy a vase from a dealer, and both of us genuinely believe that the vase is an antique, while in fact it is not, this would not be a case of mistake in identity but a mere mistake in the quality of the thing, insufficient to avoid the contract.

2. *A mistake in the identity of the other party.* Not every mistake in the identity of the person with whom a contract is made will suffice to make the contract void. The identity of the other party must be in some way a material part of the contract. It stands to reason that this kind of mistake is an unilateral one, as one must presume that a person knows his own identity. In exactly the same way in which we had to distinguish above between a mistake in the identity of the subject-matter and a mere mistake in its quality, so we also have to distinguish between a mistake in the identity of the other party and a mistake in the quality of the other party If I know with whom I am making a contract, but I mistakenly believe that he is a person of substance, while in fact he is a crook, the contract is not void for mistake in identity, and it makes no difference that the other party has misrepresented himself as a person of substance. We shall see later that such a contract may possibly be voidable on the grounds of misrepresentation, but it will certainly not be void for mistake. In *King's Norton Metal Co.* v. *Edridge*, X had notepaper printed showing some large, albeit non-existent, factory premises and a whole string of foreign agencies. Using this notepaper, he ordered and obtained from the plaintiffs a quantity of goods, which he promptly resold to the defendants, who acted in perfectly good faith. X then disappeared with the proceeds of the sale. The plaintiffs claimed the goods from the defendants, alleging that the contract which they had made with X was void and that X had therefore been unable to pass a good title to the goods to the defendants. The court held that the contract with X was not void, as the plaintiffs had known that they were selling goods to X, even though they mistakenly believed him to be a respectable businessman. The defendants were able to retain the goods. This case may be contrasted with *Cundy* v. *Lindsay*, where X was induced by a man named Blenkarn to supply goods to him. Blenkarn had intentionally signed his letter to X in such a way as to make him believe that it came from a well-known firm, Blenkiron & Co. It was held that as X had never intended to contract with Blenkarn, there was no contract between them, and X was entitled to recover the goods from an innocent purchaser who had bought them from Blenkarn. Similarly, in *Ingram* v. *Little*, the plaintiffs had been induced by a rogue, who claimed to be a man called Hutchinson, to sell their car to him in exchange for a cheque which

turned out to be worthless. The rogue sold the car to the defendant who bought it in good faith. The plaintiffs successfully claimed the return of the car from the defendant, the court holding that they had not intended to deal with the rogue, but only with Hutchinson, a respected local man, so that their mistake was one of identity and not merely of quality.

In a more recent case, however, the Court of Appeal appears to have overruled *Ingram* v. *Little*. This is the case of *Lewis* v. *Averay* where A. had sold a car to a swindler who claimed to be Richard Greene, the well-known actor. The swindler produced a cheque for the agreed price (£450) signed in Greene's name and since the owner of the car showed some unwillingness to part with it against an uncleared cheque, the swindler also produced what purported to be an identification card for Greene issued by a film studio. The owner then handed over the car and the log book. The swindler sold the car to a dealer, L., who was unaware of how the car had been obtained. When the cheque bounced, A. tried to reclaim the car from L. The Court of Appeal held that he was not entitled to do so since he had been quite willing to deal with the person who called on him and sell the car to him, even though he might not have parted with its possession against an uncleared cheque if he had not believed that the customer was a well-known actor.

3. *Mistake as to the significance of a written document.*

> Whenever a man of full age and understanding, who can read and write, signs a legal document which is put before him for signature—by which I mean a document which, it is apparent on the face of it, is intended to have legal consequences—then, if he does not take the trouble to read it, but signs it as it is, relying on the words of another as to its character or contents or effect, he cannot be heard to say that it is not his document. By his conduct in signing it he has represented, to all those into whose hands it may come, that it is his document; and once they act upon it as being his document, he cannot go back on it, and say that it was a nullity from the beginning.[1]

Where, however, the signer of the document suffered from some disability, physical or mental, and was, therefore, mistaken as to the importance of the document which he signed, he may plead *non est factum* (it is not my deed) and escape liability on it. In exceptional cases only will this plea be open to persons not suffering from such disability and it will be up to them to prove that they had not been careless in signing the document and that what they signed in fact was fundamentally different from what they intended to sign.

Thus, in *Gallie* v. *Lee*,[2] an old lady who was unable to read because

[1] Lord Denning, M. R. in *Gallie* v. *Lee*.

[2] This case went eventually to the House of Lords where it was reported under

her glasses were broken, was persuaded by her nephew to transfer the leasehold of her house to L. when in fact she thought and was led to believe that she was giving it to the nephew. L. mortgaged the leasehold with a building society who, when L. failed to pay instalments, sought to obtain possession of the house. Mrs G.'s plea of *non est factum* failed, partly because of her lack of care, but also because the transaction in which she was involved was not fundamentally different from what she had intended to do, namely surrendering the leasehold of her house.

Misrepresentation

Misrepresentation is an untrue statement of fact, made by one party to a contract to the other, either at or before the time of entering into the contract, with the intention that the person to whom the statement is made should act upon it, and when he has in fact acted upon it.

Misrepresentation must be a statement of fact and not one of law, since everyone is presumed to know the law. The statement must have come from a party to the contract (or from a person acting for him) and not from a stranger to the contract. The statement must have been made at some time before the contract has been completed, since a statement made after that time cannot have induced the other party to enter into the contract. Lastly, the statement must have been acted upon by the person to whom it has been made. If he ignores the statement and enters into the contract for some entirely different reason the statement will have no effect on the validity of the contract. If the statement has been actually embodied in the contract it becomes part of it, and if it is proved to be untrue the innocent party will have remedies for breach of contract and not for misrepresentation. Here we are concerned with those cases only where the statement is not embodied in the contract.

A misrepresentation may be innocent or fraudulent. It is fraudulent where the person making the statement knows that it is untrue or makes it recklessly, not caring whether it is true or not, or where he himself does not believe the statement to be true. Any other case of misrepresentation comes under the heading of innocent misrepresentation.

The difference between innocent and fraudulent misrepresentation was important, because of the remedies which were open to the party who had been misled into making the contract. Where the misrepresentation was an innocent one, the misled party could either refuse to perform the contract or he could ask the court to rescind it (*i.e.*, set it aside). Rescission of a contract is a remedy of equity which used to

the name of *Saunders* v. *Anglia Building Society*, the original plaintiff having died in the meantime.

be unknown at common law. At common law there was in effect no remedy for innocent misrepresentation. As the purpose of the rescission was that the parties should revert to their position before the contract was made, there could be no rescission of the contract if something had happened which made this *restitutio in integrum* (return to the previous position) impossible—*e.g.*, consumption of the subject-matter of the contract or disposal of it to an innocent third party who acquired it for value. Furthermore, as with all other remedies of equity, an action for rescission of a contract had to be introduced promptly (delay defeats equities). Thus, in *Leaf* v. *International Galleries*, L. bought a drawing which the sellers claimed to be an original Constable. This was not true, but the sellers themselves did not realize it. Five years later the buyer discovered that the sellers had innocently misled him into buying the picutre and he asked the court to set aside the contract. This was refused because of the lapse of time.

A person who has been fraudulently misled into making a contract has the above remedy, but in addition he may also claim from the other party damages for fraud.

The Misrepresentation Act 1967, provides now that a contract made after a misrepresentation may be rescinded even if the misrepresentation has become a term of the contract or the contract has been performed. It further provides that damages may be claimed by the party misled who has suffered a loss even though the misrepresentation was innocent, unless the person who made the misleading statement is able to prove that he had reasonable grounds to believe and did in fact believe until the time the contract was made that the facts represented were true (*i.e.*, that he had not been negligent in making the statement). Another provision of the Act permits the court to award damages in lieu of rescission in the case of innocent misrepresentation if in the light of all the circumstances this step would appear to be equitable.

A provision contained in any contract excluding or restricting the liability of a party for any misrepresentation made by him before the contract was entered into will not be enforced by the court unless the provision appears to be fair and reasonable in the circumstances of the case.

In the situations discussed above a person is responsible for making an untrue statement which induces another party to enter into a contract with him. The party misled will have the remedies for misrepresentation even if he could have easily ascertained that he was not being told the truth. You may always rely on a statement which has been made to you by the other party. In general, however, a person is not bound to volunteer any information and keeping silent will not be looked upon as a statement. When entering into a contract you need not volunteer to the other party all the defects from which the subject-matter of the contract is suffering. You may leave it to him to find out the defects himself There are only two instances in our law where a duty is imposed on a person to volunteer certain information and where the withholding of this information will be treated as misrepresentation.

1. Where a person has made a representation, and before the other party has entered into the contract this representation has become untrue, the person who made it is bound to correct his earlier statement. In *With* v. *O'Flanagan*, a doctor who was about to sell his practice informed the prospective buyer that the practice yielded about £2000 a year. The negotiations dragged on, and four months later, when the contract was finally signed, the takings from the practice had fallen to an average of five pounds per week. It was held that the seller should have informed the buyer of the change in circumstances and, as this had not been done, the buyer was entitled to rescind the contract.

2. In entering into a contract of utmost good faith (*a contract uberrimæ fidei*) a person has to make a full disclosure of all relevant facts to the other party. Contracts of utmost good faith are contracts where by the very nature of the contract certain facts of importance can only be known to one of the parties. The most typical contract of utmost good faith is a contract of insurance, where the insured has to volunteer to the insurer all facts that may have an influence on the insurer's decision whether to insure him at all and, if so, on what terms. Family settlements, contracts for the sale of land, contracts of guarantee, and contracts of partnership have also certain similarities with contracts of utmost good faith. In a contract for the sale of land the vendor is under a duty to disclose all defects in his title, but he need not disclose any physical defects in the property which he is selling. "Fraud apart, there is no law against selling tumble-down houses," as one judge pithily remarked. Similarly, in a contract of guarantee the creditor has to disclose to the guarantor anything which he may discover subsequently about the debtor, but this obligation does not extend to anything that may have happened before the contract has been entered into. A partner has to disclose to his fellow-partners any information concerning the affairs of the partnership business which has come into his possession.

Conditions and Warranties

Where a representation has been embodied in a contract it will become either a condition or a warranty. It is a condition where it forms a vital term of the contract, so that if this term is broken the innocent party will become entitled to treat the whole contract as discharged. Where, on the other hand, the term is not a vital one it will be a warranty, and a breach of such warranty will entitle the innocent party to damages but not to treat the whole contract as discharged.

Whether in fact a term in a contract should be treated as a condition or as a warranty depends on the intention of the parties. This intention may have been openly expressed by the parties, but, failing that, the court will have to deduce the parties' intention from all the facts of the contract. The choice of words by the parties is not relevant in this context, as they may well have used the term 'warranty' when what they really had in mind were conditions in the legal sense of the word.

Conditions and warranties may be collectively referred to as 'stipulations,' because they embody promises made by one party to the contract to the other. Such stipulations may be either express or implied ones. They are express stipulations where the party making the promises specifically embodies them in the contract. Where there is no specific mention of any stipulation, law may still imply its existence by providing that the stipulation has to be read into the contract. Implied stipulations are provided for by a number of Acts of Parliament, the most important of which is the Sale of Goods Act 1893.[1] This Act governs the sale of goods, defined as pure personalty, other than money. Five conditions and two warranties are implied in every contract for the sale of goods. The five *implied conditions*, all of which are promises by the seller of the goods, are:

1. The seller stipulates that he has a right to sell the goods or will have such a right at the time when the property is to pass. This means not only that he is the owner of the goods which he is selling (or is authorized by the owner to sell them) but also that there are no other legal obstacles, such as infringements of patents rights or copyrights, standing in the way of the sale.

2. In a sale of goods by sample the seller stipulates (*a*) that the goods supplied by him will be in accordance with the sample, (*b*) that the buyer will have a reasonable opportunity of comparing the goods with the sample, and (*c*) that the goods do not suffer from any defect which would not be recognizable on a reasonable examination of the sample.

A sale of goods is a sale of goods by sample where there is an express or implied provision in the contract to this effect. This means that the contract either specifically refers to a sample which has been considered by the parties before the contract was made or the contract has been entered into after a sample has been shown, even though there is no reference to it in the contract. The goods supplied by the seller must agree in quality with the sample, but even if they do

[1] As amended by the Supply of Goods (Implied Terms) Act 1973.

the seller will be liable for breach of condition if the goods suffer from any defect which a reasonable examination of the sample would not have revealed. The buyer is always bound to examine the sample, and if there is a defect which such a reasonable examination would have revealed he could not complain if, having ordered the goods, the goods suffer from the same defect. If the defect is one which could not be discovered by the kind of examination which a reasonable buyer would make, there is a breach of condition by the seller.

3. In a sale of goods by description the seller promises that the goods will agree with the description. Where there is a sale of goods by sample as well as by description, the goods supplied must agree both with the sample and with the description. There is a sale by description when the goods are described in the contract, whether by name, by quality, or in any other way. It is fair to say that whenever the buyer buys goods which he has not seen before the contract there must be a sale of goods by description.

4. In general, the seller is not responsible for the quality of the goods sold. The buyer should himself make sure that the goods which he is buying are suitable for whatever purpose he may want them, the general principle of the law being "*caveat emptor*"—*i.e.*, let the buyer beware. Where the seller sells goods in the course of a business there is an implied condition that the goods supplied shall be of merchantable quality, except as regards defects specifically drawn to the buyer's attention before the contract was made or if the buyer has examined the goods before the contract is made, in respect of such defects which this examination ought to have revealed. Goods are to be treated as being of merchantable quality if they are as fit for the purposes for which goods of this kind are normally bought as is reasonable to expect having regard to any description applied to them, their price and all other relevant circumstances.

5. Where the seller sells goods in the course of a business and the buyer, expressly or by implication, makes known to the seller any particular purpose for which the goods are being bought, there is an implied condition that the goods supplied under the contract are reasonably fit for that purpose, whether or not that is a purpose for which such goods are commonly supplied, except where the circumstances show that the buyer does not rely, or that it is unreasonable for him to rely on, the seller's skill or judgment.

The implied warranties by the seller are:

1. That the buyer will have undisturbed possession of the goods.

2. That the goods are free from any charge or incumbrance in favour of any third party not declared or known to the buyer at or before the time when the contract was made.

Both conditions and warranties, express or implied, may be excluded by agreement of the parties to the contract subject, however, to the following exceptions introduced by the Supply of Goods (Implied Terms) Act 1973:

1. An express condition or warranty does not negative an implied condition or warranty under the Act, unless inconsistent with it.
2. A term in a contract of sale excluding the implied condition that the seller has a right to sell and the implied warranty that the goods sold are free from charges, encumbrances, etc. would be void.
3. A term in a contract purporting to exclude the implied conditions in respect of the sale of goods by sample, by description and regarding the quality or fitness of the goods shall be absolutely void in the case of consumer sales, meaning a sale of goods (otherwise than by auction or competitive tender) by a seller in the course of his business where the goods are of a type ordinarily bought for private use or consumption and are sold to a person who does not buy them in the course of a business.
4. In the case of a sale of goods which is not a consumer sale as defined above, an attempt to exclude the conditions mentioned under (3) would not be enforceable to the extent to which it could be shown that it would not be fair and reasonable to allow reliance on such a disclaimer.

In determining whether reliance on such a term would be fair and reasonable regard should be had to all the circumstances of the case and, in particular, to:

(a) the relative strength of the bargaining position of seller and buyer, taking into account the availability of alternative products and alternative sources of supply;

(b) whether the buyer received an inducement to agree to the term;

(c) whether the buyer knew or should have known of the existence of the term;

(d) whether the goods had been manufactured, processed or adapted to the special requirements of the buyer.

It used to be believed that a condition which represented a *fundamental term* of the contract could not be excluded by the parties. The recent *Suisse Atlantique* case has stated, however, that it is not a rule of law that an exception clause in a contract would be nullified either by a fundamental breach of contract or by a breach of a fundamental term of the contract. In each case, everything depends on the construction of the contract as to whether the exception clause was intended to give exemption even from the consequences of a fundamental breach. A breach of a fundamental term entitles the innocent party to treat the contract as discharged, while a fundamental breach (which is basically the same thing as a total breach) will allow repudiation of the contract to take place only if the contractual performance would now be something radically different from what the parties had originally bargained for.

Duress and Undue Influence

Where one of the parties to a contract was not a free agent when entering into it, the contract will be voidable at his option. This situation may arise where the party has been subjected either to duress or to undue influence. A contract is entered into under duress where a party has been coerced into making it either by violence or by threats of violence or by having some of his property seized or by threats of criminal proceedings. The person threatened in all the above instances may be either the contractual party himself or someone else who is so close to him that a threat to that person would be treated as a threat to the contractual party himself. If a person enters into a contract under the threat, express or implied, of criminal proceedings the contract will be voidable by him irrespective of whether there existed some foundation for the taking of the proceedings, the reason being that it is an abuse of criminal proceedings to use the threat of them to extort contractual concessions.

A contract is voidable on the grounds of undue influence where there existed between the parties a relationship of such a kind that one of them was guided or influenced by the views of the other party. It is always possible to prove the existence of such a relationship, but in certain cases law presumes its existence. This applies to the relationships between parent and child, solicitor and client, doctor and patient, guardian and ward, trustee and beneficiary, and minister of religion and a member of his congregation. Where a contract has been entered into between any one of these persons and the other party in the pair, the contract will be voidable at the option of the weaker party. The presumption of undue influence may, however, be rebutted if it can be shown that the weaker party had independent legal advice before entering into the contract. It should be noted that there is no presumption of undue influence in contracts between husband and wife. Equity might in some circumstances be prepared to set aside a bargain where a party has taken advantage of a poor or ignorant person, such as in *Evans* v. *Llewellin*, where a poor man sold for £210 a share in an estate worth £1700.

While duress was recognized by common law, undue influence was a ground for having a contract set aside only in equity. From this follows that he who wishes to have a contract set aside on the grounds of undue influence will have to go to court as soon as possible after the influence has ceased to operate (*Allcard* v. *Skinner*).

Consideration

It is a principle of English law that a contract, except where made by deed, must be supported by consideration if it is to be legally valid. A contract is basically a form of exchange; the party receives in return for his act or promise something from the other party, and this something is referred to as the consideration. We distinguish between good consideration and valuable consideration. Good consideration consists of such things as gratitude, thanks, or love which a person may return for a promise that has been made to him. Needless to say that good consideration is insufficient for legal purposes. What law requires is valuable consideration, and that has been defined in *Currie* v. *Misa* as "some right, interest, profit or benefit accruing to one party or some forbearance, detriment, loss or responsibility, given, suffered or undertaken by the other." What this means is that, if A makes a promise to B, B's consideration for the promise may take the form either of some kind of benefit extended to A or of some detriment or forbearance suffered by B which has not directly benefited A. It stands to reason that the consideration, whatever it may be, must have been agreed upon by the parties and cannot be selected unilaterally by B.

Consideration may be *executed* or *executory*. Executed consideration is some act performed for the other party, while executory consideration is a promise made to the other party. Thus, if X in return for a book handed to him by Y pays Y £1 his consideration is executed. If he promises to pay £1 next week consideration is executory. Both types of consideration come, of course, under the general description of valuable consideration.

The parties to a contract are the persons who have provided consideration. The relationship that exists between them is that of privity of contract. A person who has not provided any consideration but who was to benefit from the contract may not bring an action for breach of contract if the contract is not performed, as privity of contract did not exist between him and the party who failed to carry out his contractual promises. In *Tweddle* v. *Atkinson*, A was about to marry B. Before the marriage A's father agreed with B's father that on the day of the wedding each of them would pay £100 to the bridegroom. A's father paid his share, but B's father did not. The bridegroom now sued the executors of B's father (who had died in the meantime) for the promised £100, but the court held that, as A had not been a party to the contract, he could not sue. The principle of privity of contract has been reaffirmed recently by the House of Lords in *Beswick* v. *Beswick*. In this case a coal merchant transferred his business to his nephew who agreed in return to retain the transferor as a consultant for the rest of his life at an agreed weekly rate of remuneration and to pay, after the transferor's death, a weekly sum to his widow. The transferor died and the young man refused to pay the weekly sum to his aunt. An action by the aunt, suing in her personal capacity as a third party beneficiary under the contract, failed because of the absence of privity of contract, but she succeeded in an action as the executrix of her husband's estate claiming for an order of specific performance to compel the purchaser to carry out the terms of the agreement.

The above principle used to be also of importance in connection with contracts containing a resale price maintenance clause where a manufacturer had fixed the prices at which his products were to be sold to the general public. Such terms were enforceable against a party who had directly contracted with the manufacturer that he would observe the official price (*Dunlop* v. *New Garage, Ltd*), but not against a party who had bought the goods from an intermediary (*e.g.*, a wholesaler) and was therefore not in direct contractual relationship with the price-fixing manufacturer. The Resale Prices Act 1964 has declared void any attempt to impose a minimum resale price on any goods, other than exempted goods, the power of declaring certain types of goods as being exempted resting with the Restrictive Practices Court.

As has been stated above, consideration is required for the validity of any contract not made by deed, even though the contract may be in writing and is otherwise in accordance with the law. The following points should be noted about valuable consideration:

1. *Consideration need not be Adequate*. There is no need for the value of the counterpromise to be anywhere near that of the promise which is supported by it as long as the consideration has some value and is not just 'good' consideration. Gross inadequacy of consideration may, however, be possible evidence of fraud, though this would have to be proved also by other facts. Behind this principle lies the reasoning that persons of full age are free to enter into any contract they like, and it is for them to determine whether they are satisfied with the bargain which they are making.

2. *Consideration must be Real*. This means that the party making the sacrifice loses something which at least at the time when he makes the sacrifice appears to him to be something of value. Thus, if a person merely promises to do something which he is bound to do already he does not make a real sacrifice and there is thus no real consideration. The best illustration of this is the case where a debtor promises to discharge his debt to his creditor by the payment of a smaller sum. Even if the creditor accepts this payment "in full settlement," he will still be able to claim the balance, as he has received no real consideration for his promise to discharge the debtor from the payment of that balance.

The creditor in *Foakes* v. *Beer*, Mrs B., agreed not to claim interest from her debtor, Dr F., if he paid the debt by stated instalments. F. did so, but after he had paid off the principal sum Mrs B. nevertheless claimed the payment of interest. It was held that she was entitled to succeed, as she had received no real consideration for her promise not to claim interest. F.'s consent to pay his debt by instalments could not be real consideration, as he was bound to pay the debt in any case.

The ruling that the acceptance of a smaller sum in settlement of a larger debt will not discharge the debt in full applies, of course, only where the creditor has not received some real consideration for his promise not to claim more. Thus, where the debt which is discharged by the payment of a smaller sum was not due yet at the time, or where payment was tendered at some place other than where the debt was payable, the debt will be discharged, as the things that have been done will be looked upon as real consideration. The creditor will also be prevented from enforcing his legal rights when it would be inequitable for him to insist upon them and the other party has relied on his promise.

The importance of the principle in *Foakes* v. *Beer* has been considerably reduced by an *obiter dictum* of Denning J. in *Central London Property Trust* v. *High Trees House*. The plaintiffs had before the War let a block of flats to the defendants. In the first year of the War many flats were unoccupied, and the defendants would probably have terminated the lease if the plaintiffs had not agreed to reduce the rent. After the War had ended the plaintiffs claimed the arrears of rent. The court held that, while the plaintiffs could at any time demand again the payment of the rent as originally agreed, they could not claim the arrears, because by their conduct in allowing a reduction they had induced the defendants to do something (*i.e.*, not terminate the lease) which they otherwise would not have done. In general terms the rule may be stated as follows: If A, without consideration, makes a promise to B which is accepted and acted upon by B and the parties intended this promise to be a legally binding one, then B will be able to set up this promise by way of defence if he is sued by A.[1] The rule in *Foakes* v. *Beer* persists, however, to the extent that B will not be able to bring an action himself against A; he can only use the promise by way of defence.

If A is already under contract to B to do something, a subsequent promise to do this made to C may be valuable consideration for a counterpromise by C, since in case of failure to carry out the promise A will be subject to two actions for breach of contract—*i.e.*, by B as well as by C. In *Shadwell* v. *Shadwell* an uncle promised his nephew, a budding barrister who was engaged to be married, that if he

[1] See note on page 122.

married his fiancée he would pay him an annuity until such time as his earnings at the bar reached an agreed amount. The court held that this was a binding contract and that the nephew's promise to marry his fiancée was real consideration vis-à-vis his uncle, irrespective of the fact that the young man was already bound to marry the girl because of having become engaged to her.

3. *Consideration must proceed from the Promise.* This point has been discussed already in connection with the principle of privity of contract.

4. *Consideration must be Legal.* This point will be discussed in a later paragraph.

5. *Consideration must not be Past.* If A makes a promise to B, B's consideration must come after A's promise. Thus, if A promises something to B in return for a service which B has rendered already B's consideration would be past and thus not sufficient to validate the contract.

It is sometimes claimed that consideration may be past where B's service has been rendered in circumstances raising the presumption that it would be paid for, the subsequent promise to pay being merely a method of agreeing on the price to be paid for the service. In fact, however, this type of situation does not create an exception to the principle that past consideration will not be valuable consideration, since we must presume that when B rendered the service to A there existed already a contract between them, albeit an implied one, that payment would be made at a reasonable figure. The consideration for the promise to pay was thus created simultaneously with the promise.

There is, however, one exception to the principle and that is bills of exchange. A bill of exchange is treated as having been given for valuable consideration even though the consideration was past (Bills of Exchange Act 1882).

The Form of Contracts

The general rule is that a contract validly entered into between parties capable of entering into contracts is enforceable irrespective of the form in which it has been made. Contracts may be divided according to the form in which they have been made into specialty contracts and simple contracts. Specialty contracts are contracts made by deed, while simple contracts are those made in any other form, whether in writing, orally (parol contracts), or even by mere conduct of the parties.

A deed is a written instrument which has been signed, sealed, and delivered. To-day, when few persons other than bodies corporate have their own seal, any kind of seal will suffice, and even a paper wafer in the form of a seal will do. The deed is not complete, however, until it has been delivered by the party executing it. Delivery can be actual, where the party executing the deed hands it to the other party in person, or constructive, where he places a finger on the seal in the presence of a witness and states, "I deliver this as my act and deed."

The main differences between specialty contracts and simple contracts are the following:

1. A specialty contract does not require to be supported by consideration. Specific performance of such a contract will not be granted, however, by the court unless there is valuable consideration to support it.

2. A right of action under a simple contract is barred after six years while the corresponding period for specialty contracts is twelve years (Limitation Act 1939; see page 110).

3. Where the parties have entered into a simple contract concerning a certain subject-matter and subsequently make out a deed to cover the same subject-matter, the simple contract is said to have been merged into the deed and thereby becomes extinct.

Deeds are used in practice on those occasions where formality is essential in order to impress upon the parties the importance of the transaction. Not all the examples which are given below relate to contracts; some of them relate to transfers (or conveyances) which follow the making of a contract and are intended to pass property rights. Deeds will have then to be used in the following cases:

1. Contracts which are not supported by valuable consideration.
2. Leases of land for more than three years.
3. The transfer of shares in a British ship.
4. The transfer of the title to land.

Where a transaction is required to be made by deed, non-compliance with this formal requirement would invalidate the transaction.

The following transactions (contracts and transfers) have to be made in writing, though not necessarily by deed. Where the transaction in these cases is effected otherwise than in writing it would again fail to be legally operative.

1. A contract of marine insurance (though not other contracts of insurance).
2. Bills of exchange, cheques, and promissory notes.
3. An acknowledgment of a statute-barred debt (see page 111).
4. Contracts under the Moneylenders Act 1927.
5. Hire-purchase contracts, if subject to the Hire Purchase Act 1965. (Replaced now by the Consumer Credit Act 1974.)
6. The transfer of shares in a limited company.
7. The assigning of a copyright.

Apart from the instances mentioned above and a few others of the same kind, we have also to consider contracts which, though they may be made in any form which the parties wish to adopt, will not be enforced by the court unless there exists written evidence of them. This means that in the absence of this special form of evidence the contract though valid will be unenforceable.

There used to be a fair number of contracts to which this evidential condition applied, but only two have survived.

1. A contract of guarantee. (Section 4 of the Statute of Frauds 1677.) This is a contract whereby one person (the guarantor) promises another that he will be responsible for the debt or wrongdoing of a third party. The guarantor's liability is conditional upon the creditor being unable to obtain satisfaction from the main debtor and differs in this way from a so-called contract of indemnity where a person promises to be responsible for the payment of a sum of money independent of another person's indebtedness. If I say to X who is about to sell something to Y, "You may sell it to him because if he does not pay I shall pay," this is a contract of guarantee. If in the same situation I say to X, "I shall be responsible for payment," this is a contract of indemnity, and this contract is enforceable even in the absence of written evidence.

2. Any contract for the sale or other disposition of land. (S.40 of the Law of Property Act 1925.) The "other dispositions" referred to above cover such transactions as leases or mortgages.

The two contracts mentioned cannot be enforced unless there is some written evidence available to prove their existence. The best possible evidence would be the contract itself if made in writing. Where the contract is not in writing other evidence will be acceptable, provided it satisfies the requirements of a "memorandum in writing" as defined by the Statute of Frauds and the Law of Property Act.

1. The memorandum must contain the names of the parties. Normally these names must appear on the same document, except that in the case of a letter the envelope may be produced as additional evidence in order to satisfy the requirement.

2. The document must describe the subject-matter of the contract, and this includes also all the essential terms of the contract. Thus, in *Hawkins* v. *Price* the plaintiff had bought a house from the defendant for £1000, vacant possession of the house to be given on completion of the contract. The only written evidence of the contract was a receipt for a deposit of £100 which the defendant had signed and given to the plaintiff. There was no reference on the receipt to the time when vacant possession would be given. It was held that the receipt was not a sufficient memorandum in writing, as it omitted a most important term of the contract.

3. The memorandum must state the consideration which has been

given, except in the case of a contract of guarantee, where this is not necessary.

4. The memorandum must have been signed by or on behalf of the person against whom it is to be used in evidence. The signature need not appear at the end of the document as long as it is clearly shown that the person against whom the memorandum is to be used has accepted responsibility for its contents.

5. Any written document which satisfies the above points may serve as a "memorandum in writing," irrespective of the purpose for which it has been issued. It could be a private letter, a receipt, or anything of that sort.

A contract which has to be evidenced in writing cannot be enforced at common law in the absence of written evidence. The equitable *doctrine of part performance* may come, however, to the assistance of a party who wishes to enforce a contract for the sale or lease of land which has been validly entered into but which is not evidenced by writing. The doctrine of part performance is based on the maxim of equity which says, "Equity looks to the intent not to the form." The conditions to be fulfilled for the application of the doctrine are the following:

1. The contract must be one for which specific performance will be granted, since equity will only force the other party to complete the contract by executing the necessary deeds. Damages would not be granted in this case.

2. The party wishing to enforce the contract must himself have partly performed the contract. The act of part performance must be exclusively referable to the contract to be enforced. This means that what the plaintiff has done can be explained only by reference to a contract. The payment of a sum of money would thus not be a sufficient act of part performance, as there are many possible reasons why a person may pay a sum of money to another.

3. The situation is such that it would be fraudulent on the part of the defendant to take advantage of the absence of writing. In *Rawlinson* v. *Ames*, A. had verbally agreed to take a twenty-one years' lease of the plaintiff's flat. In order to meet A's requirements the plaintiff had made structural alterations to the flat. When A. then refused to take the flat the court held that R. was entitled to a decree for specific performance.

4. Sufficient other evidence must be available to prove that the contract has been entered into.

Illegality

A contract which is illegal is absolutely void. It may be illegal either because it is forbidden by the law or because a court will not be prepared to enforce it on the grounds of 'public policy' or because the contract has been entered into for an illegal or immoral purpose.

Contracts declared to be Illegal by Statute

A gaming or wagering contract is illegal (Gaming Act 1845). Gaming or wagering is a contract under which a person agrees to pay a sum of money to another on the happening of some uncertain event in return for an immediate payment or for a payment which is to take place if the event does not materialize. The parties must have no interest in the subject-matter of the wager other than the stake. This is the difference between this contract and one of insurance, which otherwise closely resembles a wager. The main difference between wagers and gaming contracts is that in the latter case the bet is one on the result of a game or pastime while in the former case it is one on any other event of fact (*e.g.*, the result of an election).

An essential feature of a gaming or wagering contract is that both parties must stand to win or lose. Where, as with a football-pool competition, one side does not stand to lose, the contract is not one of gaming in the legal sense and could therefore be enforced, provided that the parties had the intention of entering into a legal relationship when they made the contract.

Contracts opposed to Public Policy

The term 'public policy' is a technical legal term and should not be identified with the policy of the government in office. The list of contracts which are deemed to be 'opposed to public policy' is by now complete, and it is most unlikely that the courts will add further contracts to the list. The following contracts may be mentioned as examples of contracts which are opposed to public policy:

1. A contract in *absolute* restraint of marriage—*i.e.*, a contract whereby a person promises not to marry at all. A contract whereby a person promises not to marry a particular other person or a person belonging to a certain class of people (*e.g.*, a Roman Catholic) would be valid, provided that the restriction was one which could be clearly interpreted by the courts.

2. A contract tending to impede the administration of justice. The main example is a contract whereby a person agrees not to prosecute a person who has committed a criminal offence—*e.g.*, promising not to prosecute a burglar provided that he returns some of the loot. We call this an agreement to stifle a prosecution. Where the victim of the offence has the choice either of prosecuting the offender for the crime or of suing him for tort, he may agree not to

take any steps against the offender—*e.g.*, in the case of an assault on his person.

3. A contract tending to injure the public service. This includes the sale of a public office or the receipt of bribes to procure certain favours from a government department—*e.g.*, the grant of honours. In *Parkinson* v. *College of Ambulance* an agreement to procure a knighthood in return for a large donation to a charity was held to be illegal.

4. A contract involving trading with the enemy in wartime is illegal, unless made with the licence of the Crown. An 'enemy' for the purpose of this contract is any person resident in enemy or enemy-occupied territory.

5. A contract of champerty or maintenance is illegal. Maintenance means assisting a person in bringing or defending a legal action where the person giving the assistance has himself no legal interest in the subject-matter of the dispute. Champerty is the same as maintenance, only that the person giving the assistance has been promised a share in the proceeds of the action.

6. A contract tending to injure the safety of the country is illegal, such as where a person enters into a contract the purpose of which is the breaking of the law of a friendly nation (*Foster* v. *Driscoll*—smuggling whisky into the United States while prohibition was enforced in that country).

7. A contract interfering with the performance of parental or marital duties is illegal, such as where a person agrees to sell his child or his wife.

8. A contract in unreasonable restraint of trade is also looked upon as illegal. At common law, contracts in restraint of trade were absolutely void, and it is only in the last two centuries that some at least of these contracts have been enforced by the courts. A contract in restraint of trade is one whereby a person accepts some limitation as to his future choice of occupation or business or as to the conduct of his business affairs. A restraint of trade may either be based on a separate contract or, more frequently, it consists of a clause inserted in a contract entered into for a different purpose. There are three main types of these contracts:

(*a*) Restraints of trade embodied in a contract for the sale of the goodwill of a business, where the seller promises that he will not compete with the buyer of the business.

(*b*) Contracts between competing business-men whereby they agree on some common price or selling or production policy (Cartel agreements).

(*c*) A restraint is also frequently embodied in a contract of employment where the employee promises that if and when he should leave his present employment he will not for a fixed period of time and within an agreed area set up in competition with his existing employer or work for a competitor.

A contract in restraint of trade is illegal and therefore void unless it is deemed to be reasonable. In order to be reasonable it must be in theory both reasonable as between the contracting parties and also reasonable from the point of view of public interest, though very rarely will a restraint held to be reasonable between the parties be held to be unreasonable on the grounds of offending against the public interest.

A restraint of trade is reasonable between the parties if it adequately protects the legitimate interests of the party on whose behalf it has been imposed but does no more than that. The court is less ready to find the restraint reasonable where it has been imposed in a contract of employment than in the other types of contract mentioned, since an employee is deemed to have a more limited bargaining power than a business-man.

An employer is entitled to protect himself against possible competition by an employee only where the employee in the course of his employment is likely to come into contact either with trade secrets or with trade connexions (*i.e.*, where he comes into personal contact with customers who might follow him when he leaves his employment). Where the employer's business has no trade secrets or trade connections of the type described the restraint can never be reasonable, as it will be deemed to have been imposed for the sole purpose of preventing competition as such. Even where there are trade secrets or trade connections, the restraint must not be wider than is necessary to protect the legitimate interests of the employer. The extent of the restraint in time and space which will be deemed to be reasonably wide is always a question of fact, depending largely on the type of business conducted by the employer. Where he is drawing his customers from a wider area, the restraint may be wider in space; where his trade secrets are likely to be of value for a longer time, the restraint may be for a longer duration. Much depends also on the exact position occupied by the employee. If he has been working in a subordinate and not well-paid capacity the court will not readily accept the reasonableness of a restraint based on acquaintance with trade secrets, as the low pay seems to be a sign that the employer did not value the services of the employee very highly.

If the restraint consists of several parts, some of which are reasonable while others are unreasonably wide, the court may at its discretion enforce those parts which are reasonable while holding the others to be void. This severance of the good from the bad is possible only where it can be achieved without the court having to rewrite the restraint for the parties. In *Attwood* v. *Lamont* the plaintiff was in business in Kidderminster as tailor, dressmaker, hatter, milliner, and haberdasher. The defendant was employed by him as a cutter in the tailoring department. He agreed that after leaving his employment he would not carry on any business competing with that of the plaintiff within an area of ten miles. The restraint was held to be unreasonably wide, as it prevented the defendant in effect from entering into business as hatter, milliner, haberdasher, or dressmaker, whereas the only restraint to which the plaintiff would have been entitled would be that referring to the defendant's acquaintance with the trade connections of the tailoring department. The court refused to enforce even such a limited restraint, however, as it would have necessitated rewriting the contract.

Contracts entered into for an Illegal or Immoral Purpose

Where a contract, legal in itself, is entered into for an illegal or immoral purpose the court will refuse to enforce it. Thus, in *Alexander* v. *Rayson* the landlord of a block of luxury flats entered into an agreement with a tenant whereby the agreed rent should be paid partially as compensation for certain services which in fact were not provided. The reason behind this agreement was that the landlord did not want the rating authority to find out the true rental value of the premises. It was held that this contract had been entered into for an illegal purpose—namely, cheating the local authority out of their rateable revenue—and for that reason the court refused to enforce it.

The Effects of Illegality

An illegal contract is not necessarily a criminal one. Illegality with reference to contracts means merely that they will not be enforced by a court of law. As soon as the court discovers that a contract is illegal it will refuse to help the plaintiff any further. There is a legal maxim which says *In pari delicto potior est conditio defendentis* (where the guilt of the parties is equal the position of the defendant is the stronger one). This means that if both parties are equally responsible for the illegality the defendant is in the stronger position, because the court will not help the plaintiff to recover anything against him. Thus, if a contractor has done some work for you for which a government licence is required and no licence has been issued, the court will not order you to pay him the agreed price for his work. An illegal contract will never be enforced by the court, but in exceptional cases the court may allow a party to recover money which he has paid on a contract which was illegal:

1. Where the guilt of the parties is not equal and the plaintiff is less to blame for the illegality than the defendant. A mere mistake

of law on the part of the plaintiff will be no help to him, as he is presumed to know the law; but a mistake of fact induced by the defendant would help. Thus, where in the above example the householder was told by the contractor that he had obtained the licence and the householder then paid a sum of money as an advance to the contractor, he would be able to recover it even though the contract was illegal because of the absence of a licence.

2. Where the illegal purpose of the contract is not carried out because one of the parties repents in time and prevents its execution, that party will be able to claim the repayment of anything which he has paid out. Repentance is, however, feasible only if the possibility of carrying out the illegal purpose still existed. If the illegal purpose could not be attained for some other reason repentance would be too late. In *Bigos* v. *Bousted*, A agreed with B that B should supply some Italian currency to A's wife, who was on holiday in Italy. This contract was illegal as it offended against the exchange control regulations. A deposited some securities with B as guarantee for the repayment of the money to be advanced. B then refused to supply A's wife with the currency and also refused to return the securities. A's action for the return of the securities failed, the court holding that the contract between A and B was illegal, and that A could not recover his securities, as "there can be no true repentance once it has become impossible to sin."

3. Where a party to an illegal contract may recover property without relying on the illegal contract—*e.g.*, by relying on their rights of ownership. (*Belvoir Finance Co. Ltd*, v. *Stapleton.*)

Discharge of Contracts

A contract is discharged when it ceases to be operative, so that all rights and obligations which had existed under it become extinguished. A contract may be discharged in five main ways:

1. *Discharge of the Contract by Agreement.* A contract, having come into existence by agreement between the parties, may be discharged in the same way in which it has been made. This means that in order that the discharge should be fully operative consideration must be given. Where neither party has as yet performed their respective promises under the contract, a mutual release will be fully operative, as the consideration for the release of one party by the other is the similar undertaking of the party to be released.

Where, however, one of the parties has already performed his undertaking under the contract and now wishes to release the other party, that party will have to provide some new consideration. We speak here of a discharge of the contract by *accord and satisfaction*, as, in addition to the accord (or agreement) of the parties, the party to be released from his original obligation is providing some satisfaction—*i.e.*, consideration—for the other party.

Another way of discharging a contract is by replacing it by a new contract either made by the same parties or made by one of them with a third party. We call this the discharge of a contract by *novation*. Let us illustrate how novation works by means of an example. Assume that A has sold a book to B for £2. A and B then may make a new contract whereby the parties agree that A should receive for the book a turkey for Christmas instead of the agreed £2. Alternatively, C may agree with A that he (C) will buy the book in question for £2, provided that A releases B from the contract and B is willing to be released.

It is always possible to rescind or amend a contract in any form, irrespective of the form in which the contract itself has been made. Where, however, a contract has to be in writing (see page 101) it is possible to rescind it orally, but it can be amended in writing only. A parol agreement to amend the terms of such a contract would therefore be disregarded by the court when interpreting the contract. While a parol amendment of a contract which by law has to be in writing will not count, parol evidence may be used to interpret the terms of the contract.

A contract is also discharged by agreement where the contract itself contains a term providing that it should be discharged on the happening or non-happening of a future event or the fulfilment or non-fulfilment of some condition. During the last War many contracts were entered into 'for the duration of the War,' and that meant that these contracts were treated as discharged as soon as His Majesty by Order in Council decreed that the War had ended.

2. *Discharge of the Contract by Performance.* A contract is discharged if both parties have performed their respective undertakings under the contract. If one party tenders performance, and this is without good reason rejected by the other party, the effect of the tender will vary according to whether goods or money had been tendered. Where goods have been tendered in performance of a contract and they are not accepted, the party tendering will be discharged from his obligation. A tender of money, not accepted by the creditor, does not discharge the debtor, but the debtor may pay the sum owed into court. If he does that, and the creditor in a subsequent action does not recover more than the money already paid into court, the creditor will have to pay the costs of the legal proceedings.

When money is tendered in settlement of a debt the money must be offered in the form of *legal tender*. Bank of England notes are legal tender for any amount, cupronickel or silver coins with denominations of more than 10 new pence are legal tender up to £10, cupronickel or silver coins with denominations of up to 10 new pence are legal tender up to £5, while all bronze coins are legal tender for up to 20 new pence.[1] The debtor must always tender the correct sum, as the creditor is not bound to provide change. Tender must take place at a reasonable time, which, if the creditor is in business, means during his normal business hours. It is the debtor's duty to see that the payment reaches the creditor, and if he sends money by post and the letter is lost he has not discharged his debt. Where, however, the creditor has asked for the money to be sent by post and the debtor sends it in this way, exercising all the usual precautions of a reasonable business-man in preventing loss (*e.g.*, registering letters containing notes, crossing cheques sent by mail), then a loss, if it should materialize, would fall on the creditor. It should also be noted that where payment is made by cheque or by any other credit instrument, then, unless the parties have expressly provided otherwise, it will always be presumed that the discharge of the debt is conditional on the credit instrument being honoured.

Where a debtor owes several sums to the same creditor and then makes a payment which is insufficient to discharge the total debt, it may be of great importance to decide which of the sums outstanding have been paid off. The reason is that some of these debts if not discharged may presently become unenforceable by becoming statute-barred (see below). When the debtor makes a payment he has the right of deciding at the time of payment which debt he wishes to discharge. If the debtor does not choose, the creditor may appropriate the payment to any of the outstanding debts, even if the debt selected is one which has already become statute-barred (see para. 3 below). Where the debtor has a 'current account' with the creditor—*i.e.*, an account the balance of which is carried forward, payments made being deducted from the balance and further debts being added to it—the presumption is that the payment made will discharge the oldest debt.

3. *Discharge of a Contract by Lapse of Time.* A contract is discharged by lapse of time only where the contract has been entered into for a specific period of time—*e.g.*, a contract of employment for one year. In all other contracts, where time is not a material ingredient of the contract, the mere passing of time will not discharge the contract.

While, then, a contract will be discharged by the lapse of time in exceptional circumstances only, a contract may become unenforceable (statute-barred) if it is not enforced within a certain period of time. The reason for this rule is that there must be an end to litigation at some time, and parties should not be put to the expense and trouble of defending actions based on stale causes. The periods of limitation are now governed by the Limitation Act 1939.

[1] Decimal Currency Act, 1969.

Actions based on simple contracts will be statute-barred six years after the cause of action first arose, while actions based on specialty contracts and actions brought in order to recover land will be barred after twelve years. The periods mentioned are reckoned from the time when "the cause of action first arose"—*i.e.*, when the plaintiff could have brought the action for the first time. This is generally not the time when the contract was made, but the time when the breach has taken place on which the action is founded, though it is possible, of course, that the contract was broken immediately it was made.

If the plaintiff was a minor or a lunatic at the time when the cause of action first arose the period of limitation will not begin to run until the disability has ended, but once the period has begun to run it will not be stopped by any subsequent incapacity on the part of the plaintiff.

Where the plaintiff failed to discover the existence of the cause of action because of the defendant's fraud or where he is bringing an action based on fraud or one asking for the setting aside of a contract on the ground of mistake, the period of limitation will begin to run from the time when the plaintiff has discovered the existence of a cause of action or from such time when, with reasonable care, he could have discovered it.

The passing of the period of limitation does not discharge a contract; its sole effect is that the plaintiff's right of action is barred. Thus, if the debtor of a statute-barred debt pays the debt at a time when he could not have been sued for it he will be unable to recover the money which he had paid as he paid a valid (though unenforceable) debt. A right of action which has become statute-barred may be revived in one of two ways:

(*a*) Where the debtor pays a sum of money on account of principal or interest.
(*b*) Where the debtor acknowledges the existence of the debt in writing.

In either of these cases a new period of limitation will commence to run from the time of the payment or the acknowledgment of the debt.

4. *Discharge of the Contract by Breach.* Strictly speaking, a contract is not discharged by a breach, but a breach gives the innocent party a right to treat the contract as discharged if he wishes to. A contract may be broken in various ways. A party may fail to fulfil his obligations under the contract or he may repudiate his liability under the contract at some time before he was due to perform his obligations or he may do something which will make it impossible for himself to perform the contract.

Every breach of contract entitles the innocent party to claim damages from the party guilty of the breach. Not every breach, however, entitles the innocent party to treat the contract as discharged. He may treat the contract as discharged only where the breach is a total one and not merely a partial breach. A breach is a total breach if it affects some vital part of the contract or if it clearly shows that the contract-breaker has no intention of performing the contract.

Where a party repudiates his obligations under the contract, the innocent party may treat the contract at once as discharged or he may decide not to do so in the hope that the other party will still perform his contractual obligations when the time for performance arrives. This second possibility is fraught with danger in that if the contract in the meantime becomes discharged for some other reason —*e.g.*, impossibility—the innocent party will have lost his remedies. If A has engaged B to work for him as from January 1 and A informs B on November 1 that he will not be requiring his services, B could treat the contract at once as discharged and sue A for damages. If he decides, however, to wait for January 1, hoping that A will change his mind and A is killed in an accident on Christmas Eve, the contract will have become discharged by impossibility and B will be unable to sue A's estate. If he had treated the contract as discharged in November, and had immediately sued A, the action would continue against A's estate.

Where a person makes it impossible for himself to perform a contract, this will be treated in the same way as a repudiation of the contract. If X has agreed to sell his house Greenacre to Y, vacant possession to be given at Easter, and early in that year X has pulled down the house, Y will be able to sue him at once for breach of contract.

Where a breach has taken place in a contract which is to be performed by instalments, it is always a question of fact whether the innocent party may consider the breach a total one and thus treat the entire contract as discharged, or whether the breach is a partial one affecting the particular instalment only. In *Maple Flock* v. *Universal Furniture Products, Ltd*, it was held that the main considerations are "first, the ratio quantitatively which the breach bears to the contract as a whole and, secondly, the degree of probability or improbability that such a breach will be repeated."

5. *Discharge of a Contract by Subsequent Impossibility.* If a person contracts to do something which according to our present scientific knowledge is impossible the contract will be void because of the absence of real consideration. If he contracts to do something which can be done, but he cannot do it, the contract will be valid and he will have to accept the legal consequences of his inability to perform. We are concerned here with the case of a contract which was pos-

sible to start with but for some reason has become impossible after it was made.

The general rule which will guide us is that parties are bound by the contracts which they have freely entered into. Thus, where I have promised to do something and it has now become quite impossible for me to perform it, the contract will not be discharged. I should have anticipated the possibility of circumstances intervening which would interfere with performance and I should have safeguarded myself by including a term in the contract providing for this contingency. In certain exceptional circumstances, however, a contract will be discharged by subsequent impossibility.

(*a*) A contract will be discharged where it becomes legally impossible (*i.e.*, forbidden) to perform it. Thus, in *Baily* v. *De Crespigny*, A had leased some land to B and had promised that on the adjoining land no buildings would be erected. A railway company, possessed with statutory powers of compulsory acquisition of land, bought the land and erected a station on it. It was held that A's contractual obligation to B had become discharged.

(*b*) A contract of personal service is discharged by the death of either party and also by the illness of the employee where that illness makes the performance of the contract impossible. It should be noted, however, that the death of either party does not discharge contracts other than those for personal services. As an example of a contract discharged by the illness of the employee we may mention *Robinson* v. *Davison*, where a pianist who had agreed to give a concert on a certain date was unable to appear because of illness. The contract was held to be discharged. Illness discharges a contract for personal services only where it makes the performance of the contract impracticable. The illness of a clerk who has to stay off work for a week does not discharge his contract, as he is employed for a period of time and not just for a single occasion.

(*c*) A contract is discharged where the contract expressly or implicitly rests on the continued existence of a certain subject-matter and this subject-matter has been destroyed. In *Taylor* v. *Caldwell* a contract for hiring of a theatre was held to be discharged when the theatre was accidentally burned to the ground. This rule applies, however, only where the contract rests on the continued existence of a particular subject-matter. Thus, if I engage a driver for my car and the car is destroyed accidentally, the contract with the driver will not be discharged unless he has been engaged specifically for the car which I originally owned.

(*d*) Where a contract has been entered into in contemplation of a future event or state of affairs and the event or state of affairs does not materialize, the contract will be discharged. *Krell* v. *Henry*, one of the so-called coronation cases, provides an illustration. These cases arose from the same situation. The coronation procession of King Edward VII had to be cancelled at short notice, because the King was not fit to undergo the strain of a long drive through London. People had hired rooms along the procession route to watch the procession. The courts held in these cases that the people who had hired the rooms could not be forced to pay rent for them, as the contracts had been discharged by the non-occurrence of the event which in the intention of both parties formed the basis of their contract.

(*e*) Lastly, a contract will also be discharged where its commercial purpose has been frustrated. It should be stated at once that the courts have been not too ready to find that a contract has been discharged for this reason, because frustration is based on the presence of an implied term in a contract whereby the contract should become discharged on the happening of certain events which the parties, if they had considered them expressly in the contract, would have agreed as affecting the very roots of the contract. The important feature of this ground of discharge of a contract is that performance must have become a thing radically different from what the parties undertook in the contract.

In *Davis Contractors, Ltd,* v. *Fareham Urban District Council* the plaintiffs had contracted to build for the defendants a certain number of houses at an agreed inclusive price. Through reasons outside the control of the parties (bad weather, shortage of labour and materials) the completion of the contract took much longer than had been anticipated. In the meantime costs had risen, and the work involved the plaintiffs in a greater cost than the price at which they had contracted to work. They claimed that original contract had been frustrated, but the court held that a mere miscalculation as to the profitability of the contract did not amount to a radical change in the obligation of the builders and the contract had to stand. Similarly, in a number of cases arising out of the closure of the Suez Canal in the autumn of 1956 (e.g., *Albert D. Gaon & Co.* v. *Société Interprofessionelles des Oléagineaux Fluides Alimentaires* where Sudanese exporters had sold local produce to European buyers at prices including cost of transport *i.e.*, on *c.i.f.* terms)—it was held that the contracts had not been frustrated by the impossibility of shipping the goods through the Suez Canal (the normal trade route from Port Sudan to European ports). It was still possible to ship the goods round the Cape, though at a higher cost, and this form of shipment did not represent a radical change in the performance of the contract. The extra cost of shipment had thus to be borne by the sellers.

Where a contract has been discharged by subsequent impossibility in any of the above ways, the financial settlement between the parties is now governed by the Law Reform (Frustrated Contracts) Act 1943. This Act provides as follows:

1. Anything paid by a party in pursuance of a contract subsequently discharged by impossibility may be recovered by the party and any sums still due will cease now to be payable.

2. If one party has incurred any expenses in connection with the contract subsequently discharged he may recover at the discretion of the court part or all of the expenses (including a proportion of his overheads) from the other party.

3. The Act does not apply to the following contracts, among others:

i. Contracts of insurance.

ii. Contracts of carriage of goods by sea.

iii. Contracts containing specific terms dealing with the effects of frustration.

iv. Contracts for the sale of specific goods which perish before the property has passed to the buyer.

Remedies for Breach of Contract

We have seen already that every breach of contract, total or partial, entitles the innocent party to claim damages from the party responsible for the breach. As an alternative to a claim for damages, the innocent party might sue for the equitable remedies of specific performance or injunction. The conditions, subject to which the court will grant these remedies, have been discussed already on pages 18–21.

The damages to which the plaintiff may be entitled may be either *liquidated* or *unliquidated*. They are liquidated when their amount has been agreed upon by the parties themselves in the contract. They are unliquidated if they have to be assessed by the court.

Where a contract contains a clause providing for the payment of agreed damages if a breach of the contract should take place, the innocent party will be able to claim the sum agreed upon irrespective of the extent of the loss which he has actually suffered. It is important, therefore, to distinguish between liquidated damages in their true legal sense and what is called a *penalty*, because a penalty clause will not be enforced by the court, and where the court holds agreed damages to be a penalty, the plaintiff will have to be satisfied with unliquidated damages. In order that the agreed damages should be liquidated damages in the true legal sense, they must represent a true and fair estimate (at the time of agreement) of the loss likely to be suffered by the plaintiff in case of breach of contract. If the agreed damages do not rest on a true and fair estimate of the likely loss they are a penalty and will not be enforced by the court. As with other technical legal terms, it does not matter what the parties have called the agreed damages—all that matters is the fairness of the estimate. Agreed damages do not become a penalty merely because the plaintiff's actual loss turns out to be much smaller than had been expected, provided that the forecast of the loss embodied in the agreed damages was a reasonable one.

The court will always hold agreed damages to be a penalty where the obvious purpose of the amount agreed upon was to terrorize the other party into performing the contract rather than the making of a fair estimate. Where the contract provides for the payment of a single sum of money in the event of any of a number of possible breaches, some of which are more serious than others, it will be a penalty. It is so also where the contract provides that a larger sum of money is to be paid on the non-payment of a smaller sum. If A has agreed to pay B £100 on January 1 and it is provided that if he should not pay on that day he would have to pay £120, the agreed damages—*i.e.*, £20—are a penalty, because the same amount appears to be payable by way of damages whether payment is delayed by one day or by one month while the real loss of the creditor cannot be the same in these two eventualities.

Where the parties have not agreed on any damages, the court will have to assess the plaintiff's loss. The basic principle is that the plaintiff should be compensated—but no more than compensated—for the loss which he has suffered as a result of the defendant's breach of contract Thus, where the plaintiff has lost some income subject to the payment of income tax as a result of the defendant's action the court, in awarding him a lump sum (not taxable)[1] by way of damages, will assess his loss on his net income (after deduction of tax) and not on his gross income (*British Transport Commission* v. *Gourley*). This rule is, however, subject to the further reservation that the defendant cannot be made responsible for all the consequences that have followed from his breach. Some of the loss suffered by the plaintiff may have been too remote in relation to the defendant's breach of contract. It becomes, therefore, important to determine the exact limits of the defendant's responsibility. The present rule as to the measure of damages recoverable by the plaintiff is based on the nineteenth-century case of *Hadley* v. *Baxendale*. Here a miller sent a broken crankshaft by a carrier to a firm of engineers for repair. He informed the carrier that it was an urgent matter and that there should be no delay in delivery, and the carrier accepted the consignment on these terms. The miller did not inform the carrier, however, that without the crankshaft the mill could not work

[1] Unless in excess of £5000.

at all, and the carrier had no reason to believe that the crankshaft was such an essential part of the machinery of the mill. The carrier delayed delivery of the crankshaft to the engineers, and the mill was idle for longer than it need have been. In an action for damages by the plaintiff the court held that the defendant was not liable for the loss of profits during the enforced idleness of the mill.

In giving their decision, the court laid down two general principles which have been followed by the courts ever since:

1. The damages to be awarded to a plaintiff for breach of contract should cover such of his losses as may be fairly considered to arise naturally—*i.e.*, in the usual course of events—from the breach of contract.

2. Where the plaintiff suffers some unusual loss, he will be able to recover damages for this loss only if it has been in the reasonable contemplation of the parties—*i.e.*, if the parties entered into the contract foreseeing the possibility of this loss if the contract should be broken.

In a way the second principle in *Hadley* v. *Baxendale* covers also the first rule, as, if no special circumstances have been brought to the notice of the defendant, he can only foresee such loss as would naturally or normally arise from the breach of contract in the circumstances as known to him.

It is not necessary for all the possible risks to be pointed out specifically to the other party; certain risks must always be presumed to be in the reasonable contemplation of the parties. Thus, in *Victoria Laundry (Windsor), Ltd,* v. *Newman Industries, Ltd* the plaintiffs had ordered a reconditioned boiler from the defendants which was to have been delivered in June but did not, in fact, reach the plaintiffs until November of that year. As a result of this delayed delivery the plaintiffs lost the profit on additional laundering work which they could have accepted if the boiler had been installed in time and they were also unable to accept a remunerative dyeing contract with the Ministry of Supply. The plaintiffs were held to be entitled to claim under the first heading, as the defendants must have realized that a laundry would be unable to do its normal work if deprived of some ordered piece of equipment, but they could not claim for the second loss, as this loss was not foreseeable when the contract was entered into.

The plaintiff who has suffered a loss as a result of the breach of contract must do everything in his power to minimize the loss. Thus, a seller who finds that the buyer of goods refuses to accept them will have to dispose of them elsewhere at the best price obtainable. If the plaintiff has failed to minimize his loss he will be unable to recover more than the amount which he would have lost if he had done so. In *Brace* v. *Calder* the plaintiff was employed by a partnership. A change in the personnel of the partnership took place, and by law this operates as a dismissal of all the employees. The remaining partners offered the plaintiff re-engagement on his previous terms of employment, but he refused to accept it. The court held that in the circumstances B. had been wrongfully dismissed, but as he had failed to minimize his loss he could only claim nominal damages.

Whenever, as in *Brace* v. *Calder*, there is a breach of contract but the plaintiff has suffered no loss he will be entitled to nominal damages only—*i.e.*, the court will award to him a few pounds for the formal breach of the contract but no more.

In discussing the law of torts we shall see that in some cases the court awards punitive or exemplary damages to a plaintiff. These damages amount to more than the plaintiff's actual loss, and their purpose is to punish the defendant for some malicious wrong. Exemplary damages are not generally awarded for breaches of contract, except for the wrongful dishonour of a cheque by a bank, where the cheque happens to be that of a trader, but not otherwise.

Payment of Interest

Where a person owes a sum of money, he will have to pay his debt as such; but interest on the debt will be payable in the following cases only:

1. Where the parties have expressly or impliedly agreed that interest should be paid.
2. Where a bill of exchange has not been paid on the date on which it has fallen due for payment.
3. Where a person has wrongfully retained money belonging to another party.
4. The court may also allow interest in an action for the recovery of a sum of money if in the opinion of the court it is just and fair that interest should be paid (Law Reform (Miscellaneous Provisions) Act 1934).

Compound interest will be payable only if specifically agreed upon by the parties.

Agency

Where a person is capable of entering into a contract, he may also enter into the contract through an agent. An agent in law is a person who possesses authority to enter into a contract on behalf of another. The contract which the agent makes is the principal's contract, and it does not matter, therefore, whether the agent possesses contractual capacity as long as his principal can validly enter into the contract.

The agent's authority may have been granted to him expressly or it may be implied by law. Where the principal has expressly authorized the agent to make a contract on his behalf the agent will be contractually bound to the principal to act for him if he had received consideration from the principal. The agent's authority, if granted by deed, is known as a power of attorney. If the agent has not received any consideration he possesses authority to act on behalf of the principal, but he need not exercise this authority. Thus, if I ask a friend to attend an auction sale on my behalf and to bid for me there, then, if I have promised him some reward for his services, he would be liable in damages to me if he failed to attend the sale. If no reward has been promised to him I could not take any action against him if he did not attend.

An agent possesses implied authority to make contracts on the principal's behalf where the principal has placed him in a position from which others can reasonably assume that the agent has authority to act on behalf of the principal. We have discussed already at an earlier stage (see page 68) the authority of a married woman to enter into contracts on her husband's behalf. A partner has similar authority to make contracts on behalf of his fellow-partners. Similarly, an employee who has been placed in a position of responsibility may be assumed to have such authority as normally goes with that position, irrespective of what instructions the principal may have given him. This means that a third party who, acting in good faith, enters into a contract with such a person believing him to be authorized by his principal will be able to claim directly against the principal. If the principal has never expressly authorized the agent to make any contracts on his behalf he will still be responsible to the third party for contracts made by the person who has implied authority to bind the principal.

As an example we may quote *Watteau* v. *Fenwick*, where the manager of a public house had been expressly instructed by his employers to order all the requirements for the business through them. In breach of these instructions he ordered some cigars and other goods from a traveller. The court held that the owners of the public house were bound by the manager's contract, although he had acted without express authority, as a third party is entitled to assume that the person apparently in charge and control of a business has authority to order goods for the business.

Where a person acting without authority enters into a contract on behalf of another, the person on whose behalf the contract was purported to be made may subsequently ratify the act of the self-styled agent. If that happens the contract will be treated as if it had been made by an agent with a valid authority. It is essential, however, that the agent should disclose to the person on whose behalf he had acted all the details of the transaction before ratification. The principal also must have had contractual capacity both at the time of ratification as well as at the time when the contract was originally made. This means that a contract entered into by a company-promoter on behalf of a yet non-existent company may not be ratified by the company when it has been incorporated, as the company obviously had no contractual capacity (being not yet legally established) at the time when the contract was originally entered into.

The Contract of Employment

A contract of employment may be either a contract of service or a contract for services. The difference between them rests in the degree of control which the employer is able to exercise over the work of the person serving him. If the employer is entitled to tell the other party what he should do, but is not entitled to tell him how he should perform his work, we have a contract for services and we should refer to the person working as an independent contractor. If, on the other hand, the employer is able to tell the other person not only what he should do, but also how he should do it, we have a contract of service, and we should refer to the person working for another as his servant or employee.

Though the control test is the basic one for distinguishing between contracts of service and contracts for services it is not easily applied where the person rendering services is a professional man—*e.g.*, a doctor or an architect. In those cases the courts have recently adopted the organization test where they asked whether or not the person rendering services is to be treated as a member of the employer's organization or business or is to be looked upon as an outsider.

The difference between a contract of service and one for services is important in the law of torts, since an employer is responsible for wrongs committed by his servants in the course of their employment even if he has not expressly instructed them to do the wrongful acts, while an employer is responsible for the act of an independent contractor only where the contractor has acted under orders from the employer. Servants and independent contractors are also personally responsible for their wrongful acts.

A servant may or may not be his employer's agent. This will depend on whether he possesses authority to bring about contractual relationships between his employer and a third party or third parties. Similarly, an agent may or may not be his principal's servant, depending on whether the principal is entitled to control the agent in the manner of performance of his duties.

The rights and duties of the parties under a contract of service depend on the terms of their contract; but if no express terms have been agreed upon the following terms will apply:

The servant must

1. Render his services personally and not by a substitute.

2. Exercise reasonable care in the execution of the employer's orders and indemnify the employer if he causes any damage to his interests through his negligence.

3. Maintain loyalty to his employer by not disclosing confidential information acquired during his employment.

4. Account to the employer for anything received on the employer's behalf.

5. Carry out all lawful orders given by the employer.

The employer for his part must

1. Pay the servant the agreed wage, and, if no wage has been agreed but the service was not intended to be an unpaid one, a reasonable wage. In those cases where the servant's pay depends on the amount of work given to him by the employer, or where his professional reputation depends on the actual performance of the work for which he has been engaged (*e.g.*, an actor), the employer must not only pay the servant but also find the promised work for him.

2. Indemnify the servant against any liabilities which he may have assumed on the employer's behalf in the course of his employment.

3. Make reasonable provision for the employee's safety by ensuring that the method of work to be followed, the equipment to be used, and the premises in which work is permanently conducted are reasonably safe for their purpose.

The employer may terminate the contract of service in any of the following ways:

1. He may give notice. The period of notice is that agreed upon, and if none has been agreed it will have to be that which is customary for the employee's occupation. In the absence of any custom reasonable notice must be given. The Contracts of Employment Act 1963 (as amended by the Industrial Relations Act 1971) makes provision for a minimum period of notice which is one week for employees who have been employed for more than thirteen weeks but less than two years, two weeks for those employed for between two and five years, four weeks for employees with a minimum of five years' service to their credit, six weeks for those with ten years' and eight weeks for those with fifteen years' service.

2. He may give the employee his wages for the period of notice in lieu of giving him notice and make the employee leave at once.

3. He may dismiss the employee summarily if the employee has been guilty of something which constitutes a total breach of his contract.

The employee may terminate his contract by giving notice on the same terms as given in (1) above. Under the Contracts of Employment Act 1963 the minimum notice which the employee has to give is one week, irrespective of the length of his employment. He may also leave his employment summarily if the employer has been guilty of a total breach of contract. He may not leave his employment summarily by paying his own wages in lieu of notice.

Since a contract of service is one of a personal nature, it will be terminated by the death of either party or by any other event which constitutes impossibility of performance.

Before the passing of the Industrial Relations Act 1971 there were no restrictions on the right of an employer to dismiss an employee provided that the dismissal was not in breach of the contract of employment. Now, however, a dismissal will be presumed to be *unfair* unless the employer is able to prove that the dismissal was related to the capability or the qualifications of the employee to undertake the work which he was employed to do, or was related to the employee's conduct, or was justified by a redundancy situation or was necessary since continued employment of the employee in his existing position would have been in breach of some statutory provision. Dismissal will always be unfair if the principal reason for it was the exercise by the employee of his rights in relation to trade union membership as outlined in the Act. Where an employee complains that he has been unfairly dismissed, the complaint is heard in the first place by an industrial tribunal who may either recommend his re-instatement or alternatively award him financial compensation. These provisions concerning unfair dismissal have been retained, notwithstanding the repeal of the Industrial Relations Act.

Addendum to page 99:
Lord Denning, M.R. redefined equitable estoppel in *Crabb* v. *Arun District Council* as follows:

> If he, by his words or conduct, so behaves as to lead another to believe that he will not insist on his actual contractual rights—knowing or intending that the other will act on this belief—and he does so act, that will raise an equity in favour of the other.

CHAPTER FIVE

The Law of Trusts

From the Use to the Trust

The modern trust is derived from the medieval concept of a use. The term 'use', which is supposed to have been derived from the Latin *opus* (need or help), was applied to an arrangement by which lawyers tried to bypass some of the rigidities of common law. We shall see (p. 137) that at common law the heir to an estate in land had to make various onerous payments to his lord. The owners of such estates were also prevented from disposing of them by will or from transferring them into mortmain. If, then, an estate owner wished to make such dispositions regarding his land, he had to do so in his lifetime by transferring the land to another person, known as a *feoffee to uses*, with instructions as to how the property should be administered for the benefit of the ultimate beneficiary or beneficiaries, known as the *cestuis que use*. Common law did not recognize the arrangement that had been entered into between the creator of the use and the *feoffee to uses*, so that if the latter, having acquired property rights in the land, refused to carry out the terms of the use common law courts would not help either the creator of the use or the *cestui que use* to make him do so. This unwillingness of common law courts to remedy an obvious injustice was one of the main reasons for the direct appeals that were made to the Chancellor, asking for his intervention. The Chancellor, acting as a judge of conscience, would not allow an open breach of trust to go without remedy and he would force the *feoffee to uses* to carry out the terms of the use.

The further history of the use was a hectic one and cannot be recounted here. In time the use became the trust and the *feoffee to uses* was renamed trustee, with the *cestui que use* now called *cestui que trust* or beneficiary.

The Nature of a Trust

A trust may be defined to-day as a relationship which arises whenever a person, called the trustee, is compelled in equity to hold property for the benefit of some persons (of whom he may be one), who are called *cestuis que trust* or beneficiaries, or for some object permitted by law in such a way that the real benefit of the property accrues not to the trustee in person but to the beneficiaries or objects of the trust.

Trust property is, then, property which is in effect owned by two persons at the same time. The trustee is the legal owner, and he is the person who will make all dispositions with the property. The beneficiary is the owner, recognized by equity, to whom the property will eventually come and who is entitled to all the income accruing from it. As between trustee and beneficiary, the property belongs really to the latter; but, as far as third parties are concerned, the trustee will be considered to be the owner.

We shall see that a trust may be created in various ways, often by means of a contract between the creator (known as donor) of the trust and the trustee. The trust differs, however, from ordinary contracts in that with contracts no third party who did not participate directly or indirectly in the making of the contract has any right to enforce the contract. This is known as the principle of privity of contract. With a trust, on the other hand, a beneficiary who took no part in the creation of the trust may enforce its terms against the trustee.

Trusts are employed widely to-day for the purpose of protecting the interests of persons who, for one reason or another, cannot look after their own affairs. This includes the following examples:

1. Trusts for the benefit of unborn children.

2. Trusts for the benefit of persons suffering from some legal incapacity—*e.g.*, minors and lunatics.

3. Trusts for the benefit of unincorporated associations.

4. Trusts to administer property in which a number of persons have successive or simultaneous interests (*e.g.*, settlements, trusts for sale).

5. Trusts for charitable purposes.

Types of Trusts

Trusts may be either express trusts or implied trusts, according to whether they have been expressly created by their donor or whether their existence is merely implied from the conduct of the parties. Express trusts again may be either private trusts or public (or charitable) trusts.

An express trust may come into existence in one of three ways:

1. By the declaration of trust, where the donor makes himself trustee of some property for the benefit of some persons or objects.

2. By a conveyance of the trust property to trustees to whom the terms of the trust are communicated.

3. By will.

In general no special form is required for the creation of a trust, except that where it is made by will, the will must comply with the formal requirements of the Wills Act 1837.

The Law of Property Act 1925, provides, however, that any declaration of trust respecting land or any interest therein must be manifested and proved by some writing and must be signed by a person who possesses capacity of creating such a trust. This capacity is coterminous with the capacity of making contracts. It has to be noted that the 1925 Act does not demand that a declaration of trust should be *made* in writing as long as there exists some evidence in writing, signed by the donor, that a trust has been created.

While, then, there are no particular formalities in creating an express trust, the trust will be valid only if it complies with the so-called *three certainties*. These are:

1. *Certainty of Words*. The donor of the trust must have imposed a clear duty on the trustee to carry out the provisions of the trust. It is not enough if the donor has requested the recipient of some property to deal with it in a certain way if he has not imposed an absolute obligation on him. Testators frequently 'request' their legatees to be generous to old servants, but this would not by itself create a trust in the servants' favour.
2. *Certainty of Subject-matter*, which must be clearly described.
3. *Certainty of Objects*. This includes the persons of the beneficiaries who must be clearly described. Note, however, the exception in the case of charitable trusts (p. 126).

Express trusts may be further divided into *executed* and *executory* trusts. An executed trust is one where the intentions of the settlor have been clearly stated, so that the trustee merely has the duty of carrying out the terms of the instrument by which the trust has been created. In an executory trust, however, something has yet to be done before the rights of the beneficiaries under the trust can be clearly ascertained, though the existence of the trust as such is certain. Executory trusts are mainly found in wills where the testator has indicated in general terms his intentions as to the distribution of his estate or part of it, but has left to his trustees the task of finding the best way of carrying out his intentions.

Another important division of trusts is that into *completely constituted* and *incompletely constituted* trusts. A trust is completely constituted if the trust property has been finally vested in the trustees, who, in the event of a trust declaration, may include the settlor himself. All trusts created by wills are treated as completely constituted, even if they are executory. Where the trust property has not yet been finally vested in the trustee or trustees, the trust is incompletely constituted. This distinction is important as far as the rights of the beneficiaries are concerned. Where valuable consideration has been supplied for the creation of the trust the beneficiaries will be able to enforce it, even if the trust is incompletely constituted, since one of the fundamental maxims of Equity is that "Equity regards that as done which ought to be done," and the settlor may therefore be compelled to perfect the incomplete trust by conveying the property to the trustees. Where no consideration has been provided, however—*i.e.*, where the trust represents a voluntary settlement—the beneficiary will be able to enforce the trust only if it has been completely constituted.

Trusts are said to be *discretionary* where the trust instrument gives a discretion to the trustees as to the application of the trust income. These trusts are useful where the settlor has the shrewd suspicion that the main beneficiary may be a profligate who would squander the trust income at the expense of his family. The trustees may then be empowered to distribute the trust income between the main beneficiary and other members of his family as the trustees see fit.

Charitable (Public) Trusts

A charitable trust is not necessarily a trust created for an object which in common speech would be called charitable. In order to be 'charitable' the object of the trust must be one of the objects named in an Act of Parliament passed during the reign of Elizabeth I.[1] It is better, however, to rely on the restatement of these objects given by Lord Macnaghten in *Income Tax Special Purposes Commissioners* v. *Pemsel*, where the following objects were enumerated:

1. The relief of poverty.
2. The advancement of education.
3. The advancement of religion.
4. Any other purpose beneficial to the community.

It should be noted that in all the cases mentioned above the trust must be public in the sense of benefiting a large number of persons and not merely one person or a small group of people. A trust for the education of a particular child would thus not be a charitable trust, but a trust for the education of children from a certain village would be. The only partial exception appears to apply in respect of trusts for the relief of poverty, because trusts for the relief of poor ex-employees of particular firms or even trusts for the relief of poor relations of the donor have been held to be valid charitable trusts.

The Recreational Charities Act 1958, lays down that it is "charitable" to provide facilities for recreation or other leisure-time occupation if the facilities are provided in the interests of social welfare. This means that the facilities must be provided to improve the conditions of life of the persons for whom they are primarily intended, *and* these persons must have need for these facilities by reason of

[1] Statute of Charitable Uses, 1601.

age, youth, infirmity, disablement, poverty, or social or economic circumstances *or* the facilities are to be available to the members or the female members (*e.g.*, Women's Institutes) of the public at large.

It remains now to consider why it is important to decide whether a trust for some object is a true charitable trust. Law has always adopted a generous attitude towards charitable trusts in the following ways:

1. The income from trust property held on charitable trusts is not subject to income tax.

2. Charitable trusts are not subject to the 'rule against perpetuities.' This ancient rule of the common law tried to ensure that property should not be tied up for excessive periods of time. As amended by the Perpetuities and Accumulations Act 1964 ,the rule provides that where property is held on a private trust, the ultimate beneficiaries must become absolutely entitled to the property *either* within a period no longer than that of a life in being at the time when the trust came into existence plus twenty-one years after the end of that life, *or* within a period not exceeding eighty years from the coming into existence of the trust. The second possibility has been added by the 1964 Act. This Act has also introduced the 'wait and see' principle in that it provides that no interest is to be treated as void under the perpetuity rule on the grounds of remoteness until it has become established that it must vest, if at all, after the end of the perpetuity period. Under the law as it existed before 1964, trusts frequently failed because the courts held it possible that a child might be born to a woman of advanced years where this would then lead to a delay in the final vesting of the property. The 1964 Act states now as a presumption that males under 14 and females under 12 and over 55 are deemed incapable of having children.

As stated already, the rule against perpetuities does not apply to charitable trusts and where the purpose of a trust is a genuinely charitable one, property may be held on trust for ever. If the trust is not deemed to be charitable and it offends against the perpetuity rule, the trust will be void and the trust property will revert to the settlor or, in the case of a will, go to the residuary legatees of the testator.

3. A charitable trust will never fail for uncertainty of object. With a private trust such uncertainty would mean that the whole trust was void. Where the trust is a charitable one, however, the court would inquire whether the donor of a trust had what is called "a general charitable intention"—which means, whether he intended to benefit charity in general while naming one particular charitable object as the direct beneficiary of his charity. If that is so, and the object named by the donor cannot be attained either because he has not described it clearly enough or because it has ceased to exist, the

court may order that the trust should be administered *cy près*—which means, in a way as close as possible to that indicated by the donor. The trustees would have to prepare for the approval of the court a scheme for the administration of the trust property for such a purpose. Assume, for instance, that a testator in his will left a sum of money to his trustees with instructions to apply the income for the purpose of awarding an annual prize to the head-boy at the testator's old school. As it happens, that school has been closed down and no longer exists when the testator's will becomes operative. The court will then have to decide whether the gift was intended to benefit the mentioned object only or whether the testator had a general charitable intent—to promote education. If the court adopt the latter interpretation of the testator's intentions the trustees will have to work out some scheme which will apply the donor's wishes *cy près*, perhaps by giving the prize to the head-boy of the school with which the testator's old school has been merged.

The Charities Act 1960, has extended the application of the *cy près* doctrine. A trust fund may now be applied *cy près* when the settlor of the trust has shown a general charitable intention and the purpose of the trust does not use up the entire trust fund, or where it would be convenient to use the trust fund in conjunction with other funds intended for the same purpose, or where the original purposes of the fund have now been adequately provided for by other means. Trust property may also be applied *cy près* where it was given with a general charitable intent, the purpose of the trust has failed or has been fully achieved, and it is impossible to trace the original donors or they have in writing waived their right to a return of their contributions. This provision is particularly important where a trust fund has been established from small collections (say through street collectors) and it is practically impossible to ascertain the people who have contributed.

4 Private trusts are enforced by the beneficiaries. With public trusts this responsibility rests with the Attorney-General.

Implied Trusts

Trusts may be implied either from the conduct of the parties or by the operation of law. The former are known as *resulting trusts* while the latter are called *constructive trusts*.

Resulting trusts arise in a variety of circumstances. For instance, where a person has been made a trustee of some property for a purpose or purposes which subsequently fail and there are no other instructions in the trust instrument as to the disposal of the property, he will be treated as the trustee of that property for the benefit of the original donor or his successors in law. If you organize a collection in your office for the widow of a recently deceased colleague and the widow dies before the money that has been collected can be handed over to her, you will be treated as trustee of the collection for the benefit of the original subscribers. The same applies, as has been shown already, where the trust on which property has been passed to a trustee is void (*e.g.*, by offending against the rule against perpetuities) or its objects are illegal.

A resulting trust also comes into existence where one party supplies money to another for the purchase of some property. The person who buys the property will then be presumed to hold the property on trust for the party who provided the money. The presumption of a resulting trust will be rebutted either where the parties have definitely agreed otherwise or where it is offset by the presumption of advancement. This means that where a husband advances money to his wife, or a parent advances money to a child of his, it is presumed that this has been done by way of gift and the wife or child will hold the property on her or his own behalf and not as trustee for the provider of the funds.

A constructive trust comes into existence where a person has come into possession of property by means of a breach of confidence. Thus, where a third party receives trust property from a trustee, knowing that it has been disposed of in breach of the trust, he will be deemed himself to hold the property on trust for the beneficiary of the trust. Similarly, where the trustee himself uses the trust property for speculation or for some other purposes which leads to an addition to his wealth, he will be deemed to hold that addition on trust for the beneficiary of the trust. The leading case on this point is *Keech* v. *Sandford*, where a trustee held a lease of Romford Market on trust for an infant. When the lease expired the lessor refused to renew it for the benefit of the infant, but indicated that he would not object to granting a lease to the trustee on his own behalf. The trustee acquired the lease for himself, and the court held that he must be deemed to be holding it on a constructive trust for the infant.

Trustees and Beneficiaries

Only a person of full age who possesses legal capacity to enter into binding obligations can become a trustee under an express trust.

The number of trustees under a trust is in general immaterial, but in a trust concerning land there may be no more than four trustees; also, when the land is sold a valid receipt for the purchase money must be signed by at least two trustees or on behalf of a trust corporation. From this we may deduce that for a trust concerning land there must be at least two and no more than four trustees, with the reservation that a trust corporation may act as sole trustee.

A trust corporation is a corporate body which had been authorized by the Treasury to do trustee work. A trust corporation may be either a corporation aggregate, such as the trustee departments which most of the large banks have set up as separate companies to undertake trustee business, or a corporation sole in the form of the Public Trustee. The office of Public Trustee was set up by the Public Trustee Act 1906, with a view to providing for the general public the services of a trustee who could not die and would thus always be available to carry out the instructions of the trust.

Where a personal trustee dies, the remaining trustees will carry on the work on their own; but where the last or only trustee dies, the duties of trusteeship fall on his personal representatives.

Any legal person may become a beneficiary under a trust. Minors may be beneficiaries even where the trust property is represented by a legal estate in land. The Crown and corporations may be beneficiaries. Aliens may benefit in the same way as British subjects. An animal could not be a beneficiary, as it is not a legal person; but a trust in favour of a home for animals has been held to be a valid charitable trust, as it is considered to be beneficial to the community.

Where the beneficiary under a trust is of full age and is absolutely entitled to the trust property, he may terminate the trust and ask the trustees to transfer to him the legal ownership of the trust property. A beneficiary may protect his interests under the trust against the trustee in the following ways:

1. By a personal action against the trustee where the latter has neglected the trust or has wrongfully disposed of trust property.
2. By following trust property which has come into the hands of a person who has accepted it either knowing it to be trust property, or even without this knowledge if he had not given valuable consideration for it.
3. By initiating criminal proceedings against the trustee where he has used trust property for his own purposes.

Duties of the Trustee

A trustee has the following duties:

1. He must administer the property prudently. In order to avoid unnecessary risks, he has to convert the trust property into authorized (by the Trustee Act 1925) trustee securities, unless the donor of the trust has expressly authorized him to hold the property in its existing form. The powers of investment of trustees have been increased by the Trustee Investments Act 1961. This Act provides that a trust fund may be divided into two halves, one-half to be invested in gilt-edged securities with the other half invested in equities (ordinary shares of joint-stock companies). This reason for this Act is that

inflation has tended to erode the value of gilt-edged securities while the value of equities tends to increase as the value of money falls, thus maintaining the real value of the capital assets involved.

2. He must not make any profit out of the trust. We have seen that where he uses any part of the property for his own purposes the gains will belong to the beneficiary while the trustee would have to make good any losses. He is not entitled to any remuneration unless he acts as a professional trustee, as most trust corporations do, or unless the donor of the trust has provided for payment to be made to him. The trustee must not put himself into a position where a clash might arise between his private interests and his duties as a trustee.

3. The trustee may not delegate his duties, except by permission of the court, but he may employ specialists (*e.g.*, solicitors) to undertake on his behalf such transactions as are generally handled by specialists.

4. He must pay over the trust property to the beneficiary when the latter becomes entitled to it and even before that time he must give information to the beneficiary about the affairs of the trust.

Where it is expedient for the more effective administration of trust property to do so, the court may vary the powers of trustees as conferred on them by the original trust instrument. The Trustee Act 1925, demanded that such an arrangement should be approved by all beneficiaries of full age. Where some beneficiaries are infants or unborn children or otherwise unable to attest, the Variation of Trusts Act 1958, has authorized the court to approve the arrangement on their behalf.

CHAPTER SIX

The Law of Property

Ownership and Possession

The term 'property' is used in English law in two different senses. On the one hand, property may mean a legal relationship existing between a legal person and some thing, while, on the other hand, property may mean the thing itself over which a legal person has certain rights. In order to avoid confusion we shall refer to 'ownership' when discussing the legal relationship between persons and things and restrict the use of the term 'property' to the description of the things which a legal person may own.

Ownership has to be carefully distinguished from possession. The main difference between them is that, while ownership is a purely legal concept, possession is largely a matter of fact. As such, possession historically predates ownership. Possession was recognized by law long before the concept of ownership had been fully developed. Indeed, the very idea of ownership as something distinct from possession becomes practical only in a fairly well-developed capitalistic economy, where the control and the use of the means of production rest in different hands.

Possession consists of physical control over a thing (which, of course, includes animals), coupled with an intention to exclude others from this control. It differs from ownership in that while ownership may in general (though there are exceptions) not be lost without the consent of the owner, possession may be lost accidentally or through the wrongful act of another person. Even a person who has acquired possession of a thing by wrongful means is entitled to have his possession protected. There are then two elements in possession, namely:

1. The *corpus possessionis—i.e.*, the continuous exercise of control by a person over a thing. The control need not be direct; I control not only the things which I have on me, but also those which another person, an agent or sevant, holds on my behalf.

2. The *animus possidendi—i.e.*, the intent to have exclusive control over the thing and to exclude others from it. A person who exercises control, but has no intention of excluding others, is said to have custody of a thing—*e.g.*, the porter carrying a passenger's bag on a railway station. It should be noted that for the purpose of proving the animus possidendi it is immaterial whether the person having

this intention has or has not a legal right to exclude others. A thief has possession of the article stolen, as naturally he does not wish to return it. Furthermore, it does not matter whether the person having possession knows of the existence or the whereabouts of the specific thing possessed where it is one of a group or collection of articles (*i.e.*, books in a library) which he controls and from the control of which he intends to exclude others.

In primitive societies possession was protected because a thing possessed by a person was treated as a kind of extension of his personality. A man's knife was protected in the same way as his hand. It was only when, with industrial conditions changing, people having certain things allowed others to use them that it became necessary to distinguish between the legal rights of the man in actual control and those of the person who had only temporarily parted with possession. Ownership may then be defined as the best right to possess. This means that the possessor's title to goods will be protected by law against the attack of anyone, except that of the owner. Possession is still protected by law to-day for the following reasons:

1. An old saying tells us that possession is nine points of the law. This is quite correct, as law will presume the person in possession to be the owner until such time as another person is able to prove that he is the owner. It is always much easier to prove possession, which is a mere matter of fact, than ownership. It would be difficult for you to prove that you are the owner of the suit you are wearing unless you are a careful man and have retained all receipts. There is little difficulty in showing that you are in possession of it.

2. Law also protects possession, because any attempt to deprive a possessor of the thing under his control would be bound to lead to a breach of the peace. Even an owner is not to be encouraged to recover his property by using self-help.

Possession may exist for a time without effective control, such as where a person has lost control over a thing without abandoning it —*e.g.*, where he has mislaid it. His possession is considered to continue until some one else takes control with intention of excluding the former possessor.

A person may also possess an article the existence of which is unknown to him. Thus it is held that a man possesses everything which is attached to or under the land which he possesses. In *Elwes* v. *Brigg Gas Co.* the plaintiff had leased land to the defendants for ninety-nine years for the purpose of erecting a gas-holder. While digging the foundations the defendants discovered a prehistoric boat which was embedded in the soil six feet below the surface. It was held that the plaintiff as possessor of the land was also in possession of the boat at the time of leasing the land to the defendants. He had no intention of parting with the possession of the boat, and had therefore a better right to possession than the defendants. Similarly, in *South Staffordshire Water Company* v. *Sharman* the defendant, together with other workmen, was employed by the plaintiffs in cleaning out a pool of water. He found two gold rings in the mud at the bottom of the pool. It was held again that possession of the rings vested in the plaintiffs.

On the other hand, a man does not possess an article which is lying unattached on the surface of his land. In *Bridges* v. *Hawkesworth* a wallet had been dropped on a shop floor. The plaintiff, a customer, found the wallet and handed it in to the defendant, the proprietor of the shop. When the wallet was not claimed by its owner the finder demanded its return from the shopkeeper. It was held that he was entitled to it because as finder of the wallet he had acquired possession.

Ownership may be acquired in three ways:

1. *Originally*, where a person stakes a claim to something which has never been owned by anyone (*e.g.*, a wild animal) or to something which has been abandoned by its previous owner.
2. *Derivatively*, either with or without the consent of the previous owner. Ownership is passed on with the consent of the previous owner where he gives or sells something to another person. As we shall see later, intention to pass the property is not enough unless accompanied by some act of delivery. Property may pass without the consent of the owner, where it is taken from him by the operation of the law, such as with businesses that have been nationalized or in connection with bankruptcy proceedings.
3. *By succession*, on the death of the previous owner.

Types of Property

Ownership may extend to a variety of things. Some of these are tangible, such as land or goods; others are rights which have no tangible existence. The confusion that may result from this may be avoided if we remember that what a person owns is not a thing as such, but certain rights to that thing. Ownership can thus be looked upon as the control over a bundle of rights which will be protected by the law. If I am the owner of a typewriter I have the right of using it, the right of disposing of it or destroying it, the right of deriving an income from hiring it out to others, and of leaving it in my will to those whom I wish to benefit. Where the owner commands the full range of rights mentioned he is said to own a *thing* (*or chose*) *in possession*. Where he has all the rights except the first one—*i.e.*, the right of physical possession—he is considered to own a *thing* (*or chose*) *in action*. Thus, my typewriter or my house are things in possession, while the copyright in this book is a thing in action. The owner of the copyright cannot do what the owner of the typewriter can do, and that is take physical possession of it.

Once we appreciate the fact that ownership is really the possession of a bundle of rights over a thing we shall also find no difficulty in distinguishing between property rights in one's own thing (*jura in re propria*) and property rights in a thing belonging to some one else (*jura in re aliena*). The latter rights are those extending to something in which the bulk of the property rights is held already by another person. If I have a right of way over my neighbour's land he is the owner of the property rights in that land, but his rights are restricted by the fact that I possess the right to walk across the land It may perhaps help if at this stage the division of property rights is illustrated graphically:

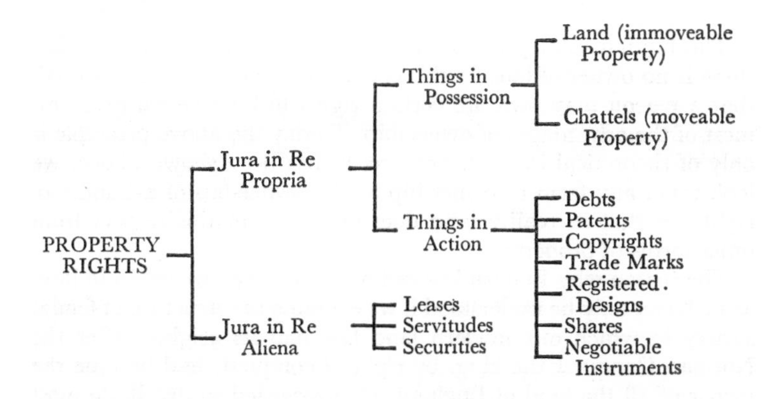

The division of choses in possession into moveable and immoveable things is one common to most legal systems. In English law, however, there exists a further division which is not to be found in the legal systems of other countries, and this is the division of property into *real property* and *personal property*. This division can be understood only by examining its historical foundations.

In early English law property was treated as real property if the courts were prepared to restore the property itself to its owner who had been dispossessed. An action for the restoration of property was known as a real action to distinguish it from a personal action, whereby a plaintiff claimed damages for the loss of property. Property which could not be reclaimed by a real action was personal property. It would not be entirely correct to identify real property with land. Only the holder of a freehold interest in land (see p. 137) is the owner of real property. A leasehold interest in land is treated as personal property, but in order to distinguish it from personal property made up of chattels it is referred to as *chattels real*, while other personal property is called *pure personalty*.

Before the property legislation of 1925 the difference between real and personal property was an important one, since in the absence of a will different classes of persons stood to inherit these properties. Furthermore, with real property, if no heirs could be found, the property went by right of *escheat* to the descendants of the person from whom the predecessor in title of the deceased owner had derived the land. With personal property, on the other hand, the absence of heirs would mean that the Crown would take the property as *bona vacantia*. All these differences have now disappeared, but specific recovery has remained a special feature of real property.

Land Law

The fundamental principle underlying English land law is that there is no owner of land in this country other than the Crown. All that a person may own are certain rights to land which give him most of the advantages of ownership. To-day the above principle is only of theoretical interest, because, as has been shown above, we look upon any form of ownership as the ownership of a bundle of rights, so that in reality land does not differ in this respect from other forms of property.

The reason why English law did not recognize ownership in land as such can only be understood if we examine the structure of feudal society in which our modern land law had its origins. After the Norman Conquest the king, by right of conquest, had become the owner of all the land of England. He proceeded to distribute most of the land to his main followers (the tenants-in-chief) in return for the promise of services, mainly military in nature. The tenants-in-chief on their part also distributed land among lesser knights (tenants-in-demesne) again in return for the promise of services; and so it went on down the scale, right to the humble peasant, who held his land from his lord but had no sub-tenants of his own. He only owed services to other without having anyone owing services to him.

The feudal society was thus based on a kind of pyramid, where only the king at the top and the peasants at the bottom were not both landlords and also tenants. Every person in this society held his land, the only real source of livelihood at the time, from some one else, except of course the king. The rights of a tenant to the land which he held from his lord were known as his *estate*. On the size of his estate depended his social position (status). The relationship between lord and tenant (at any level of the pyramid) was known as tenure and the tenant had certain duties (incidents of tenure) towards his lord. As the feudal economy used hardly any money, rent in the modern sense was practically unknown; but its place was taken by services and payments in kind. At the higher levels of the scale the incidents of tenure were generally either military (providing so many armed men in the event of a conflict) or religious (where the tenant was a dignitary of the Church). At the lower levels of the scale the incidents were partly military (involving personal service in an armed capacity) and partly were made up of personal work for the lord. In addition, the lord was generally entitled to claim one year's rent or one year's income from the land from the successor of a deceased tenant. He also claimed the wardship of the infant successor of a deceased tenant, which entitled him to the income from the land during the minority of the infant. His right of escheat has already been referred to.

The interest of a tenant in his land (*i.e.*, his estate) depended on the duration in time of his rights to the land. From this point of view estates could be divided in the way shown below.

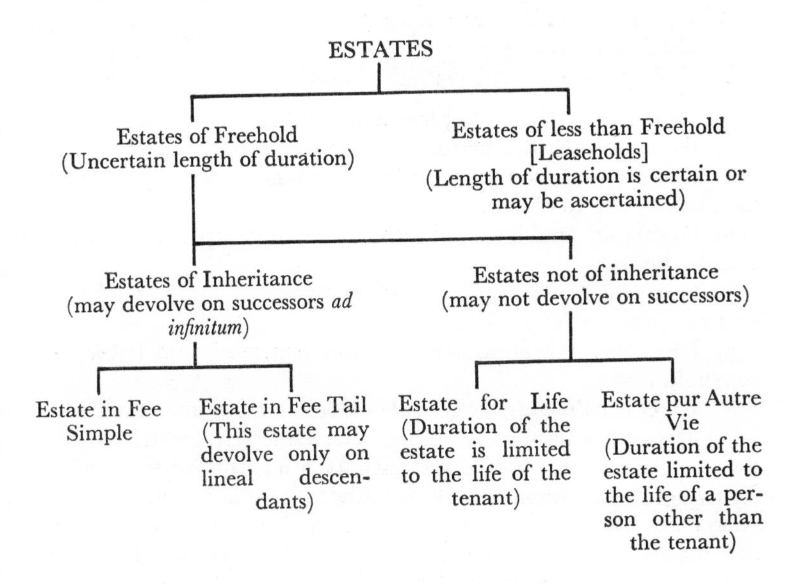

Before the property legislation of 1925 all the given estates could exist either as legal estates or as equitable estates—*i.e.*, behind the protective veil of a trust. This meant that there could be a number of legal owners of the same piece of land, whose interests followed on each other over a period of time. Thus, for instance, A could hold some land as tenant for life, legal estate in fee simple falling after his death to B. Where a number of persons were to hold land in succession, the owner whose estate would become effective only on the expiration of the estate of a previous owner was said to hold a *remainder*. A remainder had to be carefully distinguished from a *reversion*, which arose where the owner of a larger estate (*i.e.*, one existing for either an indefinite time or at least for a longer time) granted an estate in the land for a shorter period to another person on the understanding that when this period expired the land would revert to him. Remainders and reversions can exist now only as equitable interests.

It can easily be seen that land law was perhaps the most intricate part of our legal system, much more complicated than the law relating to chattels. It was for this reason that in 1925, under the guiding hand of the then Lord Chancellor, Lord Birkenhead, a thorough reform of the land law was undertaken. The reform was achieved by five Acts of Parliament—namely:

Law of Property Act 1925
Settled Land Act 1925
Administration of Estates Act 1925
Land Charges Act 1925
Land Registration Act 1925

The main aims of the 1925 legislation were:

1. To abolish the distinction between real property and chattels real, and to assimilate the law relating to land as far as possible to the law relating to chattels.

2. To simplify land law, and thus to make it cheaper and easier to transfer land.

3. To make the rules for intestate succession the same for all forms of property.

4. To abolish the antiquated form of tenure of land known as copyhold tenure.

5. To reduce the number of *legal* estates in land to two—namely, a fee simple and a term of years absolute. Other estates in land can now only exist as equitable interests. It is now no longer possible for two or more persons simultaneously to have legal estates in the same land, except for a lessor and lessee under a lease. Remainders and reversions can thus no longer exist as legal estates. Where in fact two or more persons are interested in land, the land must be either subject to a trust for sale or must be settled land.

Fee Simple Absolute

A fee simple absolute in possession (to give it its full title) is one of the two estates in land which since 1925 may exist as legal estates. The word 'fee', which is derived from the old *feodum*, represents an inheritance, and this means that this estate may be freely inherited.

The fee is 'simple' to distinguish it from a fee tail. It is 'absolute' in that it may not be subject to conditions, and it is 'in possession,' since the owner must be entitled to immediate, as distinct from future, possession of the land. A tenant in fee simple, while in theory not an owner of land, is for all practical purposes in the same position as an owner. He may do anything he likes with the land and is subject only to such restraints as have been imposed by Act of Parliament on landowners.

Estate in Fee Tail

An estate in fee tail is an estate in land which does not pass freely to any heirs of the tenant. On his death the estate would pass to his lineal descendants only. The entailment could be general—*i.e.*, worded in such a way as to allow the estate to pass to lineal descendants of either sex; or it could be restricted either to male (estate in tail male) or female (estate in tail female) descendants. The reason why estates were entailed will be discussed later. Before the 1925 property legislation entailed estates could exist as legal estates; since then they may exist only as equitable interests—*i.e.*, behind a trust.

Estate for Life

These estates can now after 1925 exist as equitable interests only. The essence of this type of estate is that it only lasts for the life of a person, who may be either the tenant for life himself (estate for life) or some other person (*estate pur autre vie*). The latter type of estate usually comes into existence when the tenant for life assigns his interest to another person who would hold the land then for the life of the original tenant.

Strict Settlements

In the days when large landowners played a more important part in our society than they do to-day family pride often induced them to think out ways and means of ensuring that the family estates should remain in the hands of the family, come what may. The most popular means of assuring this outcome was the strict settlement (governed by the Settled Land Act 1882). The strict settlement worked as follows: Let us assume that Jones, a large landowner, was about to get married. A few days before his marriage Jones would execute a marriage settlement whereby he transferred his estates to trustees on the following trusts. Jones himself was to have a life-interest in the estates. His eldest son—then, of course, still unborn—would be assured an estate in tail, subject to his father's life-interest. The new

Mrs Jones would receive in the settlement a *jointure* (an annual payment on widowhood), and provision was also made for similar annual payments (*portions*) for any other children that might be born in the marriage. The jointure and the portions were secured by means of a *rent-charge* on the land. This meant that the payments of these annual sums represented a first charge on the proceeds of the estate. The holder of a rent-charge has rights similar to those of a landlord (especially the right of distress) to enforce the payment of the amounts owing to him.

As a result of the settlement, the land became now inalienable until such time as the eldest reached majority. When this happened the son could *bar the entail—i.e.*, convert his fee-tail estate into a so-called *base fee*; but this would not provide him with an independent income as long as his father was alive. In order to retain the land in the family, Jones would persuade his son to agree to a resettlement of the land. A new settlement would be made out, providing for a life-interest for Jones senior, to be followed by a life-interest for Jones junior, to be followed by an entailed interest for his yet unborn son, with the usual jointure and portions added to it. Jones junior would receive an allowance to tide him over the period until his life-estate became operative. The effect of the settlement was that the land was now safely tied up for another generation. And so it went on.

The main defect of the strict settlement was that the life tenant had to finance all outgoings for repairs, maintenance, taxes, etc., out of his own pocket, being unable to sell any part of the estate to secure additional capital for improvements. This system could work in the days when the income from land was ample to provide for all the outgoings, but with the increase in taxes it became more and more difficult for the tenants for life to maintain their estates in decent working order. It was for this reason that the Settled Land Act 1925, introduced considerable changes in respect of settled land.

The Settled Land Act 1925

This Act applies to settled land but not to land held on trusts for sale. Where land is settled, the legal estate is now vested in the tenant for life. He holds the legal estate on trust for himself, and for all the other beneficiaries under the settlement. In two cases, however, the legal estate and the attached powers will not vest in the tenant for life but will instead go to the 'statutory owner.'

1. Where the tenant for life is an infant the statutory owner will be the personal representative of the testator if no vesting deed has been made out—otherwise, the trustees of the settlement.

2. Where there is no tenant for life the statutory owner will be any

person of full age on whom the settlement expressly confers these powers—otherwise, the trustees of the settlement.

Under the Settled Land Act, land is to be treated as settled land if it is deemed to be the subject of a settlement. A settlement is created by any document or documents which satisfy any of the following three conditions:

1. The land is held on trust for any persons by way of succession (*e.g.*, to A for life, then to B for life, then to C in fee simple).
2. The land is held on trust for an infant either in fee simple or for a term of years absolute.
3. The land has been made subject to family charges.

In order that land should be settled, two documents will have to be made out—namely, a vesting deed and a trust instrument.

The *vesting deed* must contain the following information:

1. A description of the settled land.
2. A statement that the land is vested in the estate owner on the trusts set out in the trust deed.
3. The names of the trustees of the settlement.
4. A description of any additional powers which the life tenant is to have.
5. The name of the person who is entitled to appoint additional trustees.

The *trust instrument*, which is made out at the same time, contains a description of the trusts on which the land has been settled.

If a settlement is made by will the will is treated as the trust instrument, and the testator's personal representatives hold the land on trust to execute a vesting deed in favour of the tenant for life.

The beauty of the new system of settling land is that the tenant for life can now freely sell the land if that should be necessary for commercial reasons (a good offer being received) or in order to raise money for improvements. The buyer need only see the vesting deed which shows that the tenant for life has the title to sell; the details of the trust on which the land has been settled, which are, after all, private family matters, need not be disclosed to the buyer, who has no need to see the trust deed. The purchase price of the land would, of course, not be paid to the tenant for life but to the trustees of the settlement.

The Act also lays down the powers of the tenant for life in relation to the settled land. He has in general unlimited discretion as to his management of the settled land, but there exist the following safeguards against any possible abuse by him of his powers:

1. The tenant for life has the general duties of a trustee.
2. He may exercise certain of his powers only on giving prior notice to the trustees of the settlement. This applies to any sale, lease, or mortgage of the settled land.

3. The tenant for life may exercise certain powers only with the consent of the trustees of the settlement. This includes a sale of the principal mansion house or the cutting and selling of timber from the settled land.

Trusts for Sale

Where, before 1925, the property to be settled was not land which the owner intended to cultivate and keep in the family, it was usual to use the method of a trust for sale. The property was vested in trustees on some definite trusts with a duty to sell the property and to reinvest the proceeds. The trustees were generally given the power of postponing the sale and of managing the property instead if, in their discretion, they considered this to be preferable. It is essential that the trust should impose a definite *duty* on the trustees to sell, even though they have the power of postponing the sale. Where trustees have a discretion as to whether they should sell at all there does not exist a trust for sale but a settlement.

Trusts for sale have not been basically affected by the 1925 legislation—indeed, further instances of trusts for sale have been added. A statutory trust for sale is deemed to exist where land is held by co-owners or where it is held by the personal representatives of a deceased person who died intestate.

Co-ownership of Land

Property rights in land are generally held by one person only at a time. It is possible, however, that two or more persons may own land simultaneously. Common law knew different forms of co-ownership of land, but the only ones surviving to-day are *joint ownership* and *ownership in common.*

With joint ownership, each co-owner owns the whole land, subject only to a similar right on part of the other co-owners. With ownership in common, each co-owner owns an individual share (*e.g.*, a quarter) of the land. This means that the owner in common is entitled to a share in the estate, but not in any specific part of it.

The difference between the two forms of co-ownership can be best studied by examining the situation which arises when one of the co-owners dies. If the land has been held by the co-owners in common the deceased owner's share will go to his heirs. If, however, the land has been owned jointly the right of survivorship (*jus accrescendi*) will operate, and the surviving co-owners would absorb the share of the deceased co-owner. This would continue until one owner was left, and he would then become the sole owner of the land.

The main advantage of joint ownership is that it prevents the splitting up of land into too many small parcels. With joint ownership there will always be a small number of co-owners whose consents and signatures have to be secured when the land is to be sold. Where land is held in common by a number of owners, transfer becomes difficult, as every single co-owner would have to sign the necessary deeds, and the collection of the signatures would take an unduly long time. On the other hand, of course, joint ownership is unfair in that the accident of longevity will determine who will eventually become the sole owner.

The Law of Property Act 1925 has resolved the dilemma by providing that where land is owned by a number of persons the owners, or the first four of them if there are more than four, should be treated as joint owners, holding the land on trust for the benefit of themselves and of all other co-owners as owners in common. The only form of co-ownership recognized now at common law is joint ownership; ownership in common can exist only behind a trust. The advantage of the set-up is that there are never more than four persons entitled to deal legally with the land, but beneficially the interest in the land of any co-owner will pass to his heirs in the same way as any other form of property.

The Squatter's Title

The Limitation Act 1939 (see page 110) applies also to the recovery of land. Thus where an unauthorized person (a squatter) has been in possession of land belonging to another for a period of twelve years, the owner will be unable to recover the land from the squatter. The squatter could be a person who has merely moved in without any authority, or he could be a former tenant who has stayed on after the tenancy has expired. The usual rules about the postponement of the commencement of the period of limitation where the owner is under a disability at the time when the period of limitation should have commenced apply in respect of land as in respect of other interests, and similarly the period of limitation recommences where there has been an acknowledgment in writing or a part-payment (*e.g.*, of rent).

Where the ownership of land is vested in the Crown the period of limitation would be thirty years.

When the period of limitation has expired the squatter does not acquire the fee simple. His rights to the land are negative rather than positive ones, in that he may successfully resist an attempt by the former owner to recover the land from him, without, however, being able to prove a good title to the land if he wishes to sell it. If a squatter who has acquired a squatter's title wishes to sell the land he may have to prove not only that the true owner of the land has been barred by lapse of time, but also that this person was in fact the sole and true owner, and that there are no other persons who might legitimately claim a title to the land.

What happens fairly frequently is that one landowner occupies a piece of land which in reality belongs to his neighbour, and if he has done so for the length of the period of limitation he may be able to treat this piece of land as having become part of his own plot.

Leaseholds (Terms of Years)

A lessee (or tenant) is entitled to the exclusive possession and enjoyment of the land during the period of his tenancy. In this way he differs from a mere licensee, whose possession of land is not exclusive in that he is bound to share it with others. A lodger, for instance, is not a tenant of the room which he occupies, because he is not entitled to exclude the landlord from it as a lessee could do. The estate of a lessee is a legal estate only if it is absolute and in possession. This excludes a tenancy at sufferance, which is not a legal estate because it may be determined at any time. Although we call a leasehold a term of years, this does not mean that a lease must always be for a multiple of years; it may exist as a legal estate even where it is for a shorter period, provided that the period is fixed. Even periodic tenancies, extending from month to month or from quarter to quarter, are treated as sufficiently definite to constitute leasehold. It is possible to distinguish between the following types of leases:

1. *Leases for a Fixed Period.* The commencement and the termination of the lease must be certain or ascertainable before the lease comes into effect. A lease "for the duration of the War" would thus not qualify.

2. *Yearly* (*or Weekly or Monthly or other Periodical*) *Tenancies.* These tenancies continue from year to year (week to week, etc.) until determined by proper notice. They may be created either expressly or by implication, where a person occupies land with the owner's consent and pays a rent which is calculated on an annual (weekly, etc.) basis. Such a tenancy also arises where a tenant for a fixed period 'holds over' after the expiration of his tenancy, and the landlord accepts rent from him on a yearly (weekly, etc.) basis. A periodic tenancy is determined by such notice as has been agreed upon between the parties. In the absence of agreement a yearly tenancy must be determined by at least half a year's notice. Where the tenancy commenced on one of the official quarter days, half a year means two quarters. Periodical tenancies for shorter periods are determined by notice for the full period, expiring at the end of a completed period, subject, however, to a minimum of four weeks (Rent Act 1957, s. 16).

3. *Tenancy at Will.* This arises where a person occupies land with

the consent of the owner as tenant (*i.e.*, not as servant or agent) on the understanding that either party may determine the tenancy at any time. The tenancy may be rent-free, but unless this has been expressly agreed upon the tenant will have to pay rent. This tenancy comes to an end if either party does something which is inconsistent with the tenancy or if either party gives notice. If a tenancy at will has been created without reference to rent, and rent is subsequently paid on a periodical basis, a periodical tenancy would come into existence.

4. *Tenancy at Sufferance* comes into existence where a tenant on the expiration of his tenancy holds over without the landlord's permission. The absence of the landlord's consent represents the difference between this tenancy and a tenancy at will. No rent is payable, but the tenant has to pay compensation (*mesne profits*) for the use and occupation of land. It may be terminated at any time or it may be converted into a periodic tenancy if a periodical rent is paid and accepted.

Creation of Tenancy

Since 1925 a tenancy can be created by deed only, except in the following cases:

1. where the lease is one for not more than three years and
2. where the lease is to take effect in possession—*i.e.*, the tenant is to take possession at once and
3. where the lease is one at a *rack-rent*—*i.e.*, the best rent obtainable for the land.

Duties of Landlord and Tenant

Unless otherwise agreed, the landlord has the following duties towards the tenant:

1. He has to ensure that the tenant gets quiet enjoyment of the land. This means that he guarantees to the tenant that no third party will be lawfully able to question the tenant's title to the land.
2. The landlord must not derogate from his grant to the tenant. He must not do anything which would render the land unfit for the purpose for which it is let.
3. In general, the landlord has no obligation to ensure that premises leased should be fit for habitation. There are two exceptions to this. A furnished house which is let must be fit for human habitation at the time of letting, though the landlord need not subsequently maintain it in that state. Houses let for less than £52 a year (£80 in London) must both be fit for human habitation at the time of letting and also maintained in that state subsequently. Where

a dwelling house has been let after 1961 for a term of not less than seven years the landlord must keep in repair the structure and exterior of the house, must keep in repair and proper working order the installations in the house for the supply of water, gas and electricity and for sanitation and space heating or heating water.

The main *duties of the tenant* are the following:

1. The tenant has an obligation to pay rent. Where no particular amount has been fixed, the rent must be 'reasonable.'

2. The tenant is responsible for the payment of 'tenant's taxes' (*i.e.*, all taxes, except for land tax and Schedule A income tax) and rates.

3. The tenant must not commit *waste*. This means that he must not do any deliberate damage to the property leased. Where he is a tenant for a fixed period or from year to year, he must also keep the premises wind- and water-tight.

Assignment and Subletting

Where the lessee assigns his lease he is transferring his rights under the unexpired portion of his lease to another person, the assignee, who will step for all purposes into the place of the lessee. The assignee of the lease will now have the same duties towards the lessor as the original lessee had, but the lessee will also remain liable to the lessor under the contract which he made with him.

Where the lessee grants to another person the use of the land for a period shorter than the unexpired portion of his lease, he is subletting the land. The lessee remains responsible to the landlord for the rent and for the other obligations of his lease, possessing, however, similar rights as to rent, etc., against the sub-lessee; the nature of these rights depends on the terms of the sub-lease. No legal relationship will be established between the landlord (lessor) and the sub-lessee.

Many leases contain clauses against an assignment or a sub-lease of the leased land or premises providing, as a rule, that assignment or subletting may not take place without the superior landlord's consent. Where such clauses are included in a lease, it is implied, however, that the landlord will not unreasonably withhold his consent to an assignment or sub-lease (Landlord and Tenant Act 1927). To justify a refusal to consent, the landlord would have to have a good reason, based on either the unsuitability of the proposed subtenant or on the use to which the sub-tenant proposed to put the land. In no circumstances may the landlord demand any consideration for giving his consent, except the payment of his legal expenses.

Servitudes

Servitudes differ from leases in that the owner of a servitude is not entitled to the exclusive possession of that land to which the servitude relates. The owner of a servitude has certain rights over land which is in the possession and ownership of another person. Servitudes may be either *easements* or *profits à prendre*.

An easement is the right of the owner of one piece of land to compel the owner of another piece of land to permit something to be done on his land or to refrain himself from doing something on it. The most important easements are a right of way, a right to light, a right to have a building supported by the adjoining building, and a right to discharge water (*e.g.*, from drains) on some other person's land. The main features of an easement are the following:

1. An easement can only be enjoyed in respect of land. This means that the right constituting the easement is enjoyed by the owner of one piece of land in his capacity as owner of that land and not in his personal capacity. The land in favour of which the easement exists is known as the *dominant tenement*, while the land over which the right is exercised is called the *servient tenement*. The easement must in some way help in the better enjoyment of the dominant tenement (*e.g.*, by making it more accessible) and not merely benefit the owner in some way unconnected with the dominant tenement.

2. There must be separate ownership of the dominant and servient tenements. If the two pieces of land are, or come under, the same ownership the easement will cease to exist.

3. The easement must be capable of forming the subject-matter of a grant, which means that it must relate to something which is capable of reasonable definition. There could be, for instance, no easement to allow free movement of air from one land to another except if it is passing through some defined channel.

A *profit à prendre* is a right to take something from another person's land. This includes, for instance, the right to fish in another person's stream or the right to graze cattle or collect firewood. The right to draw water from another person's river or stream is treated as an easement and not as a profit, because running water cannot be privately owned. A profit differs from an easement in the following ways:

1. An easement, as we have seen, must always be 'appurtenant to land.' A profit may exist 'in gross'—*i.e.*, it may be enjoyed by its owner or owners independent of any dominant tenement.

2. A profit may be several (enjoyed by one person only) or common (enjoyed by many people). One person, for instance, could own the right of grazing cattle on some one else's meadow, or the right might belong to a number of people—*e.g.*, the inhabitants of a village.

The following diagram shows the main ways in which both easements and profits may come into existence.

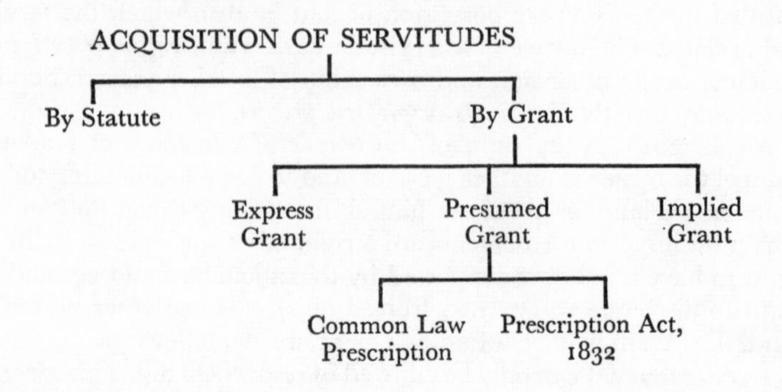

Servitudes are created by statute, when an Act of Parliament, generally a local one, grants certain rights to the undertakers of public works. The usual method of acquiring a servitude is by grant. These grants are express where the owner of the servient tenement creates the servitude by deed. A grant of a servitude (particularly of an easement) is implied where the owner of two adjoining properties sells one in circumstances where he used to exercise certain rights on behalf of the sold property over the retained property which, if the two properties had not belonged to the same owner, would have constituted an easement. Thus, if the owner of two plots of land (A and B) used to walk from A through B to the main road and he has now sold A, the buyer of A will have the right of way over B by implied grant.

A grant of a servitude may be presumed to have been made either by common law prescription, where the servitude has been enjoyed since time immemorial (*i.e.*, legally since 1189), or under the provisions of the Prescription Act 1832. This Act provides that the grant of a servitude may be presumed from long user of the right involved. The user would have to be twenty years in the case of an easement or thirty years in that of a profit. Where the servitude has been held by *oral* permission from the owner of the servient tenement the periods of prescription under the Act would be double—*i.e.*, forty for an easement and sixty for a profit. The grant of a *written* permission by the owner of the servient tenement will, however, rule out the possibility of acquiring a legal right to the servitude irrespective of the time for which it has been enjoyed.

The Rights of Light Act 1959, apart from dealing with some temporary problems which had arisen as a result of the War, has brought about a permanent change in the methods of preventing the acquisition of a right of light. Under the 1832 Act the owner of the servient tenement could avoid the creation of a right of light by statutory prescription only if he gave either his written permission or if he interrupted the enjoyment of the right for a continuous period of one year (*e.g.*, by putting up a screen). The latter method may not always be practicable as planning permission will be needed for the erection of such a structure. The owner of the servient land may now substitute for the actual screen an imaginary one, by registering in the register of local land charges a statutory notice indicating the exact siting of the screen which he would have liked to erect. If this is done the effect is the same as if the access of light to the dominant building had been obstructed for one year.

Restrictive Covenants

Where a landowner undertakes certain contractual obligations in respect of the land, these obligations are in general personal obligations, which affect only the parties to the contract and will not be binding on their successors in title. This is the natural result of the application of the principle of privity of contract, which we have considered already.

There are, however, certain contracts, or covenants, which 'touch and concern the land' and which are said to 'run with the land' so that they may be enforced by or against the successors of the original parties. The enforcement of these restrictive covenants, as they are known for short, is based on the principle of equity, that a person who acquires property with knowledge that some other person has certain rights over it will be conscience bound to observe these rights.

The leading case in which this doctrine originated is *Tulk* v. *Moxhay*, where a person bought some ornamental gardens in the middle of Leicester Square, in London, subject to the condition that the gardens would be preserved in their then condition. The buyer sold the gardens, and after they had passed through a number of hands they eventually became the property of M., who, knowing of the original condition, wanted to have the land built on. It was held that he could be restrained from doing so because, having bought the land with knowledge of the restriction on its use, he was bound to observe it.

Restrictive covenants may be enforced to-day in the following circumstances:

1. *The obligation must be restrictive—i.e.*, negative in substance. A promise not to build or not to pull down a house may be a restrictive covenant, but a promise to build or to pull down a house may not.

2. *The promise must 'touch and concern' land.* This means that it

must have been given in order to preserve the amenities or to protect the value of some other piece of land. Promises which are made in respect of land in favour of a person who is not the owner of adjoining land would not be restrictive covenants. Similarly, the promise must affect the land which is subjected to it and not merely the person who happens to be its owner at the time.

3. The person who claims the benefit of the covenant must have *retained land* which is capable of profiting by the existence of the restraint.

4. If the claimant is a person other than the original covenantee he must show that the benefit of the contract has either been *validly assigned* to him or that it has become 'annexed' to land, having been made definitely for the benefit of a particular piece of land.

5. Since the Land Charges Act 1925, all restrictive covenants must be *registered* as land charges, and it is, therefore, no longer necessary to prove that the buyer of land bought it with knowledge of the existence of the covenant, registration being treated as notice to all subsequent purchasers. For the consequences of non-registration see page 164.

The Sale of Land

Every sale of property, whether real or personal, has two elements —namely, the making of a contract and the delivery of the thing sold to the buyer. With land, actual delivery in the sense of handing over the property is impossible, and it is replaced by an act of constructive delivery in the form of the handing over of a properly executed document, known as a *conveyance*.

The contract for the sale of land, though it need not actually be made in writing, must be evidenced by something in writing—*e.g.*, by subsequent correspondence from which the making of the contract and its detailed terms may be deduced. After the contract has been made the vendor of land has to satisfy the purchaser as to his title to the land. For this purpose the vendor must show that he can trace back his title to the land for at least fifteen years. Some document at least fifteen years old will have to be produced which shows that the vendor or a predecessor in title had obtained the fee simple. If this document does not refer to the vendor himself he will also have to produce other documents, showing how his own title is derived from that of his predecessor. The history of the land over the relevant period is summarized in an 'abstract of title,' which the vendor has to deliver to the purchaser, who may check the abstract against the original documents and may put questions to the vendor to clear up any doubtful points. The purchaser will also search the land registers in order to make sure that there are no charges on the land other than those which have already been disclosed to him. When all this has been satisfactorily completed the purchaser will prepare a draft conveyance for the vendor's approval, and when this has been received the draft will be copied out as a formal deed for the signatures of the parties. Needless to say, in practice all the above jobs are performed by the solicitors of the two parties. When the conveyance has been executed the vendor will also hand to the purchaser all the documents relating to the land which he has sold, so that the purchaser should have no difficulty in proving the root of his title if he wished to sell the land.

One of the main difficulties in selling land lies in the need to examine the vendor's title and to undertake the various searches. This difficulty has been avoided in many foreign countries by making the registration of titles to land compulsory, so that a purchaser need only consult a single publicly operated register to find out whether the vendor has a good title and what charges there are on the land. The Land Registration Act 1925 introduced this system on an experimental basis in this country. Land registration is now compulsory for instance in London,[1] Middlesex, Surrey, Kent, Berkshire, Oxford, Eastbourne, Hastings, Croydon, Canterbury, Oldham, Manchester, Blackburn, Rochdale, Huddersfield, Salford, and Reading. This area can be extended by Order in Council.

The register is kept at the Land Registry in London. It includes a description holding the owner's name, a description of any charges existing over the land, and of certain other minor interests to the land. The owner of registered land receives a land certificate, and when he sells the land he has merely to make out a simple transfer deed and arrange for the purchaser's name to be substituted for his own on the register.

The reader might like to be reminded not to confuse the Land Register with the Land Charges Register, which will be discussed in the chapter on securities.

Personal Property

Personal property may be divided into choses in possession and choses in action. Choses in possession may be *chattels real* (*i.e.*, leaseholds), which we already have discussed, or *personal chattels*, the law relating to the sale of which has been codified in the Sale of Goods Act 1893. Here we are concerned with choses in action only. The one thing which all the choses in action have in common is that their owner has no right to the present possession of a tangible thing. There is no use or enjoyment attached to a chose in action other than

[1] In the area of the former Administrative County of London the system has been in force since 1898.

the right of disposing of it or drawing an income from it. The most important choses in action have already been listed, but some of them will have to be discussed at greater length.

Patents

A patent is a grant by the Crown, giving the owner of the patent (the patentee) the right to prevent other persons from making, using or selling the invention covered by the patent. The term of the patent is (providing certain renewal fees are paid) sixteen years from the date of filing a document known as a complete specification. The law concerning patents is contained in the Patents Act 1949.

A patent may be granted to the true and first inventor or to his successor in title. The title 'true and first inventor' includes not only the actual author of the invention but also a person who is the first to introduce in this country an invention made abroad. The invention must be novel, in that no public disclosure in this country has occurred prior to filing the patent application.

The subject of a valid grant of a patent must be a 'manner of manufacture.' To patent the product of manufacture one has also to disclose a way of making it. The man who first thought of electric razors could not patent the idea of shaving without soap and water; he could merely patent an electrically powered shaver. To ensure the validity of the patent, the invention, as defined by the 'claims' of the patent, must possess some utility. This does not mean that it must be a commercially practicable proposition as long as the invention is capable of serving some useful purpose.

The patentee either may produce the article himself or he may grant a licence to another person to use his patent, usually in return for an agreed royalty. He may also assign his patent to another person, in which case the original patentee may cease to have any rights to the patent.

Registered Designs

A design is defined by the Registered Designs Act 1949, as some "feature of shape, configuration, pattern, or ornament applied to an article by any industrial process or means, being a feature which in the finished article will appeal to and be judged solely by the eye, but does not include a method or principle of construction or a feature of shape or configuration which is dictated solely by the function which the article to be made has to perform." Thus, the fact that a spout is attached to a teapot would not be looked upon as a design, though the particular construction of the spout might be a matter of design.

Designs are protected if they are registered with the Comptroller of Patents. The design must always be registered in respect of a particular article—for instance, in respect of a teapot or a cigarette-case. Registration gives the owner the exclusive right of using the design for five years. After the expiration of this period the design may be further protected for an additional ten years if certain renewal fees are paid.

Trade Marks

A trade mark, under the Trade Marks Act 1938, is a mark used or proposed to be used on or in connection with goods for the purpose of indicating that they are the goods of the proprietor of the trade mark by virtue of manufacture, selection, certification, dealing with or offering for sale.

Registration of trade marks takes place also with the Comptroller of Patents who acts as Registrar. Registration is valid for seven years, but it may be renewed after that for another fourteen years. A trade mark is assignable by its owner, and it may also be transmitted to a purchaser in connection with the sale of the goodwill of a business.

Copyrights

A copyright is the sole right to produce or reproduce any particular work or any substantial part thereof in any material form whatsoever, or to perform or—in the case of a lecture—to deliver the work or any substantial part thereof in public, and if the work is unpublished to publish it. Copyright also extends to cinematographic films and to sound and television broadcasts. The law of copyright is based now on the Copyright Act 1956, which replaced the Copyright Act 1911.

A copyright is thus a form of property in intellectual work, writing, drawing, music, etc. What is protected by copyright is the actual literary or other composition, not the idea which lies behind it. Any unauthorized reproduction or performance of a work protected by copyright represents an infringement of copyright. Even those who, however innocently, distribute anything which represents an infringement of copyright (*e.g.*, booksellers selling a book containing material which infringes a copyright) are themselves guilty of an infringement.

Unlike the other types of choses in action which we have discussed, copyright does not require registration for its protection. The author owns the copyright in his intellectual works for his lifetime, and his estate owns the copyright for another fifty years from the end of the year in which he died. Copyrights in gramophone recordings and in photographs exist for fifty years from the end of the year in which the photograph or record has been first published. The owner of a copyright may assign it to another person who will then acquire all the rights of the author, but such assignment must be in writing in order to be legally valid.

Debts

A debt is also a chose in action. Like other choses in action, a debt may be assigned by the creditor to another person. This was not possible at common law, but was permitted by equity, subject to the reservation that the assignee of a debt who wished to sue the debtor had to bring his action in the original creditor's name. Since 1875 a legal assignment of debts has also been possible, and the rules applying to it are now contained in the Law of Property Act 1925.

There are three rules to be observed:

1. The assignment must be in writing.
2. Written notice of the assignment must be given to the debtor.
3. The assignment must be absolute and not by way of charge only. This means that it is impossible (*a*) to assign part of a debt, or (*b*) the whole debt on some condition, or (*c*) the whole debt or part of it by way of charge so that the assignee should become entitled to be paid out of a particular fund without the fund itself being transferred to him.

All monetary debts are assignable and so also are other rights arising under a contract. The only contractual rights which are not assignable are rights to personal services or other rights which are so tied up with personal considerations that the debtor would be at a disadvantage if assignment by the creditor were permitted. Thus a right to receive ten hundredweights of coal is assignable, but a right to receive enough coal to meet the recipient's requirements would not be assignable, as the assignee's requirements might well exceed those of the assignor.

An assignment of contractual rights is said to be 'subject to equities.' This means that any defences or counterclaims which the debtor had against the assignor will survive against the assignee. If A owes £5 to B and B owes £2 to A, B could sue A only for the balance of £3. If now B were to assign the debt of £5 owing to him by A to a third party, the assignee would also be able to claim £3 only from A.

The introduction of legal assignments has not completely destroyed the need for equitable assignments. There are to-day two kinds of equitable assignments—namely, the assignment of a right which merely exists in equity, *i.e.*, an equitable chose in action (*e.g.*, the right of beneficiary under a trust) and the assignment of a legal chose in action where the assignment does not satisfy the requirements of the Law of Property Act. Such assignments may be made quite informally, but they suffer from two disadvantages as compared with legal assignments. As has been stated already, the assignee cannot sue the debtor in his own name but must also join the assignor in the action. It has also been argued, though the point is not quite settled, that an equitable assignment of a legal chose in action requires consideration. No consideration is definitely needed for the assignment of an equitable chose in action or for a legal assignment.

Some monetary debts are embodied in written instruments which have been endowed by law with special privileges. These instruments are known as negotiable instruments.

Negotiable Instruments

A negotiable instrument is a document embodying a debt. It possesses the quality of negotiability. This quality is characterized by two main features:

1. A negotiable instrument may be transferred (and this means that the rights to the debt embodied in it are also transferred) by mere delivery without the formalities of a legal assignment. The only exception to this rule is a bill of exchange payable to order, which is negotiated by delivery coupled with an endorsement.

2. A negotiable instrument is passed on 'free from equities.' This means that the rights of the transferee are not dependent on the rights of the transferor, and the transferee may acquire a good title to the instrument irrespective of that of the transferor.

The quality of negotiability attaches to a document generally by commercial custom, though it is unlikely that further instruments would now be added to the existing list. The most important negotiable instruments are bills of exchange, cheques, and promissory notes, all three of which are governed by the Bills of Exchange Act 1882.

A bill of exchange is an unconditional order in writing, addressed by one person to another, signed by the person giving it, requiring the person to whom it is addressed to pay on demand or at a fixed or determinable future time a sum certain in money to, or to the order of, a specified person or to bearer.

A cheque is a bill of exchange drawn on a banker payable on demand.

A promissory note is an unconditional promise in writing made by one person to another signed by the maker, engaging to pay on demand or at a determinable future time a sum certain in money to, or to the order of, a specified person or to bearer.

The illustration, shown below, of a bill of exchange may help in our discussion:

Jones is the drawer of the bill, Smith the drawee, and Green the payee. Smith is under no legal obligation to pay the bill unless he indicates on the bill itself his acceptance of the obligation, generally by signing his name across the face of the bill, with or without the word 'accepted.' It is up to the holder of the bill to decide whether he wishes to present the bill to the drawee for acceptance. Until this has been done the holder does not know whether the drawee will in fact honour the bill, but if he is prepared to take the risk he need not present the bill for acceptance, except where the bill is payable so many days after demand where acceptance is necessary in order to fix the date of payment, or where the bill is payable at some place other than the drawee's residence or place of business, or where the bill itself states that it must be presented for acceptance.

£100 MANCHESTER, *January* 1, 1961

Three months after date pay to George Green or order one hundred pounds for value received.

JOHN JONES

TO EDWARD SMITH, Esq.

The bill is handed by the drawer to the payee, and the payee may hold it until maturity. If he requires the money earlier he may, however, transfer the bill to another person (negotiate it) and that person will then become the holder. The form of transfer depends on whether the bill is payable to bearer or to order. Where the bill is stated to be payable to bearer the transfer is effected by mere delivery; but where, as in our example, the bill is payable to the payee's order the payee, apart from delivering the bill to the transferee, must also endorse it. The endorsement takes the form of the endorser signing the bill on the back. He may either give the name of the endorsee (special endorsement) or may just sign his own name (endorsement in blank). In the latter case the bill may be treated henceforth as a bill payable to bearer.

We have noted already that the main feature of negotiability is that the person to whom a negotiable instrument is transferred will have a good title to it, irrespective of the title of his predecessor. With bills of exchange this applies only where the person to whom the bill has been passed is a *holder in due course* as defined by the Act. A holder in due course is a holder of a bill who took a bill which was at the time of negotiation to him complete and regular on the face of it, before it was overdue, for value and without notice of any defect in the title of his predecessor. A bill is overdue if the time for payment has passed. With a bill payable on demand this will be the case when the bill has been in circulation for an unreasonable time. With a bill payable at a fixed or ascertainable date, the bill is overdue three days (the so-called days of grace) after the date fixed. The holder in due course must have given something of value for the bill (as distinct from receiving it as a gift), and he must have had no notice of the fact that his predecessor in title had obtained the bill illegally or by fraud, if that was the case. It should be noted that a holder is deemed to be a holder in due course until the opposite has been proved.

A bill of exchange must be presented for payment immediately it falls due (see above). If the holder should fail to present the bill for payment when it falls due he will not lose his rights against the acceptor of the bill. These rights may be enforced during the normal period of limitation—*i.e.*, six years. The holder who fails to present the bill for payment will, however, lose his rights against the parties who are secondarily liable on the bill. These are all persons who have signed their names on the bill as endorsers. In order to be able to claim against these persons, the holder must not only present the bill for payment on the due date, but must also immediately give notice to them if the bill should be dishonoured by non-payment. This notice of dishonour may be dispensed with only if the holder is unable to give it because the address of a recipient is unknown, or where an addressee has in advance waived the need to give notice to him, or where the addressee who was one of the endorsers knew at the time of endorsement that the drawee was a fictitious person or was incapable of entering into contractual obligations.

Where a signature on a bill of exchange is forged, the signature will be treated as wholly inoperative, and no person, even if acting in good faith, will be able to acquire any rights under it. Similarly, any material alteration of a bill made without the consent of all the parties who are liable on the bill will mean that the bill will be void except as against the party who made or authorized the alteration.

All the rules discussed above apply also to cheques, except that a cheque, being payable on demand, cannot be presented for acceptance. Cheques may, however, be crossed. The crossing (consisting of two parallel lines drawn across the face of the cheque, with or without the words '& Co' written between them) is a direction to the banker on whom the cheque is drawn to pay it only to another banker. The holder of the cheque will thus have to pay the cheque into his own bank account and have his bank collect the cheque for him. Certain words may be written between the two parallel lines which form the crossing, and these words will further amplify the direction given to the bank. If the name of a bank is given between the lines the crossing is a special crossing and the cheque must be collected through the bank named in the crossing. It is also possible to write the words 'not negotiable' between the lines. This will not have the effect of making the cheque non-transferable, but the cheque will cease to be a negotiable instrument, so that no subsequent holder of it will be able to gain a better title than that possessed by his predecessor. Where the words 'account payee only' appear in the crossing, this will be a direction to the bank *collecting* the cheque for a customer to make sure that they collect it only for the person whose name figures as that of the payee.

CROSSINGS ON CHEQUES

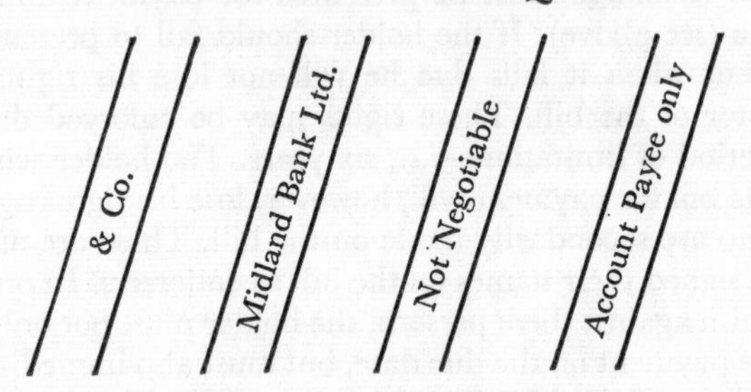

The relationship between banker and customer is primarily that of creditor (*i.e.*, the customer) and debtor (the banker). The banker has agreed to honour his customer's cheques, and for this purpose he will accept instructions signed by the customer. The banker must be presumed to know the customer's signature, and if he makes a payment out of the customer's account against a cheque which does not bear the customer's signature he will have to refund to the customer the monies thus paid out. The relationship is a confidential one, and the banker may not give information about the customer's account to any other person, except with the customer's authority or when ordered to do so by a court of law or when commanded by Act of Parliament. The customer for his part must exercise care in drawing cheques so as to make forgeries or alterations difficult, and if he has been negligent in drawing a cheque, and a third party has thus been enabled to alter the amount of the cheque, the customer will have to bear the loss (*London Joint Stock Bank* v. *Macmillan*).

In handling customers' cheques the bankers are protected by the Bills of Exchange Act 1882, as amended by the Cheques Act 1957. For this purpose we have to distinguish between the *paying banker* (the banker on whom a cheque has been drawn) and the *collecting banker* (who collects a cheque for a customer). The Cheques Act provides that a paying banker is deemed to have paid a cheque in due course even though it was not endorsed or was not properly endorsed, provided that he has observed normal banking practice in paying the cheque. This means that now when a cheque is payable to a third party, and is being collected for the credit of that party's bank account, there is no need to consider the endorsements on the cheque. In fact, even if the cheque is an order cheque, endorsements are not necessary. If, however, the holder wishes to collect the amount of the cheque over the bank's counter banking practice still insists on an endorsement. As far as the collecting banker is concerned, he requires particularly the protection of the Acts, since, if that protection did not exist, he would be liable for the tort of conversion (see page 194) to the true owner of the cheque if he were to collect a cheque for a person who was not the rightful owner. The Cheques Act provides now that if a banker collects a cheque for a customer (a person having an account with him), and the banker acted in good faith and without negligence, he will be in the same position as if he had collected the cheque for its rightful owner. The banker would, of course, be negligent if he disregarded a crossing on the cheque, particularly a special crossing or a crossing 'account payee.' He would also be negligent if he had failed to make inquiries about a new customer. The banker is supposed to know where a customer works or what business he operates so that he could exercise caution in collecting cheques for the customer where the text of the cheque (*e.g.*, the name of a payee) when related to the customer's position would induce a reasonable person to make inquiries before crediting the amount of the cheque to the customer's account.

Another important provision of the Cheques Act 1957 which may be mentioned here is that an unendorsed cheque which appears to have been paid by the banker on whom it is drawn is *prima facie* evidence of receipt by the payee of the sum for which the cheque is made out.

Promissory notes have been defined already. They differ from bills of exchange in that they contain two parties only, the maker (who corresponds to the acceptor of a bill) and the payee. The rules about acceptance will, of course, not apply to them, as the maker has signed the note at the outset.

An 'I.O.U.' is not a promissory note, as it does not indicate any time for the repayment of the debt nor does it give the creditor a right to transfer the document. It is, therefore, mere evidence of the existence of a debt. It should similarly be noted that postal orders and money orders are not negotiable instruments, because they have not been accepted as such either by statute or by commercial custom.

CHAPTER SEVEN

The Law of Securities

What are Securities?

Whenever a debt is incurred the creditor has to consider how to ensure the eventual payment of the debt. He may be satisfied with the debtor's personal promise to pay; but often, particularly when a large sum of money is involved, the creditor wishes to get a more tangible assurance of repayment. What he wants the debtor to do is to set aside some specified item of property as security for the debt so that if the debt is not repaid the creditor will nevertheless be satisfied out of the sale of the property. According to the way in which the debt is secured, we distinguish between securities created by:

1. The personal guarantee of a person other than the debtor.
2. A mortgage of an interest in land.
3. A mortgage or pledge of personal chattels.

Personal Guarantees

A person may agree to act as guarantor for the debt of another or for the performance by another of certain contractual duties. The guarantor enters into a contract with the creditor so that the general rules concerning contracts (discussed already in Chapter Four) will apply. You may recall that the guarantee, in order to be enforceable against the guarantor, must be evidenced by a note in writing, signed by the guarantor, and containing the detailed terms on which the guarantee has been given.

Mortgages of Land

A mortgage of an interest in land may be either a legal mortgage or an equitable mortgage. The creation of *legal mortgages* is now governed by the Law of Property Act 1925. The interest in land on which the mortgage is created may be either a freehold or a leasehold interest in land; it could also be a rent-charge.

There are two ways in which a legal mortgage on a freehold interest may be created—namely:

1. The mortgagor may grant the mortgagee a demise for a term of years absolute, subject to a provision that the term should cease if

the mortgagor (*i.e.*, the debtor) repays the debt secured by the mortgage within an agreed time. This time is in practice as short as six months. At common law the mortgagor was not able to pay off the mortgage after this period had expired, but we shall see that he has now an equitable right of doing so.

2. The mortgage may also be created by means of a charge by deed expressed to be by way of legal mortgage. Such a charge is treated as equivalent to a lease for three thousand years.

The owner of a freehold estate who has mortgaged his land as security for a debt may mortgage the land more than once, thus securing a number of debts on the same land. A second or further mortgage is granted in the same way as a first mortgage, except that the lease of the second mortgage is one day longer than that for the immediately preceding mortgage.

The owner of a leasehold interest in land may also choose one of two methods in creating a legal mortgage.

1. He may grant a sub-lease to the mortgagee for a term of years, subject to the usual provision that the sub-lease will cease on repayment of the principal sum secured, the sub-lease being at least one day shorter (in practice it will be ten days shorter) than the lease which is vested in the mortgagor.

2. Alternatively, the mortgage may again take the form of a charge by deed expressed to be by way of legal mortgage.

The method of creating a mortgage by deed expressed to be by way of legal mortgage has the advantage that the same form may be used for freeholds and leaseholds. A debtor owning both types of property may therefore mortgage them both by means of the same document. Where this method is used for mortgaging a leasehold interest it will also not be necessary to obtain the lessor's consent to a sub-lease as it would be if the other method had been adopted. The main disadvantages of this method are that the deed does not tell the mortgagee fully what his legal rights are and that it does not contain the provision for a cesser of the mortgage on redemption of the debt.

Equitable Mortgages

There are two types of equitable mortgages:

1. The mortgagor may have only an equitable interest in some property—*e.g.*, a life interest. He may mortgage this equitable interest by assigning it to the mortgagee with a proviso for reconveyance to him when he has repaid the debt which has been secured by this mortgage.

2. There also exist different types of informal mortgages which are enforced in equity only. An agreement in writing to create a mortgage which has not yet been acted upon will be treated by

equity as a complete mortgage, on the principle that "Equity looks upon that as done which ought to be done." The same applies also to an imperfect legal mortgage which would not be enforced at law but will be valid in equity. A good example of such an imperfect mortgage is the deposit of the title-deeds of some property by its owner with intention to create a mortgage.

Rights of the Mortgagee

The mortgagee on a legal mortgage has the following rights:

1. He may sue the debtor (mortgagor) on his personal covenant to repay the principal sum of the debt with interest without taking any steps to enforce the mortgage.

2. The mortgagee as the legal tenant of the land which has been leased to him may take possession at once when the legal time for repayment has passed. If the property mortgaged is occupied by another tenant he may instruct this tenant to pay the rent to him instead of to the mortgagor. In practice it is rare for a mortgagee to take this step, since he would be responsible to account to the mortgagor not only for such rents and other forms of income from the property which he had actually received but also for rents, etc., which he could have received with better management on his part.

3. The mortgagee may ask the Chancery Division of the High Court for a *foreclosure order nisi*. This is an order by which the mortgagor is threatened with the total loss of his redemption rights if he fails to pay the principal sum outstanding with interest within a time stated in the order, generally six months. If no payment has been made within this period the mortgagee could ask for the order to be made absolute, and this would totally deprive the mortgagor of his rights. In exceptional cases, however, the court could even then order a reopening of the foreclosure at a later date. Foreclosure is also a rare remedy for the mortgagee, since the court is not too willing to grant the order, as the property foreclosed on may be worth more than the sum or sums outstanding. The court at its discretion could order a sale of the property instead of granting the order.

4. The most frequently exercised right of the mortgagee is that of sale, provided the mortgage gives him this right. The mortgagee has a power to sell the property by public auction as soon as the legal date for redemption has passed, but he may exercise this power only if he has given the mortgagor at least three months' notice and he has failed to pay the debt or unless interest has been in arrears for at least two months or unless the mortgagor has been guilty of a breach of some essential condition of the mortgage. Out of the proceeds of the sale the mortgagee will recover the expenses of the sale,

the principal sum, and interest owing to him; and the surplus, if any, will have to be handed to the mortgagor.

5. In the same circumstances in which the mortgagee could arrange for a sale of the land he could also as an alternative appoint a receiver to take charge of the property. This would be the most likely remedy where the mortgaged property is of the investment property type—*e.g.*, a block of flats.

An equitable mortgagee has the same rights as a legal mortgagee, except that he has no right (unless specifically reserved to him) to take possession and that he may sell the property or appoint a receiver only where the mortgage has been created by deed or where the sale or the appointment of the receiver are ordered by the court.

Rights of the Mortgagor

The chief right of the mortgagor is his right to redeem the mortgage by discharging his debt. This right of redemption may be exercised on the contractual date for payment. Once this day has passed there exists no longer a legal right to discharge the mortgage, but there still exists an equitable right of doing so. Indeed, the mortgagor's interest in the mortgaged property after the contractual date for repayment has passed is referred to as his *equity of redemption.*

The reason why equity acknowledges a right of redemption even when the contractual date for it has passed is that in equity "once a mortgage always a mortgage." Property which has been transferred by way of security should not be treated as property which has been transferred beneficially. This is the implication of the well-known maxim of equity: "Equity looks to the intent not to the form." In equity, redemption of a mortgage is thus possible at any time as long as the property has not been foreclosed. The mortgagor who wishes to redeem the mortgage is expected, however, to give six months' notice of his intention of doing so or pay six months' interest in lieu. The reason for this is that money advanced on the security of a mortgage is an investment for the mortgagee, and it would not be fair to expect him to find a new investment for his capital without notice.

Equity is also the source of the rule that there must be no clog on the mortgagor's right of redemption. This means that any agreement between the parties to postpone redemption for what the court may find to be an unreasonable time would be void. What is an unreasonable time would, of course, depend on the circumstances of the case. Furthermore, the mortgage is intended to give the mortgagee security for the repayment of the debt; it should not give him any other advantages. Any other advantages which are attached to the mortgage will be void if they have been obtained by pressure—*e.g.*, a promise by the mortgagor to deal in future only with the mortgagee.

Registration of Land Charges

Where a person buys land it is of considerable importance to him to discover what charges on that land exist in favour of third parties. The reason is that if he should decide to buy the land he will acquire it subject to all legal charges and such equitable charges, of which he should have notice, and that would, of course, substantially reduce the value of the land to him. Many of the charges can be discovered by examining the land itself—*e.g.*, the existence of leases or of certain servitudes—but there are other charges which no examination of the land itself could trace. It is for this reason, and in order to simplify the investigations to be made prior to the purchase of land, that the Land Charges Act 1925 has introduced the principle of registration of land charges. Registration of these charges will give adequate warning to the buyer of the land. It also protects the holders of equitable charges against purchasers of the land who have no knowledge of these charges. The most important charges which have to be registered are:

1. *Puisne mortgages—i.e.*, legal mortgages where the mortgagee has not got possession of the title-deeds. This may happen where the mortgage is a second or further one and the deeds have been deposited with the first mortgagee.
2. *Limited owners' charges—i.e.*, charges over the land in favour of a tenant for life who pays death-duties out of his own property in respect of settled land.
3. *General equitable charges*, including equitable mortgages.
4. *Estate contracts—i.e.*, contracts entered into for the purpose of conveying or creating a legal interest in land.
5. *Restrictive covenants.*
6. *Equitable easements—i.e.*, easements created for an interest other than a fee simple or a term of years absolute.

Registration takes place at the Central Land Registry in London irrespective of where in England or Wales the land may be situated. Registration of a charge constitutes notice of its existence to the whole world, and any purchaser of land who fails to inspect the registry neglects doing so at his own risk.

Failure to register any of the first three mentioned registrable charges will mean that they will be absolutely void against any purchaser of the land or of any interest in the land. He may disregard them, and they cannot be enforced against him. Failure to register any of the other charges will have the effect that they will be void as against a purchaser of the *legal* interest in land for money or money's worth.

Apart from the Central Land Registry in London there also exist local registries kept by local authorities for local land charges, particularly those that arise in connection with charges for road construction, etc. If such charges are not locally registered they will be void as against any purchaser of the legal estate in land for money or money's worth.

Mortgage of Chattels

Personal chattels, such as furniture and other personal belongings, may also be mortgaged. What happens in this case is that the mortgagor retains possession of the chattels, but their ownership is transferred to the mortgagee on the understanding that he will reconvey the chattels to the mortgagor on the repayment of the debt. Arrangements of this type have always been looked upon by law with a certain amount of doubt, as they easily lend themselves to attempts to defeat creditors. Creditors frequently grant credit to people who appear to be living in style. They may not know that the furnishings of the house of the debtor have been already mortgaged as security for a debt. It was in order to avoid these dangers that the Bills of Sale Acts 1878–91 were passed.

The Acts provide that where the ownership of chattels is transferred, but the possession of the chattels is retained by the transferor, a document, known as a *bill of sale*, has to be drawn up in order to give effect to the transaction. There are two kinds of bills of sale—namely, absolute bills of sale and conditional bills of sale. Absolute bills of sale have to be made out where the transfer of the chattels is intended to represent a complete transfer of the ownership in them by way of sale, gift, or settlement. Conditional bills of sale are needed where goods are transferred as security for a debt subject to a proviso for redemption on repayment of the money secured. It is, therefore, conditional bills of sale which give effect to a mortgage of chattels.

The chattels, the transfer of which is given effect to by means of a bill of sale, must be personal chattels—*i.e.*, goods, furniture, and other articles which are capable of complete transfer by delivery. They include also fixtures and growing crops, provided that they have been transferred separately from the land to which they are attached.

The bill of sale must be a document on which the title of the transferee depends—*i.e.*, the right of the transferee to the ownership of the chattels must depend on this document.

Every bill of sale must be duly attested and registered. Absolute bills of sale must be attested by a solicitor, who is required by the Act to state on the bill that he has explained the legal effects of it to the grantor of the bill before attestation. A conditional bill of sale may be attested by any credible witness. The registration of bills of sale takes place with the Registrar at the Central Office of the Supreme Court, and it must be effected within seven days from the execution of the bill. A conditional bill of sale must be re-registered every five years if the mortgage is still in existence.

The effect of non-registration in the case of a conditional bill of sale will be that the bill will be totally void, and the mortgage will thus not be effective. An absolute bill of sale which has not been registered in accordance with the Act will be void against the grantor's trustee in bankruptcy or against a judgment creditor. As far as these parties are concerned, the chattels would thus still be deemed to be the property of the grantor, and they would be available for the satisfaction of his creditors.

Mortgage of a Ship

The owner of a ship may offer the ship as security for a debt owed by him. Mortgaging a ship resembles a mortgage of land rather than that of other chattels, in as much as the owner of the ship who has mortgaged her retains his ownership and possession of the ship as long as he does not default on his debt. The Merchant Shipping Act 1906 lays down that the mortgage must be effected in writing. In order to prevent the mortgagor from mortgaging the ship a second time, the mortgagee should ensure that the mortgage is registered in the ship's register kept at the port of registry. If the mortgage has been registered it will have priority as from the date of registration against any further mortgages. Failure to register the mortgage would not make it void, but the first mortgagee would lose his precedence as against further mortgagees who take the precaution of registering their mortgage. Before lending money to a shipowner on the security of a mortgage the lender should carefully examine the register. Where it is not possible for the mortgagee to examine the register he may ask the mortgagor to produce a certificate of mortgage issued by the registrar, on which the ship is described and any incumbrances are noted. Particulars of the mortgage are then noted on the certificate and are verified by a British consular official. A notice in the register that a certificate of mortgage has been issued operates as a warning to all future lenders, who are expected to await the ultimate registration of the mortgage that may be noted on the certificate. If the mortgagor defaults on his obligations to the mortgagee the latter may either enter into possession of the ship or he may sell her.

Mortgages of Choses in Action

The owner of a chose in action may also transfer these by way of security for a debt. The most important form of chose in action for the purpose of mortgages is a company share. A legal mortgage of company shares would require their transfer by the registered holder to the mortgagee, who would be registered by the company as the owner of the shares. In order to distinguish this transfer from a transfer of the beneficial ownership of the shares a written agreement would have to be signed by the mortgagee, agreeing to retransfer the shares when the secured debt has been repaid.

More frequent than a legal mortgage of shares is an equitable mortgage. This usually takes the form of a deposit of the share certificate with the mortgagee, together with the handing over to him of one or more blank transfer forms signed by the registered holder of the shares. This is coupled with an agreement between the parties that if the mortgagor should fail to discharge his debt the mortgagee will have authority to sell the shares by completing the transfer form. The advantage of the equitable mortgage as compared with the legal mortgage is that there is no immediate need for any transfer of the shares, and this saves a considerable amount of expense.

Pledges

Another way of offering chattels as security for a debt is by means of a pledge. Here the pledgor parts with possession of the chattels, but retains their ownership. A person who borrows money from a pawnbroker on the security of some chattel is pledging that chattel to the pawnbroker. The pledgor retains the right to redeem the pledge by repaying his debt. In the agreement between pledgor and pledgee a time is usually fixed for the repayment of the debt, and if the debt has not been discharged by that time the pledgee will be entitled to sell the goods. Where no time for repayment has been fixed, the pledgee may demand repayment on giving reasonable notice to the pledgor. The pledgor's interest in the pledged goods is saleable and could also be sub-pledged. Thus, for instance, a man who has pawned his watch with a pawnbroker may sell or pledge the right to redeem the watch on paying the sum borrowed together with interest to the pawnbroker.

Bailment

A pledge is a special case of a legal relationship known as bailment, and, while not all forms of bailment relate to securities for debts, this appears to be as good a place as any to discuss the problems of bailment.

Bailment consists in a delivery of goods on the condition, which may be expressed or implied, that the goods should be restored by the bailee to the bailor as soon as the purpose for which they have been bailed has been achieved.

Bailment may, but need not, be based on contract. The bailee may be accepting the custody of the goods for reward or without reward. In all circumstances, however, the bailee must have agreed to accepting responsiblity for the goods. Where goods have been left with a person without his consent, such as where goods are sent on approval to a person who has not asked for them, the recipient will in no way be responsible for their safety as long as he does not directly interfere with them.

A voluntary bailee must take care of the goods which have been entrusted to him. Where the bailee receives no reward for acting in that capacity he must take such care of the goods as he would take of his own property. Where, however, the bailee receives some form of payment, he would be responsible even for slight negligence which has led to the goods being damaged or lost.

Certain classes of bailee are subject to special obligations—for instance, common carriers, and hotel proprietors, who are, in general, absolutely responsible for the safety of the goods which have been entrusted to them.

Formerly at common law a bailee who had accepted goods from a bailor was unable to sell them if he had not been paid for his services or if the bailor failed to collect the goods from him. He has now, however, been given certain limited rights of sale under the Disposal of Uncollected Goods Act 1952. This Act applies only to goods which have been entrusted to a bailee for the purpose of repair or treatment where the bailee has not been paid and the bailor has not given any instructions as to the disposal of the goods. The bailee must have given the bailor notice that the goods are ready for delivery, and the bailor must have failed within twelve months from the giving of this notice to collect and pay for the goods. The bailee must then give a further notice to the bailor of his intention to sell the goods at least a fortnight before the date of the sale. The latter notice must be sent by registered letter. After the sale the bailee must prepare an account, and if the proceeds of the sale exceed the amount which the bailor owes to the bailee the latter will have to hand over the balance to the bailor.

Lien

Lien is a form of security for a debt which comes into existence by the operation of the law. There are three types of lien—namely:

1. Possessory lien.
2. Maritime lien.
3. Equitable lien.

A *possessory lien* is the right of a person who is in possession of goods belonging to another to retain the goods until their owner has done something for the possessor which he is legally bound to do.

A possessory lien may be general or particular. It is particular where the possessor of goods retains them until his charges in respect of work done to the goods have been paid. A shoe-repairer would have such a right in respect of shoes which he has repaired, and a common carrier also may detain goods until the freight charges due on them have been paid. A particular lien may also come into existence by agreement—*e.g.*, a joint-stock company may be given by its articles (which represent a contract between the company and its shareholders) a lien on the shares for any payments (calls) due on them.

A general lien arises either by agreement or by trade custom. Here the person who has a claim may retain any goods of the person against whom the claim exists until it has been satisfied. Solicitors have such a lien for outstanding fees on all monies belonging to their clients which come into their possession.

A *maritime lien* is a right of persons who have rendered certain services to a ship to a charge on the ship herself and her equipment for the monies owing to them. This means that where these claims (*e.g.*, for seamen's wages or salvage) have not been satisfied the ship may be 'arrested' and detained until the amounts due have been paid. A maritime lien differs from a possessory lien in that it is independent of possession.

An *equitable lien* is also independent of possession. It arises where, by operation of law, certain property is charged with the settlement of a debt, and this debt has to be satisfied by whoever happens to be or become the owner of that property. A vendor of land who has not yet been paid has a lien on the land for the purchase price.

CHAPTER EIGHT

The Law of Succession

Succession on Death

We have seen in an earlier chapter that a person retains the right of owning property only while he is alive. Law has to make provision, therefore, for the distribution of the property of a deceased person. When a person dies others will succeed to his property. Where he has left a will in which he has expressed his directions as to the distribution of his property, the rules concerning *testate succession* will apply, while where a person dies without leaving a valid will or where a person has not by his will disposed of all his property, the rules concerning *intestate succession* will have to be considered.

Personal Representatives

When a person has died his property does not pass on his death directly to those who will ultimately share it. This is so whether or not the deceased person has left a will. The whole of the deceased person's assets will devolve in the first place on his personal representatives. The term 'personal representatives' dates from the time when only the personal property of the deceased was distributed in this fashion; but to-day the personal representatives deal with both personal and real property. Their main task is to settle the deceased's debts out of his estate and to distribute the balance according to the instructions contained in the will, where there is one—otherwise in accordance with the rules of law applying to intestacies. The deceased person's estate embraces all the property of which he dies possessed, including also rights of action which he could have exercised if he had not died. Certain personal rights of action, such as the right to sue for defamation of character, will die, however, with the person who could have brought the action (Law Reform (Miscellaneous Provisions) Act 1934).

Personal representatives are called *executors* where they have been named by the deceased in the will. Where the deceased has died intestate or where the will does not name any personal representatives at all or where the named persons are unwilling or unable to act as such, the court will appoint *administrators* of the deceased's estate.

No more than four executors may act on behalf of an estate, and it is customary to appoint at least two, except where a trust corporation has been appointed to act as executor. The executors must, in the first place, obtain probate of the will. Probate is a document issued under the seal of a court of probate, and it represents the official evidence of the executors' authority to represent the estate. No one can compel a person who has been named executor to submit the will for probate (*i.e.*, prove the will), but if a person interferes in any way with the estate, so as to indicate that he has assumed the position of an executor, he will be responsible as if he had become an executor. Obtaining the probate of a will is in general a mere formality, and probate is granted then 'in common form.' Where, however, the granting of probate is opposed by some one who questions the authenticity of the will or the capacity of the testator to make a will, the dispute will be heard by a judge of the Chancery Division of the High Court. If he decides to grant probate it is said to have been granted 'in solemn form.'

Where there are no executors, the court will grant letters of administration to such persons as the court considers to be most suitable for the task, generally those who have the main beneficial interest in the estate. Where there is a will, but letters of administration have to be granted because no executor has been named, the grant of administration is said to be '*cum testamento annexo*,' as a copy of the will is attached to the letters of administration for the instruction of the administrators.

Both the grant of probate and that of letters of administration may be revoked by the court if it is subsequently discovered that they should never have been made. Provided that the executors or administrators have acted in good faith, they will not have to make good to the estate any deficiency that might have resulted through their distributing part of the estate in accordance with the instructions on which they acted. Those who had benefited from this distribution will have to refund to the estate anything which they have received out of it.

Wills

The legal systems of different countries contain different rules as to the form in which wills have to be made and as to the capacity of persons to make wills. It is therefore important to determine which law should be applied in deciding whether a will has been validly executed. The Wills Act 1963 was passed in order to give effect to the main recommendations of an international convention concluded in 1961. A will is treated as properly executed if its execution conformed to the law in force either (*a*) in the country where the will was made, or (*b*) in the country where the testator was domiciled at the time of the execution of the will or at the time of his death, or (*c*) in the country of which the testator was a national.

A will disposing of immovable property will be properly executed if made either under one of the laws stated above or in a form acceptable to the law of the country where the property is situated.

The 1963 Act came into force on January 1, 1964, and applies therefore only to wills of people who died after this date. Where, however, a person dying after this date has left a will made before 1964, which was valid under the earlier law, the validity of this will is not affected by the new legislation.

The Wills Act 1837, forms the basis of our modern law of wills. Under it, wills may be either formal or informal. A formal will must be:

1. In writing; and
2. Properly executed. The proper execution of the will means that the following requirements have been complied with:

(*a*) The will has been signed at the foot or end thereof by the testator or by some other person in the testator's presence and by his direction. Where the testator cannot write he may attach his personal mark instead of a signature. No part of the will following the testator's signature would be valid; but, according to the Wills Act Amendment Act 1852, the testator's signature need not be literally under the will, provided that it is at the end of it.

(*b*) The testator must sign the will or he must acknowledge his signature if he has signed the will already—in the presence of two or more witnesses, present at the same time. Any person, even a minor, could act as witness, provided that he is mentally capable of understanding what is expected of him. The witness need not know the contents of the will nor even that he is witnessing a signature on a will. It is advisable, however, to give the witness the latter information, as it will make it easier for him subsequently to recall the occasion.

(*c*) The witnesses must attest and subscribe the will in the presence of the testator. It is desirable but not necessary that the witnesses should sign the will in each other's presence. No special form of attestation is required by law, but in practice a specific attestation clause is used, since if it had been omitted the granting of probate might be delayed while the court made inquiries whether the formalities in connection with the execution of the will had been complied with.

If the testator subsequently wishes to make an alteration in the will without actually making a fresh will, he may do so either on the original will itself or on a separate instrument, known as a codicil.

In either case, however, the alteration will have to be signed and attested in exactly the same form as has been described above for the execution of wills. If the testator were merely to cross out something in the will and write the alteration above it or in the margin the alteration would not be valid, and the original will would still stand. If he completely obliterates the previous wording and writes in the new wording without properly executing it the old passage will be treated as revoked without the new passage taking its place.

Informal Wills

Informal wills were permitted by the Wills Act 1837, and their scope has been extended by the Wills (Soldiers and Sailors) Act 1918. Informal wills may be made by soldiers, sailors and airmen who are "on actual military service" and by seamen who are "at sea." Actual military service means that the serviceman either is engaged in hostilities or is about to proceed somewhere where he will be engaged in this way. Thus, a soldier stationed in this country in peacetime is not on "actual military service," but he will be so if he is on embarkation leave for some foreign station where he may be engaged in hostilities. The same applies also to seamen, which includes persons serving in the Merchant Navy and on other ships. They may make informal wills not only when actually out at sea, but also when they are about to leave for a voyage.

Informal wills may also be made by minors if they are on actual military service. No formalities of any sort are needed. The will may be in writing without the need for witnesses or it may take the form of an oral wish as to the disposal of property, provided always that the person making it wanted it to be a binding will. Where an informal will is made in the appropriate circumstances, the will remains valid even when the testator ceases to serve in the Forces or to be a seaman.

Capacity

Any person of full age who is of sound mind may make a will. Minors may make wills only where they are "on actual military service" or are seamen "at sea." Where the testator was sane at the time of making the will but subsequently became insane, the will remains valid.

A will may be made for the benefit of a person or of a charity. A will could not be made for the benefit of some non-charitable purpose, as there would be no one to enforce it; but the intention of the testator can be achieved by making a gift to a person on condition that he does what the testator wants done, with the proviso that if he should fail to do so the legacy will go to some other party. A testator who wants his dog to be provided for cannot leave money to the dog, but he could leave an annuity to a friend on condition that he looked after the dog, with the proviso that if he should fail to do so the annual payment would go, say, to a home for dogs.

Persons guilty of felonies may benefit under a will, except that a person found guilty of murder or manslaughter may not benefit under the will or intestacy of his victim unless he was insane when he killed the deceased.

A person who has acted as witness to the will of the deceased or the husband or wife of such a witness may not benefit under the will witnessed by him, except where the will was duly executed without his attestation.[1] The fact that a beneficiary under the will subsequently marries a witness to the will does not invalidate the bequest. The executor of the deceased may benefit under his will; but, unless the context of the will clearly provides otherwise, a legacy to an executor will be construed by the court as being conditional on the executor accepting office.

The Legal Nature of Wills

The following points are important in understanding the true nature of a will:

1. A will is said to be *ambulatory*. This means that the will has no effect until the testator has died. No benefits are conferred on anyone until this event has taken place, and it is, therefore, extremely risky to lend money to a person on his expectations under a will.

2. A will is always revocable. The testator may revoke the will at any time, and a clause in a will to the effect that it would not be revoked under any circumstances would be void.

3. The main purpose of a will is the distribution of the testator's estate; but, in addition to that, the will may provide for the appointment of executors and may also name guardians for the testator's children. Other wishes—*e.g.*, concerning the form of burial—are often added, but these are not legally binding on the executors.

4. The will need not embody all the testator's instructions. The testator may refer in the will to some other existing document in which, for instance, the legacies are detailed. Reference to a document which at the time of the making of the will was not yet in existence would not be effective.

5. The will must have been made *animo testandi*. This means that the testator had the intention of disposing of his property. Where the testator because of insanity or senility was not capable of forming any such intention, there will be no valid will.

[1] Wills Act 1968.

Legacies and Devises

A devise is a disposal of freehold land contained in a will. The disposal of any other form of property is called a legacy. Devises and legacies are said to be *specific*, where the testator has disposed of a specific object (*e.g.*, his house or his watch) to a named beneficiary. Where the gift is one which does not refer to a specific object, we call it a *general legacy*—*e.g.*, a legacy of £1000. The testator may instruct the executors to give a legacy out of a particular fund (*e.g.*, "one thousand of my ordinary shares in X Co. Ltd") and such a legacy is called a *demonstrative legacy*. It is customary in a will to give various specific and general legacies or devises and to finish up by disposing of what is left of the estate after these have been satisfied. This is known as a *residuary legacy*, and its inclusion in the will is important, because if the testator has failed to allocate the residue of his estate and there is some property left over, he would be treated as having died intestate in respect of the residue.

A legacy or devise to a person 'lapses' if he dies before the testator. Lapsed legacies or devises will become part of the residue of the estate. The will may, of course, show the intention that lapsed legacies or devises should be otherwise disposed of. There are two cases, however, where the gift would not lapse, although the legatee or devisee has predeceased the testator:

1. Where the testator has created an entailed interest in favour of the devisee (legatee), provided that descendants of the devisee (legatee) are living at the time of the testator's death.

2. Where the testator has made a gift to one of his issue (*i.e.*, one of his descendants). In that case the Wills Act 1837 raises the fiction that the child (grandchild, etc.) who had died before the testator had in fact died immediately after the testator. The purpose of this fiction is to allow the child's share in the testator's estate to be distributed in accordance with the child's will if he has left one. It should be noted, however, that this fiction does not apply to so-called 'class gifts'—*e.g.*, where the testator left the residue of his estate "to my children in equal shares." In that case, only the children alive at the time of the testator's death will share.

If a specific thing which has been disposed of by the testator in his will is no longer in existence or does no longer belong to the testator at the time of his death the gift is said to be *adeemed* and the legatee will get nothing. If the testator's estate at the time of his death is insufficient to satisfy all the legacies and devises contained in the will the following procedure will be adopted. Specific legacies and devises will be unaffected, provided that the specific objects are still part of the estate. General legacies will be *abated*—*i.e.*, reduced proportionately all round—unless the will directs that certain gifts should be satisfied before others are paid. There will, of course, be no residue for the residuary legatees to share.

Revocation of Wills

Wills may be revoked in the following ways:

1. By a subsequent will or codicil. It is customary for every will made by a person, even where it is the first one which he has ever made, to revoke expressly all previous wills. If a will does not contain such an express revocation clause it would still revoke all previous wills, but only to the extent to which they are inconsistent with the later will. Thus, if a testator in his first will leaves his house Seahaven to A and in a later will leaves the same house to B, B will get the house. But where the testator in his first will has left £1000 to A and in a subsequent will, which does not contain a revocation clause he leaves £1000 to B, both A and B will have legacies of £1000.

2. A will is revoked by physical destruction. The destruction must be intentional and must be the work of the testator himself or of some other person acting on his instructions and in his presence. The destruction may take the form of burning, tearing up, or any other form which clearly indicates that the testator wished to revoke the whole will. The destruction must, however, have been done *animo revocandi*—*i.e.*, with the intention of revoking the will. Where a will has been accidentally destroyed or where it cannot be found on the testator's death and there is no reason to believe that the testator has intentionally destroyed it, the court of probate at their discretion may grant probate even though the original of the will cannot be produced, provided that adequate evidence is submitted of the contents of the will—*e.g.*, by means of the copy kept by the solicitor who has drafted the will.

3. A will is also revoked by the subsequent marriage of the testator, except where the will states that it has been made by him in anticipation of his marriage.

A will which has been revoked in any of the above ways may be revived by a codicil which is properly executed and which states that the earlier will should stand. It is not possible to revive a will which has been revoked by a later will merely by destroying the later will. If this is done the testator would have left no will at all and he would die intestate. There exists one exception to this in the form of the *doctrine of dependent relative revocation.* Where a will has been revoked with the intention of making another one, and for some reason that other will has never been made (*e.g.*, because the testator died before executing it), the revoked will would still be treated as the will of the testator. This will be the case, however, only where the court is satisfied that the testator had not the intention of revoking the will absolutely, but merely revoked it as a first step towards making a new will, which then was never made.

Family Provision

Until 1938 a person had full freedom to dispose of his estate whether by will or under the general provisions of intestacy. He was not bound by law to make any provision for his family or other dependants and could leave all his property to some third party. In order to safeguard the interests of his family and dependants, the Inheritance (Family Provision) Act 1938 was passed. This Act, amended in 1952 and 1958, has now been replaced by the Inheritance (Provision for Family and Dependants) Act 1975 which has consolidated and amended all earlier legislation.

The dependants who may apply to the court for financial provision out of the deceased's estate are:

1. the wife or husband of the deceased;
2. a former wife or husband of the deceased who has not remarried;
3. a child of the deceased;
4. any other person who in the case of any marriage to which the deceased was a party, was treated by the deceased as a child of the family;
5. any other person who at the time of the death of the deceased was wholly or partly being maintained by him.

Any of the above persons may apply to the court for an order on the ground that the disposition of the deceased's estate by his or her will or on the basis of the law relating to intestacy or on a combination of both is such as to fail to make reasonable financial provision for the applicant. The meaning of 'reasonable financial provision' depends on the nature of the relationship between the applicant and the deceased (spouses being perhaps entitled to expect rather more than other applicants) and on the other circumstances of the case which include of course the size of the estate and the claims of other interested parties. The court in making its decision may take into account any statement, whether oral or written, as to the reasons for his actions made by the deceased.

The court, if satisfied that reasonable financial provision has not been made for the applicant, may order:

1. that periodical payments out of the estate should be made to the applicant, or
2. that the applicant be paid a fixed lump sum out of the estate, or
3. that specific items of property included in the estate should be transferred to the applicant, or

4. that specific items of property should be settled on the applicant, or

5. that certain property items (*e.g.*, a house) should be acquired for the benefit of the applicant and either transferred to him or settled on him.

In order to prevent any attempt by the deceased to defeat the aims of the Act by means of dispositions of his assets by him during his lifetime, the court may include among the assets available for meeting the claims of successful applicants any assets disposed of by the deceased in his lifetime (if such dispositions were made within six years prior to his death) provided that the applicant can satisfy the court that these dispositions have taken place with the aim of defeating a family provision claim. The donee of these assets must be a person who has received them without giving full valuable consideration for them. If this can be proved, he may be ordered to make financial payments or to transfer property to help to satisfy an order for family provision. The making of this order is not dependent on the donee still being the owner of the property in question.

Jurisdiction for hearing claims for orders of family provision rests with the county court where the value of the deceased's net estate at the time of his death did not exceed £5000 but the Lord Chancellor is empowered by the Act to raise by order at any time the above financial limit. The High Court (Family or Chancery Division) would be competent to make such order in respect of estates of a higher value.

Intestate Succession

The distribution of the estate of a person who dies intestate is governed by the provisions of the Administration of Estates Act 1925, as amended by the Intestates' Estates Act 1952, and the Family Provision Act 1966.[1] These rules apply not only where the deceased left no valid will at all, but also in respect of such portion of his estate as may not have been disposed of by his will where he left one.

The first person entitled to a share in the estate is the surviving spouse. He or she will receive in the first place all personal chattels absolutely. Personal chattels include such personal belongings as furniture, clothing, jewellery, private cars, etc., but not houses, money, or investments. In addition to that, the surviving spouse has also rights to the residuary estate, the extent of these rights depending on whether the deceased has or has not left issue.

1. Where issue has been left, the surviving spouse will be entitled

[1] The figures given under (1) and (2) below may be changed by Order of the Lord Chancellor.

to a net sum of £15,000, free of death-duties and costs, together with interest at 4 per cent from the date of death. One half of the remaining estate will also be held on trust for the surviving spouse for life.

2. Where no issue has been left, but there are other heirs falling into any of the classes described below, the surviving spouse is entitled to a net sum of £40,000 free of death-duties and with interest as above. He or she will also be entitled absolutely to one half of the remaining estate.

3. If no heirs have been left at all the personal representatives will hold the whole estate on trust absolutely for the surviving spouse.

It need perhaps hardly be added that the surviving spouse will become entitled to the above-mentioned lump sums only if the estate is large enough to yield them. If the estate is not large enough it will go entirely to the surviving spouse, as there will be no residue left.

The above rules apply also in cases of partial intestacy, but the surviving spouse would have to deduct from the £15,000 or £40,000 respectively such sums as he or she may have received already under the will.

Where the estate of the deceased contains a dwelling-house in which he and the surviving spouse have lived, the surviving spouse may require the personal representatives to appropriate that house to him or her in part satisfaction of any absolute interest in the estate of the deceased acquired under his intestacy.

Subject to the rights of the surviving spouse detailed above, the residue of the intestate's estate will be held by his personal representatives for his issue[1] on the 'statutory trusts.' This means that one half of the residuary estate will be available at once and the other half after the death of the surviving spouse. The 'statutory trusts' provide that the residuary estate should be distributed in the following way:

1. All children of the deceased living at the time of his death will share equally, provided that they have either reached the age of eighteen or are married. If any child is still unmarried and under eighteen he will not become absolutely entitled to his share until he reaches the age of eighteen or marries. The shares of children who have died before the intestate will accrue to their issue (but not to their widows), provided that the issue again are over eighteen or married.

2. The personal representatives have the power of using the income from the share accruing to a minor for his maintenance, and they also may make advances to him for the purpose of starting in business or in some other career. Such advances may be made out of capital.

[1] 'Issue' includes illegitimate children and their descendants (Family Law Reform Act 1969).

3. In assessing the share of a child, account must be taken of any advances made to him by the deceased in his lifetime. This means that such advances must be brought into 'hotchpot,' before the shares of the children are calculated. Assume that the deceased has left three children, a daughter, A, and two sons, B and C, and his estate at the time of his death is worth £10,000. His wife predeceased him. Each child will then receive one-third of the estate, provided, of course, that he or she is over eighteen or married. Now, assume further that the deceased some years before his death has given his daughter on her marriage a dowry of £3000 and has also given B £2000 to allow him to become a partner in a business. For the purpost of distributing the estate, these two sums will now be added to the £10,000 left at death, making a total of £15,000; and the share of each child will be £5000. As A has received already £3000, she will now receive only £2000; B, who has received already £2000, will get a further £3000, and C, who has so far received nothing, will get the full £5000.

4. Where a minor is contingently (*i.e.*, contingently on reaching the age of eighteen or getting married) interested in some specific personal chattels—*e.g.*, the deceased's library of books—the personal representatives may allow the minor reasonable use and enjoyment of all or some of these chattels.

Adopted, legitimated and illegitimate children will share in the intestacy of their parents in the same way as natural-born children.[1]

Where the deceased left no issue, the following classes of persons will share one half of the residuary estate (the surviving spouse having taken the other half absolutely) or the whole residuary estate if there is no surviving spouse:

1. The deceased's parents in equal shares or the surviving parent on his own.

2. The deceased's brothers and sisters on the statutory trusts as explained above. This will mean that they would share equally and that the issue of any one of them who has predeceased the intestate would share the portion going to their father or mother (or possibly grandfather or grandmother).

3. The deceased's grandparents.

4. The deceased's uncles and aunts on the statutory trusts.

Persons in any one of these classes will share in the estate only if there is no one in the preceding class who is entitled to share. If a person dies without leaving a spouse or issue or any of the abovementioned relatives, his estate will go to the Crown as *bona vacantia* —*i.e.*, goods without an owner.

[1] An adopted child loses his succession rights as a member of his natural family. (Children Act 1975.)

Gifts inter Vivos

So far we have been discussing the disposition of a person's estate in the event of his death. It is important to distinguish dispositions made by will from dispositions of property made during lifetime and intended to be effective during lifetime. Such dispositions we call gifts *inter vivos* (among the living).

A gift may be defined as a transfer of property where the transferor receives no valuable consideration from the transferee. Gifts may be made either by deed or by a transfer of the property by the donor (the giver) to the donee (the recipient of the gift) with intention that the ownership, as distinct from mere possession, should be transferred. In this latter case the gift is not complete until possession of the object has actually been transferred to the donee. The mere intention to give something is not enough, it must be coupled with an actual transfer of possession. Where a gift is made by deed the transfer of possession is not required, but the donee has the right to refuse the gift. It will be presumed, however, that he has accepted the gift unless he has clearly shown that he does not wish to accept it.

A gift is irrevocable, and English law does not follow Continental legal systems in allowing a donor to revoke a gift on the grounds of ingratitude by the donee. A gift may be conditional on the happening of some future event—*e.g.*, the giving of an engagement ring may be conditional on the girl being prepared to marry the giver of the ring.

Donatio Mortis Causa

A *donatio* (Latin for 'gift') *mortis causa* (in anticipation of death) lies half-way between an ordinary gift and a disposal of property by will. It takes place where a person gives and actually delivers a chattel to another person, on condition that the gift will not become absolute until the donor dies. A *donatio mortis causa* resembles a gift by will in the following ways:

1. The donor has the right to revoke the gift.
2. The gift lapses if the donee happens to die before the donor.
3. The gift is subject to death-duties and is also liable for the donor's debts.

A *donatio mortis causa* differs from a gift and is also liable for the gift *inter vivos* in that it takes effect, even though only conditionally, when the delivery occurs.

CHAPTER NINE

An Outline of the Law of Torts and Criminal Law

What are Torts?

English law divides legal wrongs into two classes—namely, criminal wrongs and civil wrongs (torts). Criminal wrongs are those for the commission of which the wrongdoer will be punished, while civil wrongs are dealt with by the payment of damages to the person whose interests have been harmed. It is largely a question of policy whether a wrong should be a civil or a criminal one, and whenever Parliament creates new wrongs it is for them to decide whether the situation is better met by punishing the wrongdoer or by making him pay damages to the victim of his wrongful act. Most of the crimes and torts known to English law are, however, of some antiquity, and it is too late now to argue whether they should have been dealt with differently. It is quite possible, of course, for a person to commit both a criminal and a civil wrong with the same act. In this case, with one or two exceptions, the wrongdoer will be punished and will in addition have to pay damages. An action in tort may be brought in such a case irrespective of whether a criminal prosecution has also been initiated.

The late Professor Sir Percy Winfield defined a tort as "the breach of a duty primarily fixed by the law, where the duty is one towards persons generally and its breach is redressible by an action for damages." Every tort consists, then, of the breach of a duty, and Sir Percy Winfield stressed the point that this duty had to be one laid down by the law and not one based on the agreement of the parties. This represents the main difference between torts and breaches of contract. Contracts also impose duties, but these duties are the result of the agreement of the parties, and they are owed by one party to the other and not to the general public. Winfield further stressed the fact that these breaches of duty will be visited by the award of damages so as to distinguish them from criminal wrongs. This does not mean, however, that the only remedy available to a person against whom a tort has been committed is to claim damages. There are many remedies which, at least with some torts, are available to him—*e.g.*, an injunction or self-help; but, while these remedies are available in some cases, every tort that has been committed entitles the victim to claim damages.

Specialized text-books on the law of torts discuss at great length the question whether there exists one single overriding duty imposed by law on all of us not to damage or injure our neighbours' interests without legal justification or whether there is only a series of specific duties which forbids us to commit certain specific types of wrongs. If the former interpretation is correct, then every harm done to a person would entitle him to damages, and it would be for the person who did the harm to prove that he had some legal justification. This attitude may be desirable in principle, but it does not appear to be the one taken at present by the courts; so that it seems preferable to regard the law of torts as a list of specific wrongs and remedies. Within the limited space available for this subject in the present book it would be impossible to discuss all torts, so that some selection had to be exercised. The torts chosen for discussion are basically those that affect people's property rather than their persons, though one at least of the latter type of torts—namely, defamation of character—has also been included.

The capacity of different classes of persons to commit torts has already been discussed in the chapter on legal persons. It should be noted, however, that a person may be liable for a tort not only where he himself committed it, but also where he has authorized another person to commit it on his behalf. We speak in this case of *vicarious liability*. The main instance of vicarious liability for the tort of another is the master's responsibility for torts committed by his servants. A master is responsible in this way not only where he expressly authorized a servant to do something which proved to be a tortious act, but also where he had not given express authority to the servant but the servant committed the wrong in the course of his employment. It is generally argued that where the servant does something wrong in the course of his employment the master will be responsible jointly with the servant, because he had given the servant an implied authority to do the act. This is not a satisfactory explanation, because the master will be responsible for a tort committed by a servant even if he expressly prohibited the servant to do the act which caused damage. Thus, in *Limpus* v. *London General Omnibus Co.* the employers had prohibited their servants from racing against the buses of other companies. One of the employees disregarded the order, and the plaintiff suffered injuries when the bus got out of control. The plaintiff was held entitled to claim damages from the employers. It is, of course, important to decide when a servant is acting in the course of his employment. Putting it as simply as possible, the servant is acting in the course of his employment when he does anything which he is employed to do, even though he does it in a wrongful manner. If, however, he does something which he is not employed to do at all he is not acting in the course of his employment. The employer will be responsible for the tortious acts of his servant even if these acts also constitute criminal offences or have been done by the servant for his own benefit. Thus, in *Lloyd* v. *Grace, Smith and Co.* the managing clerk in a solicitor's office gave wrongful advice to a client, as a result of which she transferred some property to him. The employers were held responsible in damages to the client, because, although the clerk had been guilty of a criminal offence, the thing which he had done—namely, to advise the client—was something which he was employed to do.

Before leaving the topic of vicarious liability, it should be noted that a master is responsible for the torts of his servants only and not for those of so-called independent contractors. A servant is a person who works for the master on such terms that the master is entitled to control not only what the servant should do but also the manner of his performance. An independent contractor, on the other hand, is a skilled man, generally working on his own account, who has been engaged to perform a certain task laid down by his employer who has, however, no control whatsoever over the manner of performing the task. A privately employed chauffeur is a servant; the driver of a taxi-cab is an independent contractor in relation to a passenger.

Malice

Malice, or evil intention, is not an essential ingredient of most torts, though there are some where proof of malice is required—*e.g.*, malicious prosecution. Otherwise, however, a person will be held responsible for his civil wrongs, even though he had no intention of doing harm to others. On the other hand, however, the presence of evil intention on its own will not make an act into a tort if there is no specific duty in existence which has been broken by the act.

The leading case on this point is *Mayor of Bradford* v. *Pickles.* The Bradford Corporation had been negotiating with P. for the sale of his land, which they required for their water-supply. As the Corporation were not prepared to pay the price which P. asked for the land, the deal fell through. As an act of revenge, P. had a shaft dug on his land; and, in consequence of that, water which was percolating under his land reached the Corporation's reservoir in a discoloured state and much of the water was lost on the way. It was held that, as there existed no duty which P. had broken, the mere fact that his act had been occasioned by an evil motive was not enough to make it into a tortious act.

General Defences

Certain defences are open to the defendant in every action for tort:

1. *Volenti non fit injuria.* This Latin maxim means that where a person has consented to the commission of a tort he may not subsequently sue for it. Thus, if I engage in a boxing contest I cannot sue my opponent for the tort of battery if he punches me on the nose. This defence may be employed only where the plaintiff not only had known of a danger but had in fact expressly or impliedly consented to accept the risk of injury. It is by no means easy to prove this. In *Bowater* v. *Rowley Regis Corporation* the plaintiff was a street-sweeper employed by the Corporation. He at first refused to take out a horse which had a reputation of being wild, but was eventually persuaded by his foreman to do so. He was thrown off his cart when the horse bolted, and sued the Corporation for damages. The defence of *volenti non fit injuria* did not help the defendants, as the court held that the plaintiff had never consented to accept the risk, though he knew of its existence. It appears, then, that the defence would only be appropriate in those cases where the plaintiff is specially rewarded—say, by danger-money—for the specific risks which he is running.

The defence will not apply, either, where the defendant has been responsible for a dangerous situation imperilling the safety of others, and the plaintiff, acting like any other reasonably courageous person, has done something in order to save a person or persons in danger and is injured. The leading case on this is *Haynes* v. *Harwood.* The defendants' servant left a horse-van unattended in a busy street. The horses ran away with the van and were approaching a group of children playing on the street when a police officer, realizing the danger, seized one of the horses and eventually managed to pull them up, being, however, seriously injured in doing so. He was awarded damages against the owner of the van on the grounds stated above. Similarly in *Baker* v. *T. E. Hopkins & Son Ltd*, where a doctor had gone down a well where two workmen had been overcome by fumes, and had died himself, the doctor's widow was awarded damages against the employers of the workmen, since it was the employers' negligence which had led to the dangerous situation that prompted the doctor's rescue attempt.

2. *Inevitable Accident.* The defendant may avoid liability for most torts if he can show that the plaintiff's injury or the damage to the plaintiff's interests has been caused by some circumstance which was totally outside the defendant's control. One example of an inevitable accident is a so-called *Act of God*, a most untheological expression, by which lawyers mean some natural phenomenon, such

as an earthquake or some unusually heavy rainfall, which could not have been anticipated or guarded against.

3. *Statutory Permission.* It is a defence in an action based on any tort to show that the tortious act has been sanctioned by an Act of Parliament or by some Ministerial order based on an Act of Parliament.

After these general comments on torts we come now to a discussion on some of the more important specific torts.

Negligence

The tort of negligence has been defined by Baron Alderson in *Blyth* v. *Birmingham Waterworks Co.* as follows: "Negligence is the omission to do something which a reasonable man, guided upon those considerations which ordinarily regulate the conduct of human affairs, would do, or doing something which a prudent or reasonable man would not do."

Three things have to be proved in order to establish that a person has been guilty of the tort of negligence:

1. A duty to take care must have existed towards the plaintiff.
2. The defendant must have broken his duty by not behaving in the way in which a reasonable person would have behaved in his position.
3. The plaintiff must have suffered some damage.

The first thing which has to be established is whether a duty to take care existed at all and whether the plaintiff was one of the persons towards whom it existed. The duty may be based either on the provision of some Act of Parliament (a statutory duty)—*e.g.*, the Factories Act—or it may be the general common law duty of every one to take care not to injure his 'neighbour.' The nearest approach to an explanation as to who should be looked upon as one's neighbour has been provided by Lord Atkin in his judgment in *Donoghue* v. *Stevenson*. He said there:

> You must take reasonable care to avoid acts or omissions which you can reasonably foresee would be likely to injure your neighbour. Who, then, in law is my neighbour? The answer seems to be—persons who are so closely and directly affected by my act that I ought reasonably to have them in contemplation as being so affected when I am directing my mind to the acts or omissions which are called in question.

In other words, I owe a duty of care to all those people whom I may foresee as being in danger of injury if I should not act as a reasonable person would have done. Thus, if the plaintiff does not belong to the class of persons which lawyers have dubbed 'neighbours'—*i.e.*, he is not one who would normally be considered to be in danger by the acts or omissions of the defendant—his action must fail. In *King* v. *Phillips*, a taxi-driver was backing his car into a narrow street and did not observe the presence of a little boy on a tricycle. He ran over the tricycle, but the little boy had jumped off in time and was running home when the boy's mother, hearing the commotion in the street, looked out of her window and saw the car just crushing the tricycle. Believing that her son had been injured, she suffered a serious shock and was ill for a long time. The taxi-driver, who had, of course, been negligent towards the child and who had to pay for the broken tricycle, was held not to have owed any duty to the child's mother, who was safely in her own house and therefore outside the range of persons likely to be in danger of injury because of the driver's negligent conduct.

Coming now to the second ingredient of the tort of negligence—namely, the standard of care to be observed by the persons owing the duty—we find that this standard depends on the person's profession or occupation. The standard of care to be expected of a doctor treating a patient is of course much higher than could be reasonably expected of a medical layman. Thus, the behaviour of a reasonable man becomes narrowed down to that of a reasonable doctor, solicitor, dentist, etc. Furthermore, the standard of care which can be expected is higher where the risk of injury following a negligent act or omission is a serious one. In *Paris* v. *Stepney B.C.* the House of Lords held that the duty of care which employers owed to an employee having only one good eye was greater than that which they owed to the majority of their employees, who had two good eyes. The one-eyed man was entitled to expect to be protected by goggles while engaged on work where it would not be negligent not to provide goggles for workers with two good eyes.

The standard of care is also higher where the persons likely to be affected by one's conduct include children. This is so because children may not realize the danger of certain situations as well as adults would. This is well illustrated by the Canadian case of *Yachuk* v. *Oliver Blais Co.* Two boys in their early teens persuaded a garage attendant to let them have a tin of petrol by spinning a tale about their mother's car having run out of petrol at some distance from the station. They poured the petrol over some timber and then put a match to it. The resulting explosion of the petrol vapour caused them serious injuries. The Judicial Committee of the Privy Council held that it had been negligent on the part of the garage attendant to entrust the children with such a dangerous commodity as petrol.

Until quite recently it was assumed that the damage which the defendant's negligent conduct had caused had to be physical damage, whether to persons or to property. It was believed that mere negligent misstatements leading to a financial loss by the person who acted believing in the statement did not create a cause of action. An excellent illustration of this doctrine was found in the Court of Appeal decision in *Candler* v. *Crane, Christmas & Co.* The plaintiff in this case wanted to invest money in a private company, but before making his final decision he desired to study the last balance-sheet of the company, which was at that time being prepared by the company's accountants. The accountants showed the plaintiff a draft balance-sheet which satisfied him as to the company's financial position, and he invested £2000 in the company. It turned out afterwards that the draft balance-sheet had been negligently drawn up, and consequently gave a misleading picture of the company's position. Within a short time the company went into liquidation and the plaintiff lost his investment. The Court of Appeal found that the accountants had been careless but were not guilty of fraud. The Court argued that Lord Atkin's definition of a 'neighbour' was never intended to apply to a person misled by an untrue statement, and decided therefore that the accountants did not owe a duty of care to the plaintiff in the absence of a contract between them.

This decision has now been overruled by the House of Lords in *Hedley Byrne & Co., Ltd* v. *Heller & Partners, Ltd.* The plaintiffs in this case were advertising agents who had placed substantial advertising orders for a client on terms by which they, the plaintiffs, accepted personal liability for the amounts involved. Before accepting this commitment the plaintiffs had inquired through their bankers from the defendants (who were the client's bankers) as to the client's credit standing. The defendants provided misleading information but safeguarded themselves by stating that the information was given "without responsibility." The House of Lords held that a negligent misrepresentation, even if given honestly, may give rise to an action for damages for a financial loss caused to a party acting on the representation, notwithstanding the fact that there existed no contract between the person giving the statement and the party for whom it was provided. The plaintiff's action failed because of the express disclaimer of liability by the defendants, but the general principle is now accepted that where a representation is made in circumstances implying that it will be acted upon, the person making the representation has a duty of care to discharge towards the other party.

It is normally up to the plaintiff to prove the three ingredients of negligence. There exists, however, an exception in those cases where the legal doctrine of *res ipsa loquitur* applies. This doctrine may be explained as follows: Where an accident happens in circumstances in which the only reasonable explanation of it is that some persons have been negligent, it will be up to these persons to prove that they were not negligent instead of the plaintiff having to prove that they were negligent. An illustration of the application of this principle is found in *Scott* v. *London and St Katherine's Docks Co.*, where a customs officer was injured when, passing by the defendants' warehouse, six bags of sugar fell on him from a crane. The court held that it was for the defendants to show that they had not been negligent; and, as they had been unable to do so, damages were awarded to the plaintiff. The same principle would also be applied in other similar situations, such as where an unoccupied stationary car suddenly runs off on its own.

The defendant in an action for negligence may rely on one of three possible defences.

1. He may deny that he owed any duty to the plaintiff, such as in *King* v. *Phillips* (*supra*).

2. The defendant may deny that he has failed to take such care as a reasonable person would have done in his position.

3. The defendant may plead *contributory negligence* on the part of the plaintiff. The defendant agrees that he has been negligent, but contends that the plaintiff has also been negligent. It stands to reason that, while a person has to take care not to injure his 'neighbour', the other party must also himself take care not to get injured. It is acknowledged now, however, that the standard of care to be expected of a person is higher where the possible consequence of his carelessness may be injury to another than where the possible consequence is injury to himself.

Before 1945 the position at common law was that, where the defendant successfully pleaded contributory negligence, the plaintiff's action was completely defeated and he would not recover any damages at all. This has been altered now by the Law Reform (Contributory Negligence) Act 1945, section 1 (*i*) of which provides:

> Where any person suffers damage as the result partly of his own fault and partly of the fault of any other person or persons, a claim in respect of that damage shall not be defeated by reason of the fault of the person suffering the damage, but the damages recoverable in respect thereof shall be reduced to such an extent as the court thinks just and equitable having regard to the claimant's share in the responsibility for the damage.

The court may thus decide on the evidence submitted that the plaintiff was to blame to the extent of, say, 80 per cent and the defendant to the extent of 20 per cent. In this case the plaintiff would recover one-fifth only of the sum at which the court assessed his loss.

We have now to consider certain instances where there exist specific duties to take care. Two will be mentioned—namely, the duties of an employer towards his employees and the duties of an occupier of premises towards the persons who come on the premises in his occupation.

Duties of an Employer

Apart from statute, an employer owes the following duties to his servants:

1. The employer has to provide reasonably safe premises. He is not absolutely responsible for the safety of the premises, as long as he has done what one could reasonably expect of him to make the premises safe. The employer will be guilty of a breach of this duty if, for instance, one of his servants is injured by a fall of plaster from the ceiling and the soundness of the ceiling has not been regularly inspected.

2. The employer must provide safe equipment, tools, and materials. Again, however, his duty is limited to doing what is reasonably possible to ensure the safety of his servants. If a man is injured through the collapse of a ladder which has not been properly maintained the employer will be liable.

3. The employer must provide a reasonably safe system of work. This is the broadest duty of all. The employer's organization must be efficient so as to avoid injuries through lack of co-ordination between departments or between various individuals engaged on separate tasks. Thus, where molten metal has to be moved about, the arrangements for warning other workers of the oncoming danger must be reasonably efficient. Under the heading of a safe system of work we also include the employer's responsibility to provide reasonably efficient fellow-workers.

Duties of an Occupier of Premises

Before 1958 the duties which an occupier of premises owed to the persons entering the premises varied according to the reasons for the presence of the visitors. A person may be present on some one's premises on the basis of a contract between him and the occupier (*e.g.*, a hotel guest). Alternatively, he could be on the premises by permission of the occupier, but without a contract existing. The law as it stood before 1958 used to distinguish in this context between *invitees* (who were present on a matter of business concerning the occupier as well as themselves) and *licensees* (who were present on some other matter, *e.g.*, the visiting mother-in-law). Lastly, a person may be on some one's premises without permission or, having entered with permission, he may have remained when the permission was withdrawn. In either event he would be a mere trespasser.

1. *Liability of the Occupier of Premises to Persons Present under a Contract.* The liability of the occupier depends in these cases on the terms of the contract, and it is quite possible that the occupier may in the contract have expressly repudiated all responsibility to

the visitor for injury or damage to his property resulting from the unsafe state of the premises or from other reasons. If, however, the contract is silent on this question, then a term will be implied in it to the effect that the premises will be as safe as reasonable care and skill could make them. The liability of a hotel proprietor to his guests regarding any property they may have brought with them is now governed by the Hotel Proprietors Act 1956. A hotel is any establishment held out by the proprietor as offering food, drink, and, if required, sleeping accommodation, without special contract, to any traveller presenting himself who appears able and willing to pay a reasonable sum for the services provided, and who is in a fit state to be received. The hotel proprietor is absolutely responsible to the traveller for any property brought to the hotel, and must make good to him any loss or damage suffered, provided:

(*a*) that at the time of the loss sleeping accommodation had been engaged for the traveller (thus excluding any person coming to a hotel merely for a meal or a drink);
(*b*) that the loss occurred with a period commencing with the midnight before and ending with the midnight after the period during which the traveller was a guest at the hotel.

The hotel proprietor's liability is limited to a maximum of £50 per article lost or damaged or £100 for any one guest, except where the property in question has been deposited with the hotel proprietor for safe custody. The liability does not cover vehicles of any sort brought with him by the traveller.

2. *Liability towards a Trespasser.* A trespasser who has come on the land of another without permission, or who has stayed on when the permission has been withdrawn, has to take the premises as he finds them. The occupier is not obliged to make his premises safe for trespassers. The occupier may not set traps (*e.g.*, spring-guns) for trespassers, and he would be committing a criminal offence, apart from being liable civilly in damages to the trespasser, if he did so. The law concerning an occupier's liability towards trespassers has been reconsidered by the House of Lords in *British Railways Board* v. *Herrington.* H., a six-year-old child, strayed from a meadow where he was playing through a broken-down fence onto an electrified railway line and sustained serious injuries. The child was undoubtedly a trespasser on the line, but the House of Lords nevertheless dismissed an appeal by the Board from a judgment of the Court of Appeal holding them liable. Lord Reid, in his judgment, argued that the occupier's liability depended on whether in the circumstances a conscientious humane man, with his knowledge, skill and resources, could reasonably have been expected to do or to refrain from doing before the accident something which would have avoided it. The

test of the occupier's liability towards trespassers is thus a subjective one since it depends not only on knowledge of the circumstances but also on the skill and resources which were at the occupier's disposal.

3. *Liability towards Other Visitors.* The law concerning invitees and licensees was in a most confused state before 1958, and a great deal of legal ingenuity was wasted on distinguishing between these two classes of visitors. Towards invitees the occupier had a duty to warn them of any unusual danger of which he knew or *ought to* know, while licensees had to be warned about hidden dangers actually known to the occupier.

The liability of occupiers of premises towards persons entering the premises is now governed by the Occupiers' Liability Act 1957. Under this Act the occupier owes a "common duty of care" to all his "visitors", except in so far as it has been modified by contract. The common duty of care is a duty to take such care as in all the circumstances of the case is reasonable to see that the visitor will be reasonably safe in using the premises for the purposes for which he is invited or permitted by the occupier to be there. In this context it is recognized that:

1. An occupier must be prepared for children to be less careful than adults.

2. A person in the exercise of his calling will appreciate and guard against any special risk ordinarily incident to it.

In deciding whether an occupier has discharged his duty regard must be had to all the relevant circumstances, so that:

1. Where injury is caused to a visitor by a danger of which he had been warned, the warning on its own will not absolve the occupier from liability unless in the circumstances it was enough to enable the visitor to be reasonably safe.

2. Where injury is caused to a visitor through faulty execution of work by an independent contractor employed by the occupier, the occupier is not to be treated merely because of this as being liable if in the circumstances he acted reasonably in entrusting the work to an independent contractor, and had taken reasonable steps to satisfy himself that the contractor was competent.

The occupier has no responsibility for risks willingly accepted by the visitor, or where liability has been excluded by contract between the occupier and the visitor. Persons who enter premises in the exercise of a right conferred by law are to be treated as "visitors" even if they have not been specifically invited.

Where premises are occupied by a person under a tenancy agreement, and the landlord is responsible for maintenance and repair, the landlord owes a common duty of care to all persons who or whose goods are lawfully on the premises as if they were there by his direct invitation.

Similarly, where under a contract between an occupier and another person, third parties acquire a right to enter and use the occupier's premises (*e.g.*, sub-contractors employed by a builder to do work in a customer's house) these third parties, although strangers to the contract, will be entitled to all the rights of visitors.

The Act applies not only to houses or land but also to other fixed or moveable structures (*e.g.*, ships or aircraft) occupied by a person.

The main effect of the Act has been to remove the difference between licensees and invitees. The position of trespassers has remained basically unchanged.

Trespass

In the early days of the law of torts the word trespass was used as a synonym for tort. To-day, however, it signifies a specific kind of tort, though we still distinguish between trespass to land, trespass to chattels, and trespass to the person.

Trespass to land is defined as the entering on land which is in the possession of the plaintiff, or remaining on such land or placing anything on it without lawful justification. It can be seen that the plaintiff in an action for trespass is the possessor and not the owner. Indeed, the owner of land could be guilty of trespass on his own property if he entered without justification and without the consent of the person in possession. Trespass may be committed either *on* land (*e.g.*, by walking over it) or *under* land (*e.g.*, by digging under it) or *over* land (*e.g.*, by flying a kite over it). As far as trespass under and over land are concerned, we must remember, however, that certain statutes (*e.g.*, the Civil Aviation Act 1949) permit such operations, subject to some reservations.

Trespass is one of the torts which is actionable without proof of loss, though, of course, if the plaintiff has suffered no loss he will not be able to claim more than mere nominal damages. He may, however, take advantage of some of the other remedies available. The occupier of land may always ask a trespasser to leave, and if he refuses the occupier may use a reasonable amount of force to eject him. In addition, where the trespass is a continuing one and there exists the likelihood that it will not stop in the future, the occupier may ask the court for an injunction ordering the trespassers to desist. It cannot be often enough repeated, however, that the trespass is not a criminal offence, so that the notice which graces so many country gates, "Trespassers will be prosecuted," is nothing but a wooden lie. The only forms of trespass which could give rise to criminal prosecutions would be trespass on railway property or on military premises.

Trespass to chattels consists of committing without lawful justification an act of direct physical interference with a chattel in another person's possession. Like trespass to land, trespass to chattels is an injury to possession rather than to ownership, and similarly it is also actionable without proof of loss. Thus, the mere act of picking up a book which is in another person's possession is trespass to goods unless, as in a public library, there exists express or implied authority to do this act. Since trespass is actionable without proof of loss it does not matter that the trespasser acted innocently and indeed without negligence.

Conversion and Detinue

While any *direct* interference with a person's possession of land or chattels is remedied by an action for trespass, an action for conversion will lie where there has been an unjustified denial of a person's *title* to chattels. The action may be brought by an owner or by a possessor or even by a person having a right to possession without ownership. An action for conversion may be additional to one for trespass where the direct interference with possession constitutes also a denial of the right to possess. Conversion consists of any denial of another person's proprietary or possessory right. Disposing of the goods of another without his consent is conversion, even though it has been done innocently. Where an auctioneer sells goods by auction on behalf of a client who was not their owner and had no right to authorize their sale, he will be liable to their true owner for conversion. It must be stressed, however, that conversion is committed only where the defendants' act is inconsistent with the *property* rights of the plaintiff. If, when I have deposited my suitcase in a cloak-room, the attendant refuses to hand it back to me, contending that it is not mine, this would be conversion, as he is denying my proprietary title to it. If, after an argument, he throws the suitcase out so that it is damaged that would not be conversion but might be a case of trespass to goods.

A person who is buying a wireless set or anything else on hire-purchase terms and who sells the article before he has paid all the instalments is committing conversion, because he does not acquire ownership until he has fully paid for the thing.

Conversion has to be distinguished from *detinue*. Detinue is the tort committed by a person who refuses to return possession of goods to some one entitled to possession, where there is, however, no denial of a proprietary title If a friend of yours borrows this book and refuses to return it until after he has sat for an examination you could proceed against him for detinue of the book.

The main points of difference between conversion and detinue are as follows: In conversion there is a single wrongful act, while detinue is a continuing cause of action which accrues at the time of the wrongful refusal to return goods and continues until delivery or judgment. An action for detinue lies only where the defendant is in actual possession. An action for conversion results in the award of pecuniary damages, while in detinue the defendant has an option whether to return the chattel or to pay its value.

Nuisance

Nuisance may be either public nuisance or private nuisance. Public nuisance is a criminal offence consisting in causing an obstruction of the public highway or in creating any danger on it—*e.g.*, by stretching a wire across it or by erecting a barricade. While public nuisance is primarily a criminal offence it is also actionable as a tort where a particular individual has suffered special damage through it.

A private nuisance is a tort, and it is caused by any unreasonable interference with the plaintiff's enjoyment of land which has led to his suffering some loss or discomfiture. The plaintiff in an action for nuisance must be the occupier of land. Thus, if my neighbour disturbs me by playing music at night I might sue him for nuisance if I am the occupier of the building, but not if I am merely a lodger in the house in which I am living.

Private nuisance may be divided into two classes—namely, (1) interference with a servitude (*e.g.*, by obstructing a person's right of way) and (2) allowing the escape of some obnoxious 'thing' on another person's land. The 'thing' may be dirt, dust, heat, noise, water, smoke, animals, or even undesirable people. A certain element of continuity must exist; a single act of escape would not be sufficient to constitute nuisance. The main difference between the two classes of nuisance is that in the former case it is not necessary to prove actual loss; but damage, whether physical or just consisting of general inconvenience, must be proved in the latter case.

The difference between nuisance and trespass is that while trespass involves some *direct* interference with another person's possession of land, nuisance is made up of acts which affect the possession of land *indirectly*. If, when weeding my garden, I threw the weeds over the wall on to my neighbour's property this would be trespass, but if I fail to weed my garden and the weeds spread to my neighbour's property that would be nuisance. Also, trespass is actionable without proof of loss, while nuisance (except where there has been an interference with a servitude) is not actionable unless damage can be proved.

The essence of nuisance is interference with the comfort of an occupier of land, though where a person has suffered injury as a result of a public nuisance he may sue the guilty party for damages irrespective of any occupation of land. Not every interference with a person's comfort will be actionable, however. An action can be sustained only where the defendant's conduct in the circumstances of the case was unreasonable. It is unavoidable that in a community such as ours, where people's homes are close together, the hobbies or activities of one person may interfere with the comfort of his neighbour. Such minor discomforts have to be borne, if not in silence, then at least without hope of legal redress. What is reasonable depends largely on the location of the property affected. The opening of a fish-and-chips shop in a purely residential area might well be looked upon as a nuisance, while the opening of the same shop in a working-class district might not be deemed to be a nuisance. Lord Justice Thesiger said in *Sturges* v. *Bridgman*: "What would be a nuisance in Belgrave Square would not necessarily be so in Bermondsey." Some form of behaviour which might normally be looked upon as a reasonable user of property may become a nuisance if it has been undertaken maliciously with the intention of harming or annoying a neighbour. In *Christie* v. *Davey*, for instance, the plaintiff was a music teacher, and her house was used for music-lessons during the day. The neighbour, who found the musical attempts of the plaintiff's pupils disturbing, took to banging and hammering on the wall between the two houses in order to disturb the plaintiff. This behaviour was held to constitute a nuisance, and the plaintiff was granted an injunction to restrain the defendant.

The court is likely to take a more lenient view of the contention that the defendant's conduct was reasonable where the plaintiff has suffered only personal discomfort than where he can show that the defendant's behaviour has caused damage to his property. If you live in a town you must resign yourself to the fact that the air which you breathe will be impure, but you might take action against the owner of a factory the fumes from which are causing damage to your property. In *Halsey* v. *Esso Petroleum Co. Ltd*, the plaintiff was the owner-occupier of a house situated opposite an oil-storage depot operated by the defendants. The depot contained a boiler-house emitting from time to time noxious acid smuts, and also giving rise to a pungent smell of oil. The defendants were held liable in nuisance for damage done by the acid smuts to washing and to the plaintiff's car, and for the smell, even though it had not affected the plaintiff's health.

The plaintiff in an action for nuisance may claim an injunction as an alternative to damages or even in addition to them. The occupier of land may also use self-help by 'abating the nuisance,' such as chopping off the branches of a neighbour's tree which overhangs his property.

Limitation of Actions

An action for damages for personal injuries suffered by the plaintiff and alleged to have been caused by the negligence, nuisance or breach of duty by the defendant (whether the duty exists by virtue of a contract or a statutory provision or independently of them) is subject to a three-year period of limitation under the Limitation Acts 1939–75. The three-year period runs from:

1. the date on which the cause of action accrued, or
2. the date, if later, of the plaintiff's knowledge.

If the person injured dies before the expiration of the period, the period shall be three years from

1. the date of his death, or
2. the date of the personal representative's knowledge, whichever is the later.

Reference to a person's date of knowledge means the date on which he first had knowledge of the following facts:

1. that the injury in question was significant (*i.e.*, would justify him in bringing an action); and
2. that it was attributable in whole or in part to the act or omission which is alleged to constitute negligence, nuisance or breach of duty, and
3. the identity of the defendant.

The Rule in Rylands v. Fletcher

The rule in *Rylands* v. *Fletcher* represents an example of a tort of strict liability. This tort deals with situations which, though they might possibly have been covered by the law of negligence, trespass, and nuisance, differ from them in some material parts. The principle was first staged in the case by which it is known. The facts of the case were as follows: The defendant had employed competent contractors to build a reservoir on his land. While digging on the defendant's land, the contractors came on some old shafts which communicated with a mine operated by the plaintiff, but this was not suspected at the time. Instead of blocking the shafts, they only filled them in with earth. When the reservoir was filled with water the water entered the plaintiff's mine through the shaft. In deciding for the plaintiff, the House of Lords laid down the following principle:

> We think that the true rule of law is, that the person who, for his own purposes, brings on his land and collects and keeps there anything likely to do mischief if it escaped, must keep it in at his peril; and if he does not do so, is prima facie answerable for all the damage which is the natural consequence of its escape. He can excuse himself by showing that the

escape was owing to the plaintiff's default; or perhaps that the escape was the consequence of a *vis major*, or the Act of God.

The rule in *Rylands* v. *Fletcher* will thus be applied where there had been a "non-natural user of land," in that something has been introduced on the defendant's land which was not there naturally. This "something" might be water, gas, electricity, plants which have been artificially sown, or, indeed, anything that may do damage if it escapes. The escape of anything which is naturally on land will, of course, not make the owner of the land liable to pay damages except where the escape was due to his negligence.

The 'escape' referred to in the rule must be the escape of the noxious thing from the defendant's land to the plaintiff's land. It was decided in *Read* v. *Lyons and Co., Ltd*, where the plaintiff was injured as a result of an explosion in the munitions factory in which she was working, that the rule could not be applied there because there was no real 'escape.'

The statement of the rule given above indicated two possible defences—namely, the plaintiff's own fault and an Act of God. Since the rule was first stated three additional defences have been added—namely, the act of a stranger (*e.g.*, where a burglar allows an escape of gas from a building which he has broken into), statutory authority, and the consent of the plaintiff to the accumulation of the dangerous matter. The latter defence is particularly important, as it may be applied where water, gas, or electricity are laid on in a building for the joint use of a number of tenants. If a water-pipe bursts, and the premises of one of the tenants are flooded, his action, either against the owners of the building or against the tenants of the premises where the burst took place, will be met by the defence that the dangerous thing—in our example, water—which has been introduced on the premises has been brought there with his consent.

Defamation of Character

Defamation of character is the tort of publishing a statement which tends to lower a person's reputation in the eyes of right-thinking members of society.

Defamation of character may be either libel or slander. It will be libel if made in some lasting form—*e.g.*, in writing or in the form of a cartoon or statue. If made in a transient form—*i.e.*, by words spoken—it is slander. The Defamation Act 1952 has laid down that any defamatory matter which is broadcast or televised should be treated as libel.

The following points should be noted:

1. The statement must be one capable of lowering the plaintiff's reputation. Mere words of abuse will not be defamatory. A state-

ment may be defamatory either openly, where any person hearing or reading the statement would appreciate that it might adversely affect the plaintiff's reputation or, alternatively, the statement may be defamatory by containing an *innuendo*, or hidden meaning, which, though not clear to every one, may affect the plaintiff's reputation in the eyes of those persons who possess some special knowledge with which to appreciate the hidden meaning. In *Tolley* v. *Fry and Sons, Ltd*, the plaintiff, a well-known amateur golfer, was depicted on a poster published by the defendants with a bar of their chocolate protruding from a pocket. A humorous verse underneath praised the merits of the defendant's chocolate. The poster had been issued without the plaintiff's consent, and he alleged now that it contained the innuendo that he, an amateur, had allowed his name to be used for reward. If he had done that it would, of course, have been improper for him to continue participating in amateur competitions. Tolley was awarded substantial damages.

In order for the statement to be defamatory it must be capable of injuring the plaintiff's reputation in the eyes of right-thinking (*i.e.*, law-abiding) members of society. The plaintiff in *Byrne* v. *Deane* had been accused by the secretary of a golf club of which he was a member that he had been responsible for a police-raid on the club-house in the course of which a gambling machine had been removed. The action failed, the court holding that right-thinking members of society would think no worse of the plaintiff for having informed the police that an offence was being committed on club premises—if, of course, he had done so, which he denied.

2. The plaintiff must prove that the statement referred to him. This may be easy where he is named; it may be more difficult where a person recognizes himself as a character in some work of fiction. In that case he would have to satisfy the court that reasonable members of society (whom he would produce as witnesses) considered him to be the character in the book, always, of course, assuming that the book or article depicted the character concerned in an unfavourable light.

3. The statement must have been published. This means that it must have been communicated to at least one person other than the plaintiff. Any defamatory statement which has been communicated to the plaintiff only (*e.g.*, in a private conversation or by personal letter) has not been published and would thus not be actionable. A statement made by one spouse to another does not represent publication. If a defamatory statement is made on a post-card sent to the plaintiff publication is presumed, as the courts take it for granted that some at least of the people handling the card in the course of transit will have read it. The same would also apply to telegrams. As far as letters are concerned, the question is whether the sender of a

defamatory letter addressed to the plaintiff should have anticipated that the letter would be opened by some one other than the plaintiff. In *Theaker* v. *Richardson* the defendant, a local councillor, sent a defamatory and abusive letter to the plaintiff, a fellow-councillor. The letter was addressed to the plaintiff by name in a manila-type envelope and placed into the plaintiff's letter-box. It was opened by the plaintiff's husband, and the jury decided that in view of the business type of envelope and the method of delivery, which made the letter appear to be a mere circular, it was to have been anticipated that some one other than the addressee would open it. This decision of the jury was upheld by the Court of Appeal. If the recipient of a defamatory letter shows it to others he will not be able to sue the writer, as any publication that has taken place has been the plaintiff's own work and the rule of *volenti non fit injuria* will be applied.

4. Slander (but not libel) is actionable only if the plaintiff has suffered some pecuniary loss as a result of the defamatory statement or if the slander falls into one of the four special classes mentioned below. The pecuniary loss need not be a specially large one; indeed, it has been held that where a person who had been slandered lost invitations to tea or dinner from people who used to invite him he had suffered a pecuniary loss, in that he had now to pay for these meals himself. The four cases where slander is actionable without proof or loss are the following:

(*a*) Where there has been an imputation that the plaintiff has been guilty of a criminal offence punishable by imprisonment.

(*b*) Where an imputation of unchastity has been made against a girl or woman.

(*c*) Where it has been alleged that the plaintiff is suffering from a contagious disease (*e.g.*, veneral disease).

(*d*) Where words have been used calculated to disparage the plaintiff in his office, business, or other occupation by imputing dishonesty, incompetence, or other unfitness for the work which he is doing.

The fact that libel is always actionable while slander is actionable in the above mentioned cases only is one of the two main differences between these two forms of defamation. The other is that libel, apart from being a tort, may also be a criminal offence, where the words used may lead to a breach of the peace. It might be noted that it is no defence in a prosecution for criminal libel to prove that the words used were substantially true.

An action for defamation of character represents a good example of the division of work between judge and jury. It is for the judge to state whether the words used of the plaintiff are capable of having defamatory implications. This is a question of law, depending on the definition of the tort of defamation. If the judge states that they are capable of having such a meaning it is then for the jury to decide whether they were defamatory in respect of the plaintiff and, if so, what damages the plaintiff should recover.

The defendant in an action for defamation has the following possible defences:

1. *Justification.* The defendant may try to prove that the statement which he made was true in substance and in fact. Surprisingly perhaps, this defence is not as often used as one might expect. The reason is that if the attempted justification fails the damages awarded to the plaintiff will be substantially higher than they would have been if justification had never been attempted, since the attempt to justify shows a total unwillingness on the part of the defendant to agree that he was wrong. He is really repeating the defamatory statement in court.

2. *Fair Comment on a Matter of Public Interest.* By a 'matter of public interest' we understand anything which is in general of interest to all persons, such as political issues, the conduct of Ministers and other public servants, the management of public institutions and of religious organizations. We include under this heading also those cases where a person voluntarily submits himself or his work to public criticism, as is done by actors, writers, sportsmen, etc. Any comment on either of these issues is privileged, in the sense that no action for defamation may be brought, however harmful the comment may be to the professional reputation of the person who is the object of it, provided always that it is a comment on facts which are undeniably true and that the comment is a fair one.

A politician may be attacked for a speech which he has made, and from what he said it may be deduced that he is in favour of revolution. This may be harmful to his career, but he cannot complain. If, however, he has never uttered the words on which the comment has been tagged, an action for defamation would succeed, as you may not put words which he has never uttered in the mouth of a person. The comment must be restricted to those parts of a person's work or life which he has submitted for public scrutiny. Attacks on the private life of a person whose actions are in some other respect a matter of public interest (*e.g.*, those of a politician or actor) would not be protected as a comment on a matter of public interest.

The comment must have been a fair one. This does not mean that the jury must agree with it. It is not the task of a jury to set themselves up as censors of the work of reviewers, editors, critics, etc. All that they have to be satisfied about is that the statement made was relevant to the facts on which the author of the statement commented and that it represented his honest opinion. If, for instance, the reviewer of a book criticizes the author for something quite unconnected with the book it would not be a fair comment—indeed, we might well say that it would not be a comment at all.

3. *Absolute Privilege.* Certain statements are absolutely privileged, in that they are not actionable irrespective of whether they are true and irrespective of whether they have been made innocently or maliciously. This applies to:

(*a*) Statements made by a member of Parliament in either House of Parliament.

(*b*) Statements made in the course of judicial proceedings by judge, juror, party, witness, or advocate.

(*c*) Any statement made by an officer of State to another in the course of their official duty (*e.g.*, an official report sent by one civil servant to another).

(*d*) Newspaper or broadcast reports of judicial proceedings in the United Kingdom, provided that they are fair and appear at the time when the proceedings are taking place.

(*e*) Parliamentary papers published on the authority of either House of Parliament.

4. *Qualified Privilege.* Statements made by one person to another are also privileged where the person making the statement had a moral, social, or legal duty to make the statement to the person to whom he made it. The privilege in this case is said to be qualified, because the statement would be actionable if the plaintiff could prove that it has been made maliciously—*i.e.*, with a motive other than that of performing one of the duties referred to above. An employer who gives a reference about a present or former employee of his to a prospective employer may use this defence if the employee brings an action for defamation of character. It should be noted that where the statement has been made in performance of a duty (and it is considered to be a social duty to give information about former or present employees) the statement will be privileged, irrespective of whether it is true. If the employer denigrated the servant's character because he did not want him to get another job, that would be an improper motive in giving a reference and would override the qualified privilege. It should be added, though, that it is very difficult to prove malice.

5. *Unintentional Defamation.* Since the Defamation Act 1952, the defendant who has innocently committed a defamation of character may offer to the person whose reputation may have suffered a full apology, together with reasonable financial compensation. Innocent defamation may arise particularly where newspapers report the happening of some events and some one happens to have the same name as a person who is referred to by the newspaper in unfavour-

able terms. It could also arise where a character in a book seems to resemble some living person. If the person to whom the apology plus compensation have been offered refuses to accept, the offer may be a defence in a subsequent action for defamation.[1]

Torts arising from Business Competition

Business competition is a form of economic warfare, and it may easily happen that one of the competing parties is ruined. Unless, however, his business adversaries have been using unlawful means to bring about his competitive defeat it will be just a further instance of what lawyers call *damnum sine injuria—i.e.*, a loss not caused by any legal wrong—and he will be unable to claim damages from anyone. Indeed, in the case of at least one tort—namely, that of *conspiracy*—it is a good defence to show that the conspiring persons were actuated solely by the motive of fostering their own business or occupational interests. Conspiracy consists of a combination of a number of persons to achieve some unlawful purpose, thus causing damage to another party. Unlawful in this context does not mean criminal; it means merely the intention of doing harm, even though by otherwise perfectly legal means. The essence of this tort lies in the fact that a number of persons are combining for this end, so that an act which would not be tortious if done by one person acting on his own may become tortious if done by a number or persons in pursuance of an agreement.

As has been stated already, where the purpose of the agreement is the advancement of the interests of the participating parties (as distinct from mere spite or some similar motive) the agreement will not be an actionable conspiracy. In *Crofter Hand-woven Harris Tweed Co., Ltd.* v. *Veitch*, mill-owners on the Isle of Lewis refused a request of a trade union for a wage increase on the ground that the mills were suffering from the competition of local crofters. In order to remove this obstacle standing in the way of a wage increase, some officials of the union called on their members who were employed in the main port of the island to refuse to handle yarn intended for the crofters. This the dock-workers were entitled to do. An action by an organization of the crofters against the trade union officials for conspiracy failed, the House of Lords holding that the predominant purpose of the defendants was to benefit the legitimate interests of their members.

There are, however, certain wrongs which may be committed in the course of business competition and which would be actionable.

1. *Malicious Falsehood.* This is the tort of publishing a false statement about a person or his property which causes damage to

[1] For the provisions of the Rehabilitation of Offenders Act 1974 see Addendum on page 213.

his material interests but which falls short of defamation of his character. As examples we might quote the spreading of a rumour about a competitor to the effect that he has died or has given up business. Neither of these statements will affect his reputation, but both may do much harm to his business. Another type of malicious falsehood is *slander of goods*, where false statements about the goods of another person are published. Sometimes such statements may be defamatory, such as where it is alleged that the sausages made by a certain butcher contain horse-meat, because that would imply that he was guilty of fraud. Even if there is no defamation of character, slander of goods will be actionable if the statement made was untrue and was made maliciously (*i.e.*, with some indirect or distinct motive), and the plaintiff has suffered some loss. A statement to the effect that a competitor's paint would not stand up to damp weather may be a slander of his goods if the above points can be proved.

2. *Passing off.* A person will be liable for passing off his goods if he does anything, whether intentionally or otherwise, which will lead reasonable people to believe that his goods are those of another producer or distributor. This might happen if a name was used identical with or closely resembling that used by another firm. It makes no difference whether the name used happens to be that of the user himself. You may always use your name for business purposes, but not in a way which is likely to mislead others into associating your goods or your business with some established firm or its goods. In *J. Bollinger and others* v. *Costa Brava Wine Co., Ltd* it was held that the sale by the defendants in this country of wine under the description of "Spanish champagne" constituted passing off, since it represented an attempt to secure for the sales of their product the goodwill associated with the word 'champagne,' and the plaintiffs, a group of French companies producing wine in the Champagne district of France, were held entitled to an injunction against the defendants.

3. *Interference with an Existing Contract.* It is a tort to induce a person to break an existing contract with another party. The person who induces another to break an existing contract must, of course, be aware of the existence of this contract. It does not matter what form of persuasion is employed. The reader should note that to induce a breach of contract is a tort, but to persuade a party either not to enter into a contract or to bring an existing contract to an end in a legitimate manner is not a tort. If A is about to buy goods from B, B's competitor C may offer to supply the goods to A at a cheaper price and thus induce A to make the contract with him. Where A has already contracted to buy the goods from B, it would still be legal for C to persuade him not to renew the contract when it expired and to buy his future requirements from C. It would be illegal, however,

for C to persuade A to break the contract with B by not carrying out whatever had been agreed upon.

A person who is sued for damages on the ground that he has interfered with an existing contract may defend himself by contending that he had a moral, social, or legal duty to do what he did. Thus, a trade-union official may ask members of his union to leave their work without notice if he has reasonable grounds for believing that continued employment in a particular factory might lead to serious illness. Similarly, a father may persuade his daugher to break her engagement if on reasonable grounds he feels that her fiancé is an undesirable person.

Damages

Damages awarded for a tort may be divided into two classes; they may be either *nominal* or *substantial*. Substantial damages are awarded where the plaintiff has suffered some loss and their purpose is to compensate him for that loss. Nominal damages are awarded where the plaintiff has not suffered any loss but has been the victim of a tort which is actionable without proof of loss (*e.g.*, trespass or libel). Nominal damages are then awarded not by way of compensation for loss but only as recognition of the fact that the plaintiff's legal rights have been infringed.

Substantial damages may be *general* or *special*. Special damages are expenses actually incurred or some loss actually suffered as opposed to general damages (*e.g.*, damages for pain and suffering or for loss of expectation of life) which will have to be assessed by the court.

Since the purpose of damages is to place the plaintiff into the position in which he would have been had he not suffered from the defendant's tort, the court will, in assessing damages, bring into account any payments of income tax or surtax to which the plaintiff would have been liable if he had not suffered the loss which forms the basis of the action. Thus, in *British Transport Commission* v. *Gourley*, G. had suffered injuries through the negligence of B.T.C. This meant that the income which he could have expected to earn during the remainder of his working life was largely lost. The damages which the court awarded to him were based, however, not on the gross income which he lost but on the net income after deduction of income tax and surtax since he had lost only the net income and not the full income before deduction of tax. It should be noted that this principle applies not only in assessment of damages for tort but also in respect of damages for breach of contract.

While the purpose of substantial damages is in principle the compensation of the plaintiff, the law of tort also recognizes occasionally *exemplary damages*. These are damages awarded in addition to mere compensation for the loss suffered by the plaintiff, their purpose being to provide a partial redress for a hurt to his feelings which he has suffered and also perhaps to punish the defendant for having caused this hurt. Judges may exercise their discretion in granting exemplary damages, and they will generally award such damages only where the defendant has been guilty of some grossly callous behaviour towards the plaintiff.

We have stated already that the purpose of substantial damages is to compensate the plaintiff for the loss which he has suffered as a result of the defendant's wrong. Many consequences may, however, flow from the defendant's act, and it is obviously impracticable to hold him responsible for all of them, some of them being, in legal language, "too remote." The attitude of the law to this question of remoteness of damage has undergone significant changes in the last few years. Until recently the general principle was that laid down by the Court of Appeal in *Re Polemis and Furness, Withy and Co.* The facts were these: F. had chartered P.'s ship and had loaded her with, among other things, some cases of petrol. There was a slight leakage from some of these cases, and petrol vapour spread in the hold of the ship. A porter employed by F. negligently kicked a plank down the hold, a spark was struck, and the ship went up in flames. The Court held F. liable for the loss of the ship. The argument proceeded on these lines: In order to decide whether the defendant is liable at all for negligence, it is necessary to prove that some damage was foreseeable from his negligent act (or, as in this case, the negligent acts of his servants). It certainly was to be expected that some damage would be caused if a plank was dropped into the hold of the ship. The extent of the damage as it turned out to be had not been foreseeable; but, once liability had been established, the defendant was held responsible for all the direct consequences of his acts.

The rule in *Re Polemis* was reconsidered by the Judicial Committee of the Privy Council in *Overseas Tankships* (*U.K.*), *Ltd* v. *Morts Dock and Engineering Co., Ltd* (the *Wagon Mound No. 1* case). A quantity of furnace oil had escaped from the *Wagon Mound*, a ship owned by O., and was carried by wind and tides towards a wharf belonging to M. The Australian courts were satisfied that it was not foreseeable that oil spread on water could catch fire; but in fact some cotton waste floating on the oil was set afire by molten metal falling from the wharf. The oil began to burn, and the flames seriously damaged the wharf and some equipment on it. The Australian courts had followed *Re Polemis* and decided the case in favour of the wharf-owners. It was foreseeable that the escaping oil would cause some damage, and consequently O. was held responsible for the full damage which actually resulted. The

Judicial Committee reversed the decision of the Australian courts and in doing so held that *Re Polemis* was not good law. The Judicial Committee found that the test of foreseeability should be applied in dealing with the problem of remoteness of damage in the law of tort in the same way in which this principle is applied in the law of contract. In reading the judgment of the Judicial Committee Lord Simonds said: "It was a principle of civil liability . . . that a man must be considered responsible for the probable consequences of his act. To demand more of him was too harsh a rule, to demand less was to ignore that civilized order required the observance of a minimum standard of behaviour." He added that his ruling was not intended to reflect on the rule of strict liability as exemplified by *Rylands* v. *Fletcher*.

The facts as given above brought forth a second action as well. In *Overseas Tankships (U.K.), Ltd* v. *The Miller Steamship Co. Pty* (referred to as the *Wagon Mound No. 2* case) the owners of two ships which had been damaged in the conflagration sued O., the owners of the *Wagon Mound*, in negligence and in nuisance. The Judicial Committee of the Privy Council, in deciding the case in M.'s favour, made two important points. They decided that the test of foreseeability applied to nuisance as well as to negligence, but they also held that O. was liable to M. in negligence since, although the risk of fire had been small, this did not justify O. in taking no steps to eliminate it. It would appear that this finding of fact contradicts that made in *Wagon Mound No. 1*, but this is not so. The fire had been caused by oxy-acetylene welding operations being continued on the wharf after the oil had been noticed and the plaintiffs in that case would therefore have been met by the defence of contributory negligence which at that time formed a complete defence under the law of New South Wales.

In *Smith* v. *Leech Brain & Co., Ltd* the Queen's Bench Division had also to deal with the problem of remoteness of damage. The plaintiff in this case was the widow of a workman employed by the defendants. Through the defendant's negligence a piece of molten metal flew out of a tank and injured the workman's lip. This apparently insignificant burn caused, however, the man's death since at the time he was suffering, unknown to himself and others, from pre-malignant cancer. The burn activated the cancer, and he died. Although the man's death was clearly not a foreseeable result of the accident, Lord Parker, C.J. nevertheless held the defendants liable and awarded damages to the widow for the loss of her husband. He approved of the decision in *Wagon Mound* but argued that this case had overruled *Re Polemis* only where the actual damage differed from the foreseeable one not only in extent but also in type. In the present case, the fatal injury to the workman differed from the foreseeable one (a burn) in extent, but not in type, both being personal injuries, and the defendants had to accept responsibility for the man's death.

To sum up, then: the defendant is responsible for any damage which he should have foreseen as the probable consequence of his tortious act. He is not responsible, however, where the loss, though resulting in a way from the defendant's wrong, has been aggravated through some cause over which the defendant had no control. In *Liesbosch* (*owners*) v. *Edison* (*owners*), a dredger sank after a collision with another ship, whose faulty navigation was responsible for the collision. The owners of the dredger had a contract for some dredging to perform, but because of shortage of funds they were unable to replace the dredger at once and had to hire another dredger. This meant that the loss which they suffered was larger than it need have been. The defendants were held liable to pay damages for the loss of the dredger only, the additional loss being held to have been caused by the impecuniosity of the plaintiffs, a circumstance for which the defendants could not be held responsible.

It is also generally held that a defendant is not responsible for a mere *economic loss* resulting from his tortious act but only for the direct physical consequences of his actions. This view found the approval of the Court of Appeal in *Spartan Steel and Alloys Ltd* v. *Martin & Co.* (*Contractors*) *Ltd.* Through the admitted negligence of the defendants' employees damage was done to an electric cable supplying power to the plaintiffs' factory. The plaintiffs were without power supplies for some thirteen hours. As a result of that, molten metal had to be poured out of their furnace, thus reducing its value, and they were unable to undertake further melts during the period of interruption of power supply. The plaintiffs were awarded damages for the loss in value of the metal actually in the furnace at the time including the loss of profit on its potential sale, but they were denied damages for the loss of profit on subsequent melts which could not be undertaken. While the physical damage to the melt in the furnace at the time and the reduction in value of the melt and the loss on its resale were foreseeable, the loss of profit on subsequent melts was not really foreseeable.

The Law Reform (Married Women and Tortfeasors) Act 1935 provides that where two or more persons are jointly responsible for a tort (*joint tortfeasors*) and one of them has been held liable to pay damages to the person suffering damage from the tort, the tortfeasor who paid the damages may claim contribution from the others. The amount recoverable will be fixed by the court, taking into account what is just and equitable in the circumstances having regard to the extent of the responsibility of each of the tortfeasors for the tort which they jointly committed. The court may exempt a person completely from contribution if his share in responsibility is deemed to be negligible; on the other hand, the contribution may amount to a complete idemnity where the party against whom the claim for contribution is made was really primarily responsible for the commission of the tort. Thus, where, as in the example given on page 194, an auctioneer has sold goods for a client who was not the owner, and is held liable in damages for conversion, he should be able to claim a full indemnity from the client on whose behalf he acted.

THE NATURE AND FUNCTIONS OF CRIMINAL LAW

What is a Crime?

It has been pointed out already in the introduction to this chapter that the line of division between a tort and a crime is a fluid one. There is nothing in the act itself which clearly determines whether legally it should be deemed to be a crime or a tort. Changes in the law, following in general on changes in public outlook, have made and unmade many criminal offences. Attempted suicide used to be a criminal offence, but it no longer is so, while trafficking in drugs was at one time within the law, but now constitutes a criminal offence.

Most crimes deal with actions which the general public disapproves of and would wish to see punished, but this is not necessarily always the case. At times, the law may be running ahead of public opinion and make punishable as criminal offences certain actions—*e.g.*, in connection with the violation of traffic codes, which the general public or a large section of it may not consider to be all that blameworthy. Sometimes it is argued that crimes are acts which are morally wrong. This may have been true in the past but it certainly is not true today. Many acts which are clearly immoral are not punishable at all and while lawyers and philosophers have hotly debated the issue as to whether morality, whatever it may be, should be protected by the law, the majority view today appears to be that except in extreme cases this is not desirable. There is thus really nothing very specific about criminal wrongs. The position was well stated by the late Lord Atkin: 'The criminal quality of an act cannot be discovered by intuition; nor can it be discovered by reference to any standard but one: is the act prohibited with penal consequences?'

This reasoning leads us thus to at least one possible definition of a crime, namely as an *act which is capable of being followed by criminal proceedings leading to some form of punishment.* Even this definition, however, is by no means fully satisfactory since some forms of criminal punishment resemble closely the sanctions of civil law—*e.g.*, a fine as compared with the award of monetary damages for a tort or a breach of contract. Even imprisonment imposed as a punishment is not really different from imprisonment used as a means to enforce a court order—*e.g.*, an injunction, in civil proceedings. One has to look therefore not just to the form which the sanction takes, but to its purpose. Is its basic purpose that of compensating or redressing a civil wrong by possibly inflicting some harm on another, or is it basically that of punishing an individual whether or not this punishment directly benefits another party.

Crimes and Torts

The main differences between civil wrongs (torts) and criminal wrongs (crimes) are as follows:

1. Only the person injured may sue for a tort, while a criminal prosecution may be initiated by the victim of the wrong, a public official or anyone else who wants to see the crime punished.

2. An action arising out of a tort may be discontinued or settled out of court by the plaintiff at any time. The Crown has no right to intervene in such proceedings. A criminal prosecution once started may not be settled out of court by the victim and the proceedings may be stopped only by the Crown by entering a plea of *nolle prosequi* which the representative of the Crown may do even without the consent of the victim of the offence.

3. The plaintiff in an action for tort need not enforce the judgment of the court, while the prosecutor in criminal proceedings has no power to pardon the offender. This privilege rests solely with the Crown, since every criminal offence is considered to be a wrong against the Crown.

Criminal Liability

The prosecutor in criminal proceedings has to prove that the defendant's conduct

(1) has caused a certain event forbidden by criminal law (the so-called *actus reus—i.e.*, forbidden act) and

(2) that the defendant's conduct was accompanied by the prescribed state of mind (*mens rea—i.e.*, guilty mind).

The burden of proof rests on the prosecution and a man cannot as a rule be found guilty unless both *actus reus* and *mens rea* were present, though we shall see later that some exceptions to this principle have developed in the recent past.

The *actus reus* includes all those elements of a crime other than the accused's state of mind. Thus, in connection with theft, the court will have to be satisfied not only that the accused appropriated some property, but that this property belonged to another. The appropriation must have been dishonest, but this is a reference to the accused's state of mind at the time of the appropriation. What will have to be proved depends of course on the definition of the particular crime with which the defendant is accused. Unless there is an *actus reus* there can be no crime, since a person cannot be convicted solely because of the state of his mind. The mere intention to kill is not punishable as such, there must have been a killing. The conduct of the accused must be willed and not involuntary such as where a person's mind has no control over his actions because of insanity, drugging or a similar reason. Inaction may in some instances also be treated as an *actus reus* but only where there exists a legal duty to act. It is no offence, whatever the morality may be, to allow another person to drown, but it could become an offence if the person who failed to act was in some way (*e.g.*, as a nursemaid) responsible for the safety of the person whose life was lost.

The meaning of the *actus reus* is fairly clear, but it is more difficult to define accurately the *mens rea*. The requirement that the defendant must have had a guilty mind does not mean that he must have felt guilty at the time of committing the act in question. He may well believe that what he is doing is the right and proper thing to do in the circumstances. The fanatic who kills for a cause may well believe his actions to be well justified, but he nevertheless has a guilty mind. In law the attitudes of the actor towards his act may take three possible forms, namely:

1. *Intention.* A person intends those consequences of his act which he desires to achieve, or which he knows will almost certainly follow on his act, or which will follow inevitably from the aim which he is trying to attain. Thus, it will not be possible for a person to plead that he did not intend to kill his victim if he shot him with a pistol at short range.

2. *Recklessness.* A man is reckless in respect of the consequences of his action if he foresees the probability of their occurring, but does not desire them. This could happen if a person discharges a fire-arm into a crowd of people, perhaps in order to frighten them away, but realizing that it is probable that he may kill someone in doing so.

3. *Negligence.* A man is said to act negligently if he brings about a consequence which a reasonable man would have foreseen and avoided. Thus, a person would have acted negligently if while out hunting he were to discharge his rifle at an animal without first making sure that there was no human being in the way who could be injured.

What particular state of mind is required will vary from crime to crime, or putting it in other words, the same *actus reus* combined with a different state of mind will lead to a different type of criminal offence—*e.g.*, the killing of a person (homicide) may be murder, manslaughter, voluntary or involuntary, or it may be justified homicide and thus be no criminal offence at all.

Public Welfare Offences

With some criminal offences our law imposes on the public a *strict liability—i.e.*, the *actus reus* on its own is sufficient to constitute the offence without the prosecution having to prove a particular state of mind on part of the accused. Strict liability is not imposed in the case of the most serious offences carrying the most severe punishments. It has however found its way into many statutory offences created by Acts of Parliament passed during the last half century or so with a view to controlling some particular aspect of our daily lives. This does not mean, of course, that every offence established by statute is one of strict liability. The statute in question has to be interpreted very carefully, but the absence of the word 'knowingly' in the definition of the offence in question will generally lead us to assume that it is an offence of strict liability. Where the wording of the relevant section of the statute leaves the question somewhat open, it is often a matter for the courts through their decisions to determine whether or not the offence is to be treated as one of strict liability and the courts may well be guided by the degree of social danger which they believe to be inherent in the offence. This has been true particularly in connection with offences involving dangerous drugs and those dealing with serious breaches of traffic regulations. It should be remembered, however, that strict liability does not mean absolute liability. The defendant will still be able to use the defences of automation, insanity, duress, etc.

The increasing importance of what have become known as public welfare offences is due to the steadily rising responsibility of the State for the maintenance of certain standards needed for the proper functioning of a modern industrial society. This includes such things as safety in factories, standards of housing accommodation, the quality of foodstuffs and drugs placed on the market, social security regulations, etc. The sanctions imposed for the breach of these standards are generally fines, but other sanctions, including terms of imprisonment, are not unknown. These public welfare offences differ from the traditional criminal offences mainly by not calling for the proof of *mens rea* on the part of the accused. The difference between these two types of offences has been well described by the late Professor W. Friedmann as follows: 'In the balance of values, it is generally considered more essential that violations of traffic rules or food laws should be strictly punished, in the interests of the public, rather than that the degree of individual guilt should be measured in each case.'

There are two other important factors to be considered. These public welfare offences are numerous and if in each case the guilt of the accused were to be as carefully considered as it is in cases of homicide or larceny, an impossible burden would be cast on the courts. Furthermore, many of these offences may be imputed to corporate bodies where, because of the very nature of a corporation, the question of guilt would be one impossible of solution. The purpose of the sanctions imposed for a breach of public welfare regulations differs also from that of sanctions levied on offenders charged with one of the traditional criminal offences. The main aim of the sanctions in the former case is that of achieving a certain standard of behaviour, a more careful approach to one's business or other commitment. This attitude was well expressed in *R.* v. *St. Margaret's Trust Ltd* where the Court of Criminal Appeal stated that '. . . the importance of not doing what is prohibited is such that the method of business must be rearranged so as to give the necessary knowledge. . . .' What is emerging from this type of offence is a form of punishing negligence without fault. Its purpose is to compel businessmen and others to apply stricter standards of enquiry and control to transactions which may endanger public safety and welfare.

Addendum

The Rehabilitation of Offenders Act 1974 has changed the law of defamation in respect of the defence of justification. A person convicted of an offence becomes 'rehabilitated' when the offence is 'spent'. The rehabilitation period varies in accordance with the gravity of the offence as reflected in the sentence imposed and amounts to either 5, 7 or 10 years. Once a conviction has become 'spent' a defence of justification in defamation proceedings will fail if the publication is proved to have been made with malice. The defence of absolute and qualified privilege and of fair comment remain however unaffected. Employers and others are thus still protected if they give references referring to spent convictions, unless they were actuated by malice. Any evidence about a spent conviction which a court rules not to be admissible can only be reported without the risk of a libel action in a *bona fide* law report or some other publication intended for *bona fide* educational or professional purposes. Otherwise it will not be a defence to show that the publication was a fair report of judicial proceedings.

APPENDIX ONE

Glossary of Legal Terms

(The reader is reminded that this glossary contains only such legal terms as can be explained shortly. Legal concepts which require lengthier explanation are described in the text of the book. The definitions given here are intended to help the reader in refreshing his memory; they would not be sufficient by themselves to cover examination requirements. For these purposes, explanations and illustrations as found in the text would be needed.)

Abatement. General legacies are abated (*i.e.*, reduced proportionately) when at the time of the testator's death his estate is insufficient to meet general legacies after all specific bequests have been met.

Accord and Satisfaction. The release of a party from his contractual obligation, the creditor accepting something else in satisfaction of the outstanding debt.

Account Stated. An admission that a sum of money is due, from which is implied a promise by the debtor to settle the debt.

Act of God. Some natural phenomenon against which no human foresight could have provided.

Actus reus. The guilty action.

Ademption. A bequest of a specific thing contained in a testator's will is adeemed (becomes null and void) if the thing concerned no longer forms part of his estate at the time of his death.

Administrator. A person appointed by the court to administer the estate of a deceased party where no executors have been appointed or where they are not prepared to act.

Adoption. The establishment of the relationship of parent and child by a court order.

Amicus curiae. A friend of the court.

Animus Possidendi. The intention of excluding others from the possession of something.

Animus Testandi. The intention of making a will.

Ante-nuptial. Before marriage.

Bailment. The delivery of goods on a condition, expressed or implied, that they shall be restored to the giver (bailor) as soon as the purpose for which they have been bailed has been achieved.

Base Fee. An estate in land which is subject to some qualification and which will cease when this qualification is at an end.

Bequest. A gift of personal property by will.
Bona Vacantia. Goods without an apparent owner.

Case Stated. The statement of the relevant facts for the opinion of a higher court.
Certiorari. An order by a superior court addressed to an inferior court, commanding it to hand over a case for trial.
Cestui Que Trust. The beneficiary under a trust.
Chose. A thing or chattel.
C.i.f. Contract. Contracts for the sale of goods, where the price quoted includes the insurance premium and freight charges.
Civil Law. Law other than criminal law.
Codification. The bringing together in one Act of Parliament (code) of the law (statutory and other) dealing with one subject-matter.
Condition. A condition in a contract is a promise which goes to the root of the contract so that a breach of it by one party will entitle the other party to treat the contract as discharged.
Consolidation. The bringing together in one Act of Parliament of the subject-matters of a number of Acts of Parliament.
Conversion. A tort consisting in the unjustified denial of a person's title to chattels.
Conveyance. A method of transferring property, mainly in land. The term is also used to describe the document by means of which the transfer is effected.
Corporation Aggregate. A corporation consisting of a number of persons.
Corporation Sole. A corporation consisting only of one member at a time.
Corpus Possessionis. The actual control over a thing possessed by a person.
Courts of Staple. Courts held in medieval times in certain ports which had the privilege of exporting specified goods from this country.
Criminal Law. The part of law concerned with the punishment of offences.
Crown. The corporation sole, represented by the Queen, in whose name the administration of the country is carried on.
Curia Regis. The King's Council or the King's Court.
Custom. A rule of conduct established by long observance.
Cy Près. As close as possible to the intention of the donor of a charitable trust.

Deed. A legal document which has been signed, sealed, and delivered.
Delegated Legislation. Lawmaking by some person or body acting under powers delegated by Parliament.
Demise. The grant of a lease of land.
Detinue. The tort of refusing to return possession of a chattel to the person entitled to it.
Devise. A gift of real property by will.

Domicile. The country in which a person is permanently resident.

Dominant Tenement. Land in favour of which a servitude exists.

Donatio Mortis Causa. A gift of personal property in anticipation of death.

Duress. A person acts under duress if he is compelled to do something by force or by threats.

Easement. A right of one landowner to use the land of another for some purpose.

Equity of Redemption. The equitable right of a mortgagor to redeem the property after the legal right to redeem has expired.

Escheat. The reversion of land to the owner of the superior title to it. Abolished in 1925.

Estate. An interest in land.

Ex Parte. An application in judicial proceedings made by one party in the absence of the other.

Execution. The act of bringing into effect a judgment by compelling the defendant to pay or to do what the court has ordered.

Eyre. Periodical circuits of the country by the king's judges, first established in 1176.

Fee. An interest in land capable of descending to heirs.

Fee Tail. An interest in land capable of descending to the direct issue of the owner.

Feme Covert. A married woman.

Feme Sole. A single woman.

Fiat. "Let it be done." The consent of the Attorney-General to certain proceedings requiring the permission of the Crown.

Fieri facias. A writ of execution in favour of a judgment creditor, addressed to the sheriff, commanding him to collect the debt from the goods of the judgment debtor.

Foreclosure. A court order preventing the redemption of a mortgage.

Frustration. A contract is frustrated if it has become impossible of performance for some reason outside the control of the parties.

Garnishee Order. A court order addressed to a debtor ordering him to pay the debt not to his creditor, but to some other party nominated by the court.

General Damages. Damages which the law presumes to follow naturally from the kind of wrong complained of.

Gloss. A comment.

Ignorantia Juris non Excusat. The ignorance of the law is no excuse.

Illegitimate. Not born in wedlock.

In Pari Delicto Potior est Conditio Defendentis. Where both parties are equally guilty, the defendant is in the stronger position.

In Personam. An act directed against specific persons only.

In Rem. An act operative against the world at large.

Injunction. A court order by which a person is ordered to do or to refrain from doing something.
Innuendo. A hidden or latent defamatory meaning of words.
Inter Vivos. During life.
Interim Injunction or **Interlocutory Injunction.** An injunction granted temporarily while proceedings are still in progress.
Intestate. Without leaving a will.
Intra Vires. Within the powers, the opposite of **Ultra Vires.**
Invitee. A person entering premises on business concerning himself and the occupier.

Joint Tortfeasors. Two or more persons responsible for a tort.
Jointure. A provision made by a husband for the support of his wife after his death.
Jura in re Aliena. Rights to a thing belonging to another person.
Jura in re Propria. Rights to a thing belonging to oneself.
Jus Accrescendi. The right of survivorship. The survivor of joint owners becomes the sole owner.

Laches. Unreasonable delay in enforcing an equitable right.
Legacy. A gift of personal property by will.
Legal Tender. Money which a creditor is bound to accept in settlement of a debt.
Legitimate. Born in wedlock.
Legitimation. Making an illegitimate child legitimate by the subsequent marriage of his parents.
Licensee. A person entering premises by permission, but not on business in which he and the occupier are both interested.
Liquidated Damages. Damages for breach of contract agreed on by the parties at the time of entering into contract.

Mandamus. A prerogative order issued by a judge of the High Court ordering a person or body to carry out some public duty imposed on them by law.
Maxims of Law. Legal principles expressed in an easily memorized form.
Mens rea. A guilty mind as an essential of a crime.

Nationality. Citizenship of a particular State.
Naturalization. Acquiring the nationality of a State otherwise than by birth.
Nisi Prius. "Unless before." A trial at nisi prius used to be a trial of an action at the Assizes.
Nolle prosequi. A formal statement entered on behalf of the Attorney-General that he does not wish to proceed with a criminal prosecution.
Nominal Damages. Damages awarded for a breach of contract in circumstances where the plaintiff has suffered no measurable loss.
Non est factum. It is not his deed. Mistake in signing a document.

Obiter Dictum. A saying by the way. Any part of a judgment which is not an essential part of it.

Option. A right conferred by contract to buy something.
Order in Council. An order, made by the Queen, by and with the advice of Her Majesty's Privy Council.

Parol. An informally made contract.
Per Incuriam. Through want of care.
Penalty. Agreed damages for breach of contract which do not represent a true and fair estimate of the loss likely to be suffered in the event of a breach.
Personal Property. Property which is not real property. Generally, chattels and other moveable goods, though leasehold interests in land are also included.
Petition of Right. The method existing before the Crown Proceedings Act 1947, whereby the subject could claim relief against the Crown.
Piepowder Courts. Commercial courts existing in the Middle Ages.
Polygamy. Having more than one wife.
Portion. The provision made by a parent for his child.
Precedent. A judgment of a court of law which is quoted as authority for some legal proposition.
Prerogative Orders (Writs). Orders made by superior courts in order to prevent inferior courts and administrative bodies from doing injustice to a subject.
Prima facie case. A case supported by sufficient evidence so as to cast the burden of disproving it on the defence.
Private Law. Law which is concerned with the relationship of citizens to each other. The opposite of **Public Law.**
Profit à Prendre. The right of taking something from the land of another person.
Prohibition. An order issued by the High Court to restrain an inferior court from exceeding its jurisdiction.
Prohibitory Injunction. An injunction which prohibits the continuation of something.
Public Law. Law which is concerned with the relationship of the individual to the State. This includes criminal, administrative, and constitutional law.
Public Policy. Certain acts are treated by law as illegal because they oppose public policy. Public policy is identified with the broad interests of the community, but the headings of public policy will no longer be added to.
Puisne Judges. Judges of the High Court, other than the Lord Chief Justice, the Lord Chancellor, and the President of the Family Division.
Puisne Mortgages. A legal mortgage which is not protected by a deposit of the title-deeds.

Quorum. The minimum number of persons who have to be present to constitute a valid meeting.

Rack Rent. The best rent obtainable for land.

Ratio Decidendi. The reason for a decision.
Real Property. Freehold estates in land.
Remainder. What is left out of an estate in land if a smaller estate has been granted out of it.
Rent Charge. A rent payable in respect of land to a person other than the landlord.
Res Ipsa Loquitur. The thing speaks for itself.
Restitutio in Integrum. Restoration to the previous position.
Reversion. The right of the owner of an estate to have the estate eventually restored to him when an estate existing for a shorter period has expired.

Servient Tenement. Land over which a servitude exists.
Simple Contracts. Contracts not made by deed.
Special Damages. Damages which are not presumed by the court and the presence of which will have to be specially proved.
Specialty Contracts. Contracts made by deed.
Specific Performance. A court order, ordering a person to carry out a promise which he has made.
Specific Recovery. Proceedings for the recovery of land from some one who is wrongfully in possession of it.
Squatter. A person occupying land without the authority of the man in legal possession.
Stare Decisis. Standing by one's decision.
Subpœna. A writ issued by the court requiring the person to whom it is addressed to be present at a specified place and time under a penalty.

Uberrimæ Fidei. Of the utmost good faith.
Ultra Vires. Outside the powers.
Undue Influence. Where a person has not been allowed to exercise his judgment freely on a matter he is said to have been subjected to undue influence.
Unenforceable. Something which cannot be proceeded for in a court of law, usually because it lacks the required form.
Unincorporated Association. Associations of persons, pursuing some common objective, which have not been given legal personality.
Unliquidated Damages. Damages which will have to be ascertained by the court.

Vicarious. On behalf of another.
Vis major. Also known as *force majeure.* **See Act of God.**
Void. Of no legal effect.
Voidable. A contract which may be made void at the option of one of the parties to it.
Volenti non fit Injuria. That to which a person consents cannot be complained of by him as an injury.

Warranty. A promise embodied in a contract which is not considered as going to the root of it.

Waste. The causing of lasting damage to land.

Writ. A document in the Queen's name and bearing the seal of the court, ordering the person to whom it is addressed to do something.

APPENDIX TWO

Selected Examination Questions

Chapter One. The Nature and Sources of English Law

1. State what you understand by 'delegated legislation' and explain the *ultra vires* doctrine as applied thereto. (C.I.S.)

2. To what extent is it true in your opinion to say that English judges make the law? Explain the relative advantages and disadvantages of the English system of case-law. (C.I.S.)

3. Write a note on legislation as a source of law. Explain the leading rules that govern the interpretation of a statute. (Corp. of Sec.)

4. "The general result of the fusion of law and equity has been not to alter substantive law but merely to alter and simplify the procedure." Discuss the statement, and consider whether it may be taken as accurate. (C.I.S.)

5. (*a*) Describe the equitable remedies available for the enforcement of a contract. How do they differ from common law remedies? (*b*) In what circumstances can the equitable remedies be granted to enforce a contract of personal service? (Bankers)

6. What do you understand by "the Law Merchant"? To what extent was its development separate from that of the common law of England? (Corp. of Sec.)

7. The Lord Chancellor has been described as "The Keeper of the King's Conscience." Discuss this statement and illustrate your answer with reference to the jurisdiction of the Courts of Equity. (Corp. of Sec.)

8. "The rules of Equity are only a sort of supplement or appendix to the Common Law; they assume its existence but they add something further. In this way Equity is an *addendum* to the Common Law." Explain this statement and mention some of the main spheres of modern equity. (C.I.S.)

9. "Where in a lawsuit a question arises for the first time as to the meaning of an Act of Parliament, the judge will decide the meaning in accordance with the recognized rules of interpretation" (Geldart). Comment on this statement. (C.I.S.)

10. "In spite of the enormous bulk of the Statute Law, the most fundamental part of English law is still Common Law." Comment on this statement and explain the difference between Statute Law and Common Law. State the position where there is a conflict between the provisions of an Act of Parliament and a rule of Common Law. (C.I.S.)

Chapter Two. The Judicial System of England and Wales

1. How does the present relationship of the Queen's Bench Division and the Chancery Division of the High Court of Justice differ from the relationship between the common law courts and the Court of Chancery as they existed before the Judicature Acts of 1873 and 1875? (Bankers)

2. Describe the composition and jurisdiction of the following courts:
   (*a*) The House of Lords.
   (*b*) A Divisional Court of the Queen's Bench Division.
   (*c*) A Crown Court.

3. Give an outline of the present organization of the Supreme Court of Judicature and of the principal types of actions which may be heard by that court. (Corp. of Sec.)

4. In which divisions of the High Court would the following proceedings be brought and to which courts would an appeal lie from the judgment of the High Court:
   (*a*) An action for the recovery of a stolen motor-car;
   (*b*) An action for the administration of a trust fund;
   (*c*) A prosecution for the theft of cash from a shop;
   (*d*) An action to prove a will in solemn form? (Bankers)

Chapter Three. Legal Persons and Legal Relations

1. How may a contract for the supply of goods be entered into so as to be binding on:
   (*a*) A partnership;
   (*b*) An unincorporated association;
   (*c*) A limited company;
   (*d*) A person who was drunk at the time when the goods were ordered? (C I.S.)

2. "The King can do no wrong." What does this mean? In your answer consider what, if any, remedies there are against the Crown for breach of contract. (C.I.S.)

3. What is the difference in law between a partnership and a limited company? In your answer deal also with the position of a limited partnership. (C.I.S.)

4. Explain the distinguishing features of:
   (*a*) A corporation aggregate.
   (*b*) A corporation sole.
   (*c*) An unincorporated association.

State how you would classify:

(*a*) The Bishop of London.
(*b*) The Public Trustee.
(*c*) The National Union of Railwaymen. (C.I.S.)

5. To what extent is a husband responsible for goods ordered by his wife? Explain the position of a tradesman who supplies groceries on credit to a married woman (*a*) where her husband has supplied her with sufficient ready money to pay for all the ordinary household needs; and (*b*) where her husband has published a notice in the local newspaper to the effect that he will no longer be liable for his wife's debts. (C.I.S.)

6. Mention four ways in which a person may acquire British nationality; and explain the position of (*a*) an alien woman who marries a British subject, and (*b*) a British woman who marries an alien husband. (C.I.S.)

7. Explain the legal position of a married woman in each of the following circumstances:

(*a*) Where she has obtained goods on credit without informing the tradesman who supplied the goods that her husband had forbidden her to pledge his credit.

(*b*) Where she bought on credit a travelling case worth £50 for use on her honeymoon.

(*c*) Where the day before her marriage she entered a neighbour's garden and picked some of his flowers and made them into bouquets for the use of her bridesmaids. (C.I.S.)

8. Why, and in what circumstances, is it important to distinguish nationality from domicile when determining the position of a person whose rights and responsibilities under English law are under consideration?

A, who was born in Austria and is now residing in England, has been employed by the Crown for four years in Kenya. He desires to acquire British nationality. Explain the legal position, and describe the means whereby A may acquire British nationality. (C.I.S.)

Chapter Four. The Law of Contract

1. What is the effect of misrepresentation on a contract?

S offers to sell his house to B for £5000. He knows there is dry rot in the house, but does not disclose this to B. B buys and after he has completed the purchase he discovers the existence of dry rot. B wants to repudiate the purchase or, if he cannot do that, to recover the expense to which he will be put in eliminating the dry rot. What remedies, if any, are open to him? (C.I.S.)

2. State the principal rules applicable to the making, acceptance, and revocation of offers by means of the post.

F, by letter written on November 1, offered to sell machinery to G in Madrid and requested a reply by cable. G received F's letter on November 5 and immediately telegraphed to F his acceptance. On

November 3 F wrote a letter to G revoking his offer and the revocation reached G on November 6. Is there a binding contract? (C.I.S.)

3. (*a*) On January 1, 1950, Henry agreed orally to sell his house to George for £3500 "subject to contract." The next day they exchanged letters confirming this arrangement (the letters also contained the words "subject to contract"). On January 3, 1950, Richard offered Henry £3700 for the house. If Henry accepts this offer can George take any proceedings against him?

(*b*) (i) Peter agreed in writing to buy a second-hand car from John for £750. The car was delivered a year ago, and Peter has not yet paid. A month ago John met Peter and told him he would take £500 in full settlement. John has now changed his mind and wishes to know whether he can sue Peter for the full £750.

(ii) Would the position be the same if John's agreement to take £500 had been in writing and signed by him? (Bankers)

4. (*a*) Peter sold George a second-hand car, expressing the sale to be with all faults. Peter knew that the car had a defective gear-box, but kept silent as to this. Explain whether George has any right of action in respect of the defect.

(*b*) John took out a policy insuring his motor-van against fire. In answer to a question on the proposal form: "At what address will the vehicle usually be garaged?" John inserted the correct address. He did not mention that the garage was a wooden shed with a thatched roof adjoining a busy railway line. A spark from an engine has set fire to the garage and destroyed the van. Explain whether John can recover under the policy. (Bankers)

5. George advertised his car for sale at £350. Harry wrote agreeing to pay the price if George would guarantee to replace all the parts which became defective within three months. George immediately wrote back, "I accept your offer, but can give no guarantee. Instead, I reduce the price to £300." Harry received his letter a week ago, but George has received no reply.

Explain whether George can sell the car to Tom, who has just offered him £325 and does not require a guarantee. (Bankers)

6. Softcrete agreed to build a house for Eager, to be completed ready for occupation by June 1, 1954. The contract provided that if it was not completed by this date Softcrete would forfeit £50 for every week's delay "by way of liquidated damages." Owing to Softcrete's negligent failure to order certain materials in time, the house was not completed until six weeks after June 1. The damage actually suffered by Eager was £20 a week, for hotel bills and storage of furniture during the six weeks.

Consider whether Softcrete is liable to forfeit the full £50 a week agreed upon. (Bankers)

7. (*a*) What do you understand by a contract *ubberrimæ fidei*? How does such a contract differ from other contracts?

(*b*) George took out a life-insurance policy. The proposal form contained the questions: "What is your profession or occupation?" "Do you indulge in motor- or motor-cycle racing?"

George answered truthfully: "Bank cashier"; "No." The form contained no other questions about his pursuits, and George did not inform the insurers that he was a keen mountaineer.

He has been killed by a fall while on a climbing holiday in North Wales. Are the insurers liable on the policy? (Bankers)

8. (*a*) Does a breach of contract committed by one party necessarily discharge the other party from the contract?

(*b*) How, if at all, may a breach of contract be committed before the time when performance falls due?

9. In what circumstances and on what principles will a covenant in restraint of trade be enforced by the court?

M., who is employed as a travelling representative by a bakery company whose registered office is in Cork, has promised the company that he will not, within three years of the termination of his employment, be engaged in a similar business within a radius of twenty-five miles of Cork.

Would M.'s promise be enforced by the court? (C.I.S.)

10. By what means may a promise be made legally binding? State the effect of the following promises:

(*a*) A promises B that, if B will refrain from suing him for trespass, he will pay £50 to B.

(*b*) C promises D that, in view of D's having rescued C from drowning, he will pay £500 to D.

(*c*) E promises F, who owes him £100, that, if F will pay him £75 at once, he will treat the debt as cancelled.

(*d*) G promises to take H for a sailing cruise in his yacht next summer. (C.I.S.)

11. P reads an advertisement in a newspaper offering for quick sale a desirable residence near London for £5000. P, without inspecting the property, accepts the offer by telephone and agrees to complete the purchase fourteen days later. Before the date for completion arrives, P discovers that the house has no garage and he declines to complete the purchase. Explain the legal position. (C.I.S.)

12. Smith, a trader in a small way of business, obtained goods on credit from Jones by sending an order on letter-paper headed with the name of an established firm, Bates & Co., and giving and address for delivery near to the premises of the real Bates & Co. If Smith has sold the goods to Clark, who took them in good faith, can Jones recover the goods from Clark? Would your answer be different if instead of using letter-paper headed with the name of Bates & Co., Smith had sent the order on paper headed with a fictitious name? (Bankers)

Chapter Five. The Law of Trusts

1. What is a trust? How is a trust created?

A testator by his will leaves his dwelling-house Holmlea to his trustees on trust for his son, to be conveyed to him when he is twenty-five. The son is anxious to have the house before he is twenty-five. Is there any way by which he can do so? (C.I.S.)

2. How is a trust created?

X owns both Blackacre and Whiteacre. He conveys Blackacre into the name of his son Y, and Whiteacre into the name of his friend Z. In whom is the beneficial ownership of (*a*) Blackacre and (*b*) Whiteacre vested? (C.I.S.)

3. State what you understand by a 'trust' and explain how a trust of (*a*) a valuable picture and (*b*) a freehold farm may be created. Would a trust arise in the following circumstances:

(*a*) A conveys his freehold house into the names of himself and of B.

(*b*) Upon the expiration of a lease of a block of flats which C holds in trust for D, the landlord refused to grant a new lease to C in his capacity of trustee, whereupon C induced the landlord to grant a new lease to C in his personal capacity. (C.I.S.)

4. (*a*) Explain the essential features of an express private trust.

(*b*) How may such a trust be created? (Bankers)

5. Explain fully the effect of the following transactions:

(*a*) Pursefull's old nurse, Maud, asked him to help her buy a country cottage. He gave her the whole purchase price, she used it to buy the cottage, and the fee simple of the property was conveyed to her.

(*b*) Pursefull also gave his son, Simon, aged twenty-two, who was about to be married, enough money to buy a house. Simon used the money for this purpose, and the fee simple of the house was conveyed to him. (Bankers)

6. State what you understand by a trust; and explain how during the settlor's life-time a trust may be created of the following: (*a*) a freehold house; (*b*) shares in a limited company; (*c*) a professional man's library and office furniture. (C.I.S.)

7. (*a*) Define an "incompletely constituted trust," a "resulting trust," and a "constructive trust."

(*b*) What are the rights of the beneficiaries of an incompletely constituted trust? (Bankers)

Chapter Six. The Law of Property

1. State the means whereby the legal ownership of the following may be transferred:

(*a*) A leasehold dwelling-house.
(*b*) A debt.
(*c*) A plot of freehold land.
(*d*) A cheque made payable to P or order. (C.I.S.)

2. Coke is the owner in fee simple of a large country estate.

(*a*) He has let Blackstone Hall, part of the estate, to Littleton. L. has assigned the lease to Hale, who has in turn assigned it to Bracton.

(*b*) Coke has let Whiteacre Farm, another part of the estate, to Giles, who has sub-let it to Thistle.

The above assignments and sub-lettings were carried out with Coke's consent. Who are the persons against whom Coke may now recover the rents of Blackstone Hall and Whiteacre respectively? Explain the principles involved. (Bankers)

3. Explain the difference between (*a*) a tenancy at will; (*b*) a tenancy at sufferance: (*c*) a tenancy from year to year; (*d*) a lease for years. (C.I.S.)

4. State the rules whereby ownership may be distinguished from possession, and discuss the legal position of the parties in the following cases:

(*a*) Sykes drives away Brown's motor-cycle from a car park.

(*b*) Jones leaves his shoes with the shoe-maker to be repaired.

(*c*) Smith lends his lawnmower to Robinson for a week.

(*d*) Miss Eve drops her purse on the floor of a shop while making a purchase; the proprietor of the shop picks up the purse, and appropriates the contents thereof. (C.I.S.)

5. Your house and the house next door have been built for twenty-five years. Your next-door neighbour has recently demolished his house with the intention of using the whole of his land as a lawn-tennis court. In consequence of the withdrawal of support, your house is beginning to collapse. Discuss the legal position. (C.I.S.)

6. (*a*) Explain the nature of the following transactions in respect of interests in land:

(i) a conveyance of the fee simple;

(ii) a grant of a lease.

(*b*) Give an example of the application to lease of the maxim "Equity looks on that as done which ought to be done." (Bankers)

7. Explain the difference between an easement and a profit à prendre.

In which category would you place the following rights?

(*a*) a right to fish in your neighbour's lake;

(*b*) a right to light over your neighbour's land to the south windows of your house;

(*c*) a right to walk across your neighbour's field to the shopping centre;

(*d*) a right to graze your cattle on the village green? (C.I.S.)

8. (*a*) In what circumstances does a bill of exchange require to be presented for acceptance?

(*b*) A drew a cheque payable to B or order. B endorsed the

cheque in blank and gave it to C who handed it to D for cash. When D presented the cheque it was dishonoured and it appears that A is insolvent. Advise D how to recover the amount of the cheque.

(*c*) Is there any difference in the effect of crossing a cheque "not negotiable" as compared with similarly crossing a bill of exchange? (Bankers)

9. (*a*) State the various methods whereby the ownership of land may be acquired other than by purchase from the owner thereof.

(*b*) For the last ten years S has grown vegetables on a plot of unfenced land adjoining his own garden and throughout the same period he has taken possession of and used sundry garden tools which he has found in a shed on the said plot. T, claiming to be the owner of the said plot and tools, now calls upon S to give up possession of the said plot and to return the said tools.

Explain the legal position. (C.I.S.)

Chapter Seven. The Law of Securities

1. In a mortgage of land what power has a mortgagee (*a*) to compel the mortgagor to redeem the mortgage, (*b*) to foreclose, (*c*) to sell the mortgaged land? (C.I.S.)

2. (*a*) What do you understand by a mortgagor's equity of redemption? On what general equitable principle is this right based?

(*b*) In 1952 Barebones mortgaged his house (worth £3000) to Skinflint to secure repayment of a loan for £2000 at 7 per cent interest, and the mortgage deed provided that no part of the loan should be repaid for forty years.

Barebones has been left a legacy, and wishes to pay off the whole of the debt immediately in order to save further interest. Discuss whether he can do so. (Bankers)

3. How is a mortgage on land carried out? What remedies are open to a mortgagee if the mortgagor makes default in payment of principal or interest? (C.I.S.)

4. (*a*) Geoffrey is the owner in fee simple of a house worth £5000. He wishes to borrow £100 on the security of the house from John and may later wish to borrow a further £500 from Malcolm. Both lenders are likely to insist on a legal mortgage. By what means can the transaction be carried out?

(*b*) Would the position be any different if Geoffrey did not own the fee simple, but held the house on a lease for 99 years from March 25, 1950? (Bankers)

5. State the appropriate method of securing a loan on any FOUR of the following types of property:

(*a*) A leasehold shop;
(*b*) An antique table;
(*c*) A freehold farmhouse;
(*d*) A British tanker;
(*e*) A bill of lading;
(*f*) Shares in a public company. (C.I.S.)

Chapter Eight. The Law of Succession

1. Explain what is meant by an intestacy.

T dies possessed of a house worth £2000, personal chattels worth £500, and investments worth £3000. He leaves a widow and one child. He makes a will leaving the house to his child, but making no further disposition to his property. How does his property pass on his death? (C.I.S.)

2. Explain concisely what is meant by (*a*) dying intestate and (*b*) dying testate.

A testator by his will gives a legacy to the wife of one of the attesting witnesses and, after executing it, alters the amount of a legacy given to X from £1000 to £500. What is the legal position? (C.I.S.)

3. In what circumstances is a will revoked?

B died in December 1954, having given by his will all his estate to his nephews and nieces. B left surviving him (*a*) his widow, (*b*) a married daughter (a widow with three young children), and (*c*) a son aged ten. Can any steps be taken by any of the persons mentioned to interfere with the disposition of B's estate as directed by his will? (C.I.S.)

4. By his will, made in 1947, Jorrocks bequeathed the following legacies:

(*a*) To Sponge, my grey mare Daisy;
(*b*) To Lucy Glitters, my pack of foxhounds;
(*c*) To Facey Rumford, £300 out of my 30 per cent War Stock;
(*d*) all the residue of my estate to my dear wife.

At the time of Jorrocks' death in 1952:

(*a*) he had sold Daisy and bought another mare with the proceeds;

(*b*) half of the original foxhounds had died and had not been replaced;

(*c*) he had sold some of his War Stock, so that only £250 remained, and had spent the proceeds.

What will the respective legatees (who are all living) receive? Explain the principles on which your answer is based. (Bankers)

5. (*a*) What form is required for a valid will?

(*b*) Will the intentions of a testator of full capacity, properly expressed in a valid will, and all of which are lawful and possible to carry out necessarily be enforced by the law? (Bankers)

6. Define and give an example of each of the following:

(*a*) a residuary devise;
(*b*) a specific legacy;
(*c*) a demonstrative legacy;
(*d*) a general legacy.

T by his will gives to his niece Mary his grand piano. Six months before his death T sells his grand piano, and purchases a valuable second-hand grand piano.

What are Mary's rights under the will? (C.I.S.)

7. State the circumstances in which and by what means a will is revoked.

(i) Six months after making his will a testator decides to reduce from £500 to £300 a legacy given to his nephew B; he alters his will accordingly, and places his initials in the margin of his will.

(ii) Knowing that his friend D, to whom he has given a legacy of £400, has since died, a testator strikes out D's name, and substitutes therefore the name of D's widow, and places his initials in the margin of his will.

What is the effect of the said alterations? (C.I.S.)

8. Frederick made a will in 1950 by which he left all his estate to Mary. In 1955 he married Jean and in 1956 he made another will (witnessed by Jean and Henry) by which he left half his estate to Jean and half to his brother George. Frederick has just died leaving an estate worth £4000 and Mary, Jean and George survived him. Who is entitled to Frederick's estate? (Bankers)

Chapter Nine. An Outline of the Law of Torts and Criminal Law

1. (*a*) Define defamation. What are the chief differences between the two forms which defamation may take?

(*b*) Ten years ago Alexander was released from a term of penal servitude. He has 'gone straight' ever since. George, who bears him a grudge, tells his present employer that Alexander is an ex-convict. The employer consequently gives him notice of dismissal. Explain whether Alexander can sue George for damages. (Bankers)

2. (*a*) Faithful, a clerk in Long and Short's Bank Ltd, while paying out notes to Purseful, a customer, negligently upsets a bottle of ink and ruins Purseful's new suit. Can Purseful sue Faithful or the manager of the branch or the Bank itself?

(*b*) Would it afford the Bank or the manager any defence if the manager had instructed the clerks not to leave any ink on the counter and to use only fountain pens?

(*c*) If a similar accident occurred to Purseful at a post office could he sue the clerk, the local postmaster, or the Crown? (Bankers)

3. The owner of the Hardrock Quarry kept upon his land a quantity of dynamite for use in quarrying operations. Without any negligence on the part of anyone, this dynamite exploded and injured Roughcast, a builder, who was at that moment in the owner's office at the quarry discussing the purchase of stone. The blast from the explosion also damaged a neighbouring farm-house owned by Hayseed. Explain whether Roughcast and Hayseed respectively can recover damages in tort against the owner of the quarry. (Bankers)

4. Is it true to say that English law provides a remedy for all harm that is intentionally inflicted by one person upon another? Consider

whether John has any remedy against Adolphus in the following cases:

(*a*) John has been long established as the only stationer in Littledown. Adolphus opens a similar business in the same street, and holds a series of sales of stationery at cheap prices, as a result of which several persons who would otherwise have continued to buy stationery from John buy it from Adolphus, and John's profits fall considerably.

(*b*) Adolphus knows that the governors of Littledown school have entered into a binding contract with John for the supply of stationery to the school. Adolphus offers to supply the stationery at a reduced price; the governors accept his offer, and refuse to accept delivery from John. (Bankers)

5. (*a*) In connection with the law of tort, what do you understand by:

(i) inevitable accident;
(ii) contribution between joint tortfeasors?

(*b*) How may a corporation incur liability in tort? (Bankers)

6. If T does the following acts—namely:

(*a*) leaves open the gate of F's field, which adjoins a trunk road; as a result thereof F's pedigree bull strays on the road, and is killed by a passing lorry.

(*b*) damages troughs provided on F's land for the feeding of F's pigs.

(*c*) posts on F's fence a bill advertising a local horse show; has F in each case any remedies against T? If so, on what grounds? (C.I.S.)

7. Henry, aged 17, was driving his car, with his wife Hilda in the passenger's seat, when the car collided with a motor-cycle ridden by Kenneth which was coming in the opposite direction. The collision was caused partly by the fact that Henry was driving too fast and partly by the fact that Kenneth was not in proper control of his motor-cycle. Henry, Hilda, and Kenneth were injured in the collision and Henry's car mounted the pavement and injured Peter, a pedestrian who was passing by. Advise Henry, Hilda, Kenneth, and Peter. (Bankers)

8. Why are some wrongful acts visited by punishment while others lead to the award of damages to the injured party?

9. What is meant in criminal law by:

(*a*) mens rea;
(*b*) actus reus;
(*c*) recklessness?

APPENDIX THREE

Bibliography

The books listed below may be of help to the reader who requires additional information on certain of the topics covered in the present book. He should remember, however, that most of the books referred to are written for the use of law students and contain, therefore, more detail than is normally expected from students in professional examinations.

General Books

P. S. James: *Introduction to English Law* (Butterworth).
G. Williams: *Learning the Law* (Stevens).

History and Sources of Law

A. K. R. Kiralfy: *The English Legal System* (Sweet and Maxwell).

Family Law

P. M. Bromley: *Family Law* (Butterworth).

The Judicial System of England and Wales

P. Archer: *The Queen's Courts* (Penguin Books).
R. M. Jackson: *The Machinery of Justice in England* (Cambridge University Press).

Law of Property and Law of Mortgages

F. H. Lawson: *Introduction to the Law of Property* (Oxford University Press).

Law of Trusts

D. B. Parker and A. R. Mellows: *The Modern Law of Trusts* (Sweet and Maxwell).

Law of Torts and Criminal Law

Winfield on Tort (Sweet and Maxwell).
R. Cross and P. A. Jones: *Introduction to Criminal Law* (Butterworth).

Law of Contract

G. C Cheshire and C H. S. Fifoot: *The Law of Contract* (Butterworth).
G. C. Chesire and C. H. S. Fifoot: *Cases on the Law of Contract* (Butterworth).

Law of Succession

S. J. Bailey: *The Law of Wills* (Pitman).

Law Dictionary

H. N. Mozley and G. C. Whiteley (ed. J. B. Saunders): *Law Dictionary* (Butterworth).

Table of Cases

[The year given after each case is the year of the court's decision. The letters and figures shown after the date of the decision refer to the places in the various series of law reports where the text of the decision may be found. Where the year is shown in square brackets, the year represents an essential part of the reference to the reports, because the series of reports mentioned is one which is not numbered consecutively; while where the year is shown in round brackets, the series of reports is one which is numbered consecutively. Candidates studying law for professional examinations will not be expected, when quoting a case in an examination answer, to refer to more than its name. They are advised, however, to underline the name, as this is common legal practice. The page references given here, are of course, to the present book.]

Table of Statutes

Table of Statutes

Index